# CONVERSION
## *The Last Great Retail Metric*

authorHOUSE®

*AuthorHouse™*
*1663 Liberty Drive*
*Bloomington, IN 47403*
*www.authorhouse.com*
*Phone: 1-800-839-8640*

*First published by AuthorHouse 7/13/2011*

*ISBN: 978-1-4634-1422-1 (sc)*
*ISBN: 978-1-4634-1421-4 (hc)*
*ISBN: 978-1-4634-1420-7 (e)*

*Library of Congress Control Number: 2011908617*

*Printed in the United States of America*

*This book is printed on acid-free paper.*

For Lena

&

Corine+ Taylor+ Cole

# Table of Contents

# The Last Great Retail Metric

## The last? Great?

You're probably thinking, "Yeah, right." You're skeptical of such claims, and you should be. Nobody says he's going to write the Last Great American Novel. One must have the courage of his convictions to make such an apparently outrageous claim.

I do have the courage of my convictions – and the experience to back it up. The latter is what this introductory chapter is about: the 17-year journey that led me to the incontrovertible conclusion that most retailers and the retail industry in general have overlooked this simple but critically important metric. I claim that conversion is the Last Great Retail Metric, and I'll prove it in the chapters that follow.

Nobody argues against conversion. It's very important, maybe even the most important thing you should focus on to improve sales performance in your stores. But the idea of "converting" shoppers into buyers is such a favorite piece of retail shop talk that we should officially classify it as a cliché. Maybe that's part of the problem. This vital metric has been so misused and underused that it's lost its value and consequently failed to find its rightful place on the dashboards of retail executives and managers alongside comp sales and average ticket. I hope to change that.

## Yet to be fully exploited

But *last* great metric? Yes, because it is the one metric that most retailers today have yet to fully exploit or leverage. Conversion is not just a critical, vital, useful, or insightful retail performance metric – it has the potential to be transformational, and that is what makes it a truly *great* metric.

There is a concomitant metric: While improving "customer conversion" is the overarching solve-for, you can't talk about conversion without also talking about store traffic – these concepts are inextricably tied in a number of important ways. So I will also talk a lot about traffic and, yes, it too needs to find its way onto dashboards.

## Conclusion first

So, with this in mind, allow me to state the conclusion of the book: *all retailers need to measure traffic and customer conversion in their stores. If you don't, you're flying blind.*

Retailers who measure traffic and conversion and effectively use the insights from this data as part of their operations have a significant competitive advantage over those who do not. Given that traffic and conversion are so fundamental to retailing, I strongly assert that these metrics should be as pervasive in retailing as point-of-sale – they're that critical.

When I wrote *When Retail Customers Count* in 2005, it was the first and only book dedicated to the topic of traffic and conversion analysis. It was, in effect, the primer on traffic and conversion – a basic guide for retail managers. What was surprising to me — and this is largely why I wrote it — was that no one had previously told the traffic and conversion story.

I was stunned. Why hadn't this already been done?

As I found out, traffic counting and conversion have been part of retailing for decades, but they have never been a meaningful topic in the dialog about how to improve retail, and for the most part, they're still not today. Oh sure, they get passing mention in trade publications here and there, and with the advent of video analytics, the traffic and conversion messages are seeping into the narrative somewhat more often lately, but usually as just a side note.

## Conversion should be the headline!

In the six years since the publication of my first book, I have spent a considerable amount of time traveling all over North America, meeting with retailing executives, educators, consultants, and industry experts to talk about traffic and conversion. I have sent out hundreds and hundreds of books, giving them away as a way to open a dialog with retail executives.

And it worked! I have had countless dialogs.

What I discovered was almost as surprising (and disturbing) as when I realized no one had written the traffic and conversion story in the first place. Most retailers still don't get it, and while some of the more thoughtful consultants, educators and industry experts I've met are sympathetic, the retail support industry is collectively ambivalent. If a retailer has traffic and conversion data, great, this is really useful; if they don't...oh, well.

In my first book, I believed the lack of adoption of traffic and conversion measures by retailers was merely a question of education or communication, but I have come to realize that the reasons for the apparent apathy are more complex than I had thought.

## Some did get it.

As I reflect on the meetings I've had with retail executives, I can make no generalizations about why most don't use traffic and conversion as part of their operations, because there's just not one simple reason.

From the majority of my discussions with retailers, it would have been easy to have just written the whole thing off – retailers just don't get it, so why bother? Traffic and conversion will never be as pervasive as POS – move on.

But, as I said, it just wasn't that simple. You see, over the course of these countless meetings, I also stumbled upon some who did get it. In fact, they got it so much that they shattered my hypothesis that the retail industry was never going to collectively get it. Not only did they support my belief that traffic and conversion analytics should be as pervasive as POS in retailing, but they insisted that they could not run their businesses today without it. And they couldn't understand how other retailers could either!

To speak with retailers who understood the importance of traffic and conversion so profoundly was nothing short of a revelation. It was analogous to visiting a faraway foreign land trying to get directions from people who spoke no English, and to then finally find someone who speaks English – perfectly and eloquently.

Awesome.

To a great extent it was this disparity between the retailer Haves and Have-Nots that compelled me to write this book. Why is it that some retailers are using traffic and conversion to great advantage, while so many (the majority, in fact), aren't? What do these retailers know that the others don't? How did they get there? Why do so many retailers struggle with these fundamental measures?

## Why I am so obsessed with conversion

You may be wondering what the source of my conviction might be – fair question. A bit of background here might help.

In 1993 I was a college student studying business and the part-time marketing manager for a local computer store. I was struggling with trying to measure the impact of our advertising. Advertising wasn't cheap, and I wanted to know what it was delivering.

I found it quite remarkable that the sales results didn't always represent what was actually happening in the store. For example, we would run a promotion, and the store would be very busy – it wasn't hard to tell, as it was a single-location store. At the end of the day, we would anxiously count the money in the cash till and hope for the best. Often, we were underwhelmed with the results. The owner would say, "Is that all we did in sales today? I thought we would have done better — I guess that promotion didn't work very well."

You see, that's what bugged me. The advertising did work. It drove prospects into the store. I saw it with my very own eyes. I also saw people wander around the store, not get served because our Sales Associates were all busy helping other customers — and then leave, without making a purchase. My advertising was working, but I had no way to prove it.

One day it occurred to me that if I could track the number of people coming into the store, I could prove that my advertising worked. It was still the early days of the Internet, so I scoured retail trade publications at the university's library, looking for someone who sold traffic counters. In a dusty old copy of *Chain Store Executive* magazine, I saw a small ad for a company who offered electronic traffic counters – bingo!

As soon as I got back to the office, I called the company and was delighted to learn that they had what I was looking for. The traffic counter would cost about $2,500 – a bargain, I thought, compared to what we spent on advertising and promotions annually. So I gathered up all my research and went to pitch the idea to the store owner.

I thought I had a compelling argument. Spend $2,500 to help us understand if the $250,000 we were spending on advertising annually was making a difference. No-brainer, right? Wrong! The owner's reaction still stings after all these years: *"You want to spend $2,500 on this gadget? We could do a radio remote for that kind of money. No way."*

I was completely dejected. Here I had found a way to answer some very critical questions about our business, and instead of being commended on the initiative, I was treated to my first, real-world, "penny wise, dollar foolish" management decision.

I was so convinced that traffic data would deliver the important insights we needed, I wasn't going to let the lack of executive support or budget get in the way. I went to one of my engineering buddies who worked in the technical service department and asked him if he could build me a basic counter –an infrared beam at the front door, some kind of data collection device, plus a way to look at the data. The answer: sure, no problem.

## Traffic data, revelations, new clients

With about $300 of parts from a local Radio Shack (which I paid for out of my own pocket), my pal built me a primitive traffic counter. From the moment we installed our counter in 1993 to this day, I have been hooked on traffic data and all the great insights it can reveal, like customer conversion rates.

After several months of using and learning about traffic and conversion data with our home- grown counter, it occurred to me that other local retailers may also be looking for traffic and conversion insights, so in 1994 HeadCount Corporation was officially born. We started the company as a small sideline while we finished college, and I even got permission from the store owner to pursue HeadCount in my spare time – that is, when I wasn't in school or working for him.

We scraped some money together, and I started knocking on doors of local retailers – not much success. In fact, I discovered that it was a very hard sell. Most retailers had the same reaction as my owner – what, $2,500 for a traffic counting gadget, no thanks!

Even after I explained all the great ways we were using the data — measuring advertising impact, scheduling staff better, and calculating something called "conversion rate" — these retailers were unconvinced. I wondered, "What the hell is wrong with these people?"

After endless tries, I finally sold a couple of units. Hurray for us! I'm not crazy...see, other retailers get it.

I sold one unit to a sporting goods store and another to a small furniture retailer. Sales were very slow — more than slow, actually. I didn't have any new sales beyond these two. As I worked up the courage to knock on more doors, I would periodically call on my only two customers and see how things were going. Much to my surprise, I discovered that they weren't.

Hi Bob, how's the traffic data working out for you? What have you learned? How are you using the data? I would ask. The response floored me: "Uh, traffic data...yah, right, we should really look at that stuff – in all honesty, we haven't looked at that stuff for a long time."

## What the...?

"Why did you buy the traffic counter if you're not going to look at the data?" I wondered to myself. This was my first experience with the widespread fact that having a traffic counter doesn't mean you're actually using the data in a meaningful way. Sadly, this has been a recurring theme even to this day.

The first incarnation of HeadCount was an abject failure. I simply couldn't convince enough retailers to buy our traffic counters and so, despite stumbling upon a few more sales here and there over the years, the HeadCount business just wasn't much of a business.

My college buddy/business partner and I moved on – he went on to an engineering career, and I eventually became the Vice President of Sales and Marketing for the Canadian arm of finance software company Intuit, makers of Quicken, TurboTax, and QuickBooks.

Intuit was a great company to work for. The company was always searching for customer insights to make better products. Collecting data, analyzing results, making informed decisions – very analytical. It wore off on me.

In 2003, I had been with Intuit for almost eight years and I felt it was time for a change. My boss, the CEO Bruce Johnson, suggested a one-year sabbatical. I accepted and set out to clear my head and recalibrate life. It didn't last long.

## Mall insights

With a little money in the bank (thanks to some good fortune with Intuit stock options) and time on my hands, I found myself whiling away the early days of my sabbatical wandering the gigantic West Edmonton Mall (at the time the world's biggest). As I strode the expansive walkways, I noticed that most retailers didn't have traffic counters.

It had been about ten years since HeadCount was born, and apparently not much had changed – retailers obviously still didn't see the importance of tracking traffic and measuring conversion. "What's wrong with this picture?" I wondered.

Just before I left Intuit, we were working on a difficult problem: how do you turn shrink-wrap software like QuickBooks into a service?

QuickBooks is fantastic small business management software, almost too good. Every year we would release a new version, but as the years went on, it became more and more of a challenge to convince existing users to upgrade to the latest version. They loved the existing version and just didn't see the need to buy an upgrade.

We figured that if we could somehow turn QuickBooks software into a service, then we would have something that customers would continue to pay for as it continued to evolve.

While we never completely solved this before I left on sabbatical, the thinking was still very much fresh in my mind while I wandered the mall. Turning software into a service was difficult, but what about traffic counting and conversion analytics?

Thinking back to my early experiences with HeadCount, I realized that retailers often struggled with working with the data, and they sure didn't like spending money on buying traffic counters. So, instead of selling traffic counters, what if we install our own traffic counters, then we collect the data, analyze it, interpret the results, and provide the retailer with detailed management reporting from store-level, districts, and regions, all the way up to executive dashboards – and we do it all as a monthly service?

## HeadCount *redux*

Based on this new model, HeadCount was reincarnated as an analytics company specializing in retail traffic and customer conversion analytics. Three months into my sabbatical, I called my boss and informed him that I wouldn't be returning from my sabbatical. I had found what I wanted to do: pursue retail traffic and customer conversion analytics and re-launch HeadCount.

Without the need to buy expensive equipment, it was easier to get retailers onboard with HeadCount, but surprisingly it was still a very hard sell. Nonetheless, we landed a small number of clients and, now as newly minted traffic and customer conversion analysts, we pored over the data, creating reports, revising them, improving them.

We looked at their data as if it were our own, trying to find the critical insights and what they meant. For example, we would map the conversion rate sags that were occurring in the stores at particular times of the day — and encourage the retail managers to review staffing schedules during these periods. It worked. Conversion rates and sales improved.

We would overlay advertising and promotional schedules on traffic and conversion charts to help clients' marketers understand the impact of their promotions. We even overlaid weather data so that our clients could truly understand the impact weather was having on their business, if any. We learned so much about analyzing traffic and conversion data and began to develop our own methodologies and approaches to this new science of traffic and conversion analysis.

And as far as we could tell, no one was doing it the way we were — and they still aren't today.

## When Retail Customers Count

In 2005, as a way to engage retail executives in the dialog about traffic and customer conversion analysis, I wrote *When Retail Customers Count* – the first book dedicated to traffic and customer conversion. The book served as an important platform on which we built HeadCount into the leading traffic and conversion analytics company it is today.

Our client list expanded to include some of the leading retailers in North America. The more clients we had, the more data we had to analyze, the more advanced and refined our unique brand of traffic and conversion analytics became – and it continues to evolve to this day.

## HeadCount today

Over the last eight years, my dedicated team of traffic and conversion analysts and I have analyzed literally thousands of retailer data sets and have produced countless traffic and conversion reports and presentations. Our clients have come to rely upon these reports to understand what's going on in their business, how their stores are performing, and, more importantly, how they can perform better.

It's now been over six years since the publication of *When Retail Customers Count*, and now there's so much more to say – new insights, methods and techniques for analyzing this critical data, and new ways for putting it to practical use.

This stuff just seems to get better and better.

Yet the juxtaposition of these great advancements in the analysis and use of traffic and conversion data with the persistent obliviousness of retail executives is excruciating. Most retailers today still don't track traffic or measure customer conversion in their stores, and they're doing themselves a significant disservice. This book is my way of making the case for traffic and conversion – hopefully, in a compelling and interesting way.

# Deeper exploration

Unlike my first book, **this book is a deeper exploration of how all retailers can leverage these powerful analytics to improve sales performance, minimize costs and gain a competitive edge**. Going far beyond the ABCs of traffic and conversion analytics, this book uncovers why retailers struggle with these vital metrics and how you can overcome the challenges — and put the insights that come from traffic and conversion data to practical use in your business today.

# Rest of the book

I wrote this book with retail executives in mind. While you will find a multitude of charts, graphs and tables, please don't think this is a book about "analytics." The graphs and charts help me tell the traffic and conversion story in a vivid, visual way that words alone could not convey. All of the examples contained in this book are based on real retailer data. As is so often the case, reality is far more interesting than fiction ever could be.

In Part I, I'll provide important context about these metrics and challenge the skeptics head-on. This section will describe the many unique and powerful insights that only traffic and conversion analytics can deliver – insights that even the most sophisticated business information or CRM system cannot.

Also, I'll use traffic and conversion to poke gaping holes in the industry's collective belief that year-over-year, same-store (or "comp") sales is the metric by which success or failure is measured. And, for those who believe that mystery shopping and customer satisfaction surveys provide all the in-store insight you need to deliver the ultimate customer experience, I'll show you how wrong you can be. Finally, I will discuss the sometimes confusing topic of retail traffic counter technology – in non-technical terms.

As compelling as I think my arguments are, I'm not asking you to rely solely upon the words of a conversion evangelist like me. So I've invited some additional voices to join the choir in singing the praises of conversion. I call them *Conversion Champions*, and you need to hear what they have to say. Their remarks and opinions appear in Part I.

In Part II, I'll demonstrate how critical insights can be extracted from traffic and conversion data. From the pitfalls of calculating conversion rates to pinpointing what a missed opportunity looks like, you'll see it all here. And I'll show you how traffic and conversion analytics can have a profound impact on two of the most important areas of your business: staffing and advertising.

In Part III, I'll talk about accountability, leverage and action. Having more metrics, even great ones like conversion, won't make your business better. *The magic is in turning the insights into action and this can happen only if the insights are "consumed,"* so I'll talk about what it takes to create a "conversion culture."

Ownership is another important topic. Who among your executive team should "own" traffic and conversion? Apolitically and uncompromisingly, I'll describe how each and every executive seated around your boardroom table should — no, make that must — use traffic and conversion insights to help him or her contribute to better performance in each area of responsibility.

Finally, I'll present the best practices in the use of traffic and conversion analytics, and, as part of this discussion, I'll also talk about why so many of you have struggled with this – there are many reasons, and you are not alone.

# Why you should read this book

*Conversion: The Last Great Retail Metric* is for everyone who makes decisions in retail organizations – from the CEO and each of the executives seated around the boardroom table to all those who aspire to be there. The ideas presented in this book will change the way you think about performance and will offer new ways for you and your team to leverage the powerful insights that come from traffic and customer conversion data, in order to *make better decisions, optimize expenses, drive sales performance in your stores and give you a competitive edge.*

This book isn't for just big retailers or retailers in specific categories. It's for all retailers, regardless of the number of locations you have or what you sell. If you already have traffic counters in your stores, great, this book will show you how to get more out of your investment. If you don't have traffic counters in all your stores, or you are struggling to drive results in your business with traffic and conversion analytics, this book was written especially for you. And while I wrote this book with retailers in mind, I hope that retail educators, consultants, and industry experts will also be convinced that it's time traffic and conversion be given the full credit that they are rightly due, regarded not as nice-to-haves, but as must-haves.

Traffic is vital. Conversion is great. Read on.

# Part 1

## Traffic and Customer Conversion – Context

# Chapter 1.1

## What this tells you that you don't already know

*What will this tell me I don't already know?* This is what many retailers ask me. They simply don't believe that counting traffic and measuring customer conversion will tell them anything they don't already know. Or, I guess, anything else worth knowing.

The answer lies in the basic dynamics of retail. Consider: Every day customers visit your stores <u>intending</u> to make a purchase. Your advertising was successful – it got prospects to <u>your</u> store despite the myriad of choices they have. Congratulations. These prospects wandered the store, looked at products, engaged one of your sales associates, and they may have even made it all the way to your check-out, but then, for some reason, decided not to buy. The sale is lost. And worse, you will never even know.

To repeat: *Every hour of every day, prospects visit your stores but leave without making a purchase – despite the fact that they intended or were predisposed to buy.* Over the course of weeks, months and years, these lost prospects add up. Customer "leakage" can represent hundreds of thousands, even millions of lost sales opportunities. These "unconverted" prospects are not captured in your POS data; they rarely fill out your customer service surveys – they just leave. And you will never know.

And worse: Not only do these lost prospects represent an immediate lost sale, but even more insidiously, you'll never know how many other people they tell about their unsuccessful trip to your store.

Traffic and conversion analytics fundamentally answer two very simple but critical questions: How many people visit your stores? And what percent of these visitors actually makes a purchase?

For some of you, this might seem a little underwhelming – how can knowing the answers to these two simple, innocuous questions possibly make any difference in your business? If you have never tracked traffic and conversion in your stores, you have no idea just how profoundly these basic but truly great metrics will transform you and your company. Not only will they make a difference, they will change the way you measure performance, make decisions and generally, run your business.

As one retailer put it, "I couldn't image running my retail operation without traffic and conversion data." What does he know that most retailers don't?

It seems to me that in the over-analyzed world of business today, the simple has been overlooked. Traffic counts and conversion rates are simple measures, and that's in part what makes them so useful and essential "Sophisticated" and "important" have somehow come to mean that the data must be incomprehensible and voluminous. This insane thinking has caused retailers to lose focus on what's truly important and what they intuitively know – *driving prospects into the store and then serving them in a way that translates into a sale is what retailing is all about.*

Why, how and where this basic message got lost, I cannot tell. But it has, and retailers of every size, shape and description are starting to rediscover traffic and customer conversion, the "corn flakes" of retail analytics.

# Decision making – the glut and the gut

Retailers are awash in data. As information systems have evolved, retailers have embraced technology and the multitude of systems that provide better, faster information. With a cornucopia of information at your fingertips, the theory goes, you will be able to make better decisions, run your businesses better and deliver better performance.

While the technological advances in information systems used by retailers and the resultant ability to produce mountains of data are irrefutable (and no doubt have had a positive impact on retailers' ability understand their businesses), the downside has been a torrent of data and information flowing into the executive suite. So prolific and continuous is the amount of data available to retail executives today that the problem has evolved from how to get the data to what to do with all the data. To which I would add – is this even the right data?[1]

Despite the unprecedented penetration of technology and the flood of data available to retailers, decision making still largely depends on an executive's gut rather than the information glut. While gut will always naturally play a role in executive decision making, retailers need the right data to help guide and validate decisions.

## Retail metrics – the critical few vs. irrelevant many

What are the critical metrics that retail executives rely upon to make decisions? With data dashboards brimming with a dizzying array of indices and stats, all presented in massive PowerPoint decks, with screen transitions that create a kaleidoscope of curious, colorful and important looking graphs and charts, what is the executive (and the cascade of functional and front-line managers, for that matter) to rely upon?

One way to solve the 'meaningfulness' problem of having too much data has been, perversely, to summarize it and package it in an interesting and engaging way, in the hope of making it somehow more relevant. In many cases, to the detriment of all stakeholders, style prevails over substance.

While it would be entirely heretical to advocate the elimination of the mass of "quant-metrics" that retail executives have become addicted to, it is completely rational and reasonable to propose a distillation of the multitude of metrics to a critical few.

Traffic and Customer Conversion, two of the most fundamental and insightful metrics in retailing – great metrics, in fact – should be given their rightful place on the dashboards and in the collective consciousness of retail executives.

# Improving your average

In his seminal work, *Why We Buy—The Science of Shopping*,[2] Paco Underhill perfectly relates conversion rate to batting average. I have not found a better metaphor than this. As Underhill rightly pointed out, you can know that a batter averages 100 hits, but did he achieve this from 100 at bats or 1,000?

Excellent question.

Traffic and conversion analysis are to retailing what at-bats are to baseball – they're fundamental. This notion of batting average (or as I like to refer to it, performance versus opportunity), is, at a very fundamental level, what traffic and customer conversion analysis is all about. How did you do relative to the sales opportunity you had?

To the many retail executives who have asked me, "What does this tell me I don't already know?" I always start with performance vs. opportunity for three reasons: first, it's tremendously thought provoking; second, it's mildly antagonistic; and, third, measuring traffic and customer conversion is the only way to tell how you're performing against opportunity. All thoughtful retailers who are serious about their business should know how the business is performing and what's driving the results. So, when I ask a retail executive how his stores are performing compared to the sales opportunity, I often get a long glare, like a schoolmaster trying to stare down a petulant student.

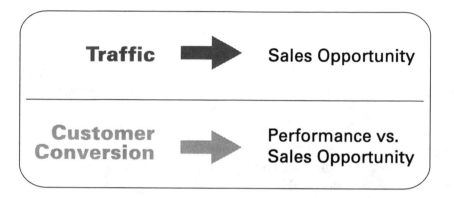

## The Framework

Store sales performance is relative. How does anyone know what good or great performance is, without a comparison to what was possible? You can't. But every day retailers do ask, "How are sales today?" Well, at the most basic level, sales are simply a function of three variables: (1) the number of prospects who visit your store, (2) the percentage of these visitors who make a purchase and (3) how much each one buys. That's it.

**Prospect Traffic x Conversion Rate % x Average Sale = Sales**

The absolute simplicity of this formula is difficult for some retailers to fully accept. For example, when the above formula was presented to the CEO of a large chain of men's clothing stores, his reaction was curious: "This stuff is too basic for us, we're a sophisticated operation, and we have PhDs on staff...this might be fine for a small retailer, but not a company like mine."

I've learned not to be surprised by what I hear from retail executives, but I mean, come on! How can a notion like performance versus opportunity apply only to small retailers and not "sophisticated" ones? It didn't make any sense and still doesn't. The epilogue to this story is that I did eventually conduct a study for this chain, and the executive was blown away by the insights.

The simple framework in the diagram below is a good visual representation of the essence of this book. The whole process starts with some form of traffic stimulus, like advertising. If your advertising is effective, it will deliver prospects to the store – a measurable traffic response. Once at the store, these prospects will have an experience of some kind, and if it's a positive one, the result will be a sale. The point is, there's a lot of stuff that happens between the moment a prospect first crosses your store's threshold and the consummation of the sale, and it behooves you to understand it.

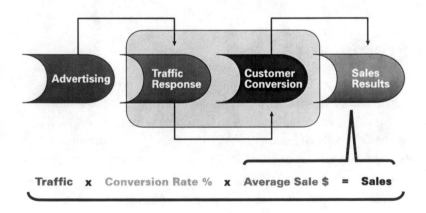

While it would be an overstatement to say that no retail executives understand the importance of traffic and customer conversion as critical performance metrics, the evidence strongly suggests that the majority of you either don't appreciate the true greatness of these metrics or significantly underestimate their value. In any event, you need to take another look at these two performance metrics and what they can help you learn about your business's performance.

## Business Intelligence has become Unintelligible

While I have no argument with the Business Intelligence industry, the problem seems to be that for many retailers, the sophisticated tools and systems offered by the purveyors of these systems are fundamentally beyond what most can put to practical use.[3]

Transaction data that comes from your point-of-sale (POS) system is the primary fuel that drives the business intelligence engine. These powerful tools enable you to slice and dice your transactional data in a multitude of ways to help you manage inventory, optimize distribution, and even deploy your staff – the value is undeniable. However, there's one glaring flaw: a reliance on sales transaction data as the primary input. *What can our business intelligence systems tell us of the sales we lost, when the only data it has at its disposal is the sales we made?*

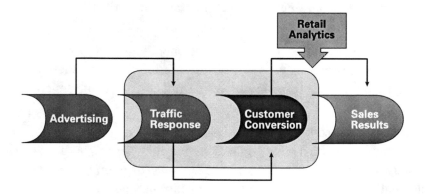

The pressure to be smarter, faster and better has never been more intense. Investing in business intelligence seems...intelligent. According to recent industry surveys business intelligence is the number one technology investment priority for retailers, and it's estimated that by 2014, retailers will spend in excess of $20 billion on this and other retail technologies.[4]

But the mere fact that you invest a huge sum in information systems and business intelligence doesn't mean you're seeing the value. In fact, more often than not, you don't. According to one survey of retailers, there was a huge gap between the value retailers expected to get from these systems and the actual value realized.[5] Given the money, time and attention the retail industry is collectively devoting to business intelligence and analytics, why aren't retailers getting more value?

## Traffic and Customer Conversion – meat and potatoes analytics

Analytics is a hot topic. Businesses across the board are turning to analytics to look for ways to perform better and gain a competitive edge. But don't take my word for it: investigate it for yourself. I highly recommend two books: *Competing on Analytics: The New Science of Winning* by Thomas H. Davenport and Jeanne G. Harris and *Analytics at Work: Smart Decisions, Better Results* by Davenport, Harris and Robert Morison.[6]

While your head will spin excitedly as you read about all the great ways analytics can be leveraged in your organization (mine did), I am merely suggesting that, for retailers, analyzing traffic and customer conversion should be at the very top of your analytics wish list.

Traffic and customer conversion analytics focus on what happens before the transaction is recorded in your POS system – if it ever is. That's what is especially powerful about traffic and conversion: Together, they tell us something about the sale we almost had; they give us a perspective on what might have been.

It all starts with traffic. If prospects don't visit your store, you have no chance at making a sale, so understanding prospect visitation is vital to understanding the opportunity. If you rely on advertising as a primary traffic catalyst, then your advertising impact can and should be largely measured by its ability to drive prospect traffic into your stores.

Once these prospects have arrived, then what happens? If they have a successful customer experience, then the end result should be a sale. But, if for whatever reason, the prospect does not buy, you will never know. What makes customer conversion truly great is that *it is the only measure that can quantify your sales potential.* It measures what your POS can't see – your missed opportunities, about which most retailers have almost no information.[7]

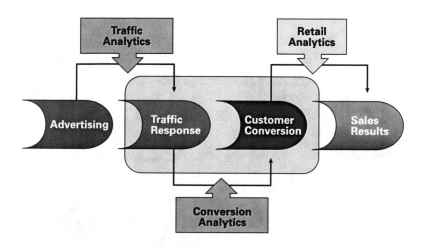

The idea of measuring store traffic is not new. Electronic traffic counters have been available since the 1970's; terms like "conversion rate" and "close rate" have been part of the retail lexicon for decades. So why, then, are they the most misunderstood and underused analytics in retailing today? For retailers who take great pride in their sophisticated information systems, analytical prowess, and ability to regurgitate vast quantities of data, I have two simple questions: how many prospects visited your stores yesterday and what percentage of the visitors actually made a purchase? Even the most brilliant analyst cannot script a query to extract answers to these fundamental questions if the system doesn't contain traffic and conversion data.

# What online retailers always knew

Without the physicality of the store environment to rely upon for insights, it seems that online retailers had no choice but to focus on the data they capture from the website – their virtual store. So perhaps it's not surprising that when it comes to analytics, brick-and-mortar retailers are playing catch-up.[8]

Two of the most fundamental metrics in online retailing are website traffic and conversion rate.[9] If your chain has a website (seriously, does anyone not?), you have likely seen a dashboard with a stat or KPI referring to website traffic and conversion. If your chain has a call center, again, calls received will undoubtedly be a KPI that is very familiar to you. Traffic and conversion play such key roles in understanding the performance of these e-channels, so why do they get so little attention as measures for the brick and mortar businesses? These great metrics are at least as important, if not more so, for brick and mortar stores.

**Retail Store KPIs**

- Comparable Store Sales — "Comp Sales"
- Sales per square foot
- Sales per employee
- Average sale value
- Units per sale
- Margin
- Inventory turnover

- Customer satisfaction
- Repeat purchase
- Market/Category Share

**Web Key Performance Indicators**

- Site visits
- Unique visits
- Page views
- Time spent on site
- Buyer conversion rate

Ironically, even the most computer illiterate retail executive can recite website traffic and conversion statistics like a Google pro, but when it comes to measuring traffic and conversion in his own stores, somehow the logic doesn't apply — or at least doesn't seem as compelling.

During a meeting I had with a major department store chain, the CEO was absolutely gushing with pride about a recent press acknowledgement listing his chain's website as one of the most visited retail websites in the country. At the time, his website was getting about 30,000 visits a month. This may not seem like a big number today, but at the time it was truly impressive.

Then I showed him the results of a traffic study we conducted for his marketing team. On the basis of the traffic counts logged in a sample of his stores, we estimated that chain-wide, his brick and mortar stores received <u>hundreds of millions</u> of visits annually. You tell me: which is more important?

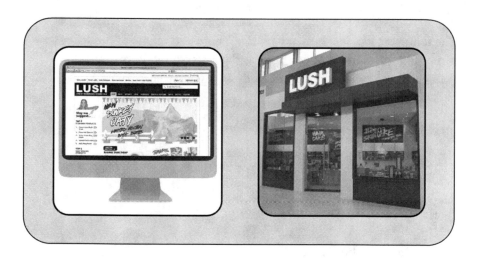

Measuring store traffic is essentially the same as measuring website traffic: we're measuring the number of people who "hit" the front door instead of the main page on the website. And just as there can be mis-hits to the website when people make a wrong keystroke and end up on your website unintentionally, there are mis-hits to your storefront as well. These mis-hits are traffic counts that don't represent true prospects, e.g., children visiting the store with their parents. The fact that there are mis-hits doesn't mean you shouldn't measure them, just as you do for your website. It's funny — executives will often question the accuracy of the electronic store traffic counts, but they never seem to question the validity of the hits to their websites – obviously, every web hit is legitimate. Not!

Store traffic is just as important as website traffic. I would argue that it's even more critical. While websites can be scaled up relatively inexpensively  by adding servers and bigger hard drives to handle the extra volume, increases in store traffic mean you need to hire more staff – a big and costly decision.

## Questions that only measuring traffic and conversion can answer

The following list, far from exhaustive, represents some of the more important questions that confront and confound retailers – but that traffic and customer conversion analysis can answer.

- How are we performing compared to the sales opportunity?
- Which are my best performing stores?
- Where and when am I losing sales?
- Does my advertising work?
- Is staff scheduled optimally?
- Are my sales associates effective?
- Are my store hours right?

I realize that some of you may still be skeptical. That's OK, I understand. You've been around retailing a long time, and you've seen and heard it all. Perhaps you've even dabbled in traffic and conversion in the past. All I ask is that you keep an open mind and give me an opportunity to make the case for why traffic counting is vital and customer conversion is the last great retail metric.

Before I tell you everything I know about traffic and customer conversion, there are some people I would like you to meet. They are a collection of retail executives, experts and academics whom I call Conversion Champions – and you really need to hear their stories.

# Chapter 1.2

## Conversion Champions

In my discussions with literally hundreds of retail executives over the years, I continue to be surprised when I come across one who truly does "get" traffic and customer conversion. And what's really strange about our conversations, besides our vehemently agreeing about its importance, is the fact that they are surprised that I'm surprised they get it. They seem to be just as perplexed as I am that all retailers don't use traffic and customer conversion analytics today.

It has been and continues to be an ongoing obsession of mine to try to understand these curious retail leaders who somehow innately understand the importance of measuring traffic and customer conversion in their stores and use these data to run their businesses on a daily basis. When I ask them, as retailers, to help me understand why they get it while the majority of their colleagues apparently don't, they can't seem to provide a reasonable explanation for it either – they almost seem even more surprised than I am. "Most retailers aren't doing this? Really?"

So it's clear that this is just not a "retailers don't get it" thing — because some retailers really do, furthermore, it's not necessarily any particular type or size of retailer who gets it more than others. Sure, some retail categories (apparel, for example) have a higher penetration rate of traffic counters than others, but owning traffic counters and really using the insights in a meaningful way are two entirely different propositions.

Some of the most sophisticated users of traffic and customer conversion analytics are small chains or even mom-and-pop businesses; some of the most closed minded and behind the curve are the biggest and supposedly sophisticated mega-chains. I have developed some theories as to why retailers haven't collectively embraced traffic and customer conversion, and I explain more fully in Chapter 3.4 *Why some retailers get it –and others don't*. If you're dying to know, feel free to jump ahead.

For the time being, however, I'd like to further examine some of these most curious retailers who have somehow found their way – this exclusive group I call *Conversion Champions*. How did they get there? What were the challenges? How did they overcome them? Why do they think traffic and customer conversion are important? The answers are in their own words.

While I've come across maybe a dozen retailers on whom I would bestow the extraordinary title of "champion," I have no doubt that there are more than a dozen. Perhaps two dozen, but not more than three. When you consider that there are thousands of retail chains in North America, representing over 1.5 million retail establishments, this is truly an exclusive group.

I am profoundly grateful to the three Conversion Champions you are about to meet and who agreed to share their stories. I hope you are as well.

Not everyone I reached out to would agree to talk to me on the record. I respect that. However, I have also modified my definition of what a Conversion Champion truly is – it's not only someone who is a leader in the understanding and application of traffic and conversion: it's an executive who also has the confidence and conviction to tell others. So, in this regard, I submit to you that the list of potential Conversion Champions is even more exclusive than I had first thought.

First, Eric Wagstaff, Director of Organization Development for footwear retailer ALDO Group. Next, Diane Blois, Vice President Human Resources for music and entertainment retailer HMV. And finally, Peter Scully, Senior Vice President of Sales and Operations for Black's Photo Corporation.

Now, on to the *Conversion Champions*.

# ALDO Group

You would be hard pressed to visit a major mall in North America without seeing an ALDO store. With over 900 stores in North America alone and more than 1,500 stores in some 50 countries world-wide, ALDO Group Inc. has become a $1.5 –billion-a-year global force in footwear retailing.

In a category with no shortage of big competitors and new ones sprouting up every day, being fleet-of- foot has certainly been part of what's made ALDO Group so successful. From adjusting shoes styles, and product mixes to store concepts, staying ahead of ever changing trends is critical.

ALDO management isn't afraid of change – in fact, they thrive on it. If something isn't working, they change it – fast.

It takes nothing less than constant renewal to successfully keep up with the fickle, fashion conscious 18-30-year-old market that ALDO serves so effectively.

With lighting fast product development cycles, world-wide direct manufacturing sources, and a highly efficient supply chain, ALDO Group executes brilliantly. Nowhere is this more apparent than in their retail stores where traffic and conversion play an important role.

Unlike the other conversion champions featured in this chapter, for ALDO Group, conversion is a team sport. There are many people who could be designated as a conversion champion. So, instead of featuring just one leader, ALDO preferred to share their experiences about traffic and conversion as a collective, with Eric Wagstaff their Director of Organizational Development as our guide.

## We need to understand our business better

ALDO Group is a company constantly striving to improve and deliver better business results. They also believe in basing decisions on data; ALDO Group is a data driven organization, and they had plenty of it to analyze.

To run the business, management looked at all sorts of detailed transactional data including comparative same-store sales, sales trending, and sales by key category down to the SKU. As adept as ALDO management was at analyzing sales and transactional data, they realized that this didn't provide the insights they needed. It wasn't enough to know what was sold, management wanted to understand the *underlying sales drivers* and that's when they turned to traffic and conversion.

The decision to install traffic counters in the stores started as a small project with only about 20 locations at first. But things changed quickly. An edict from the company's visionary President put traffic counting and conversion on the entire organizations' collective radar screen, and there was no turning back. The company went from a 20 store pilot to chain-wide rollout in less than two years.

## Getting "clean" data

According to Eric Wagstaff there were a number of issues that the company had to overcome if they were going to get managers to use traffic and conversion data. The first challenge: count accuracy. "We had problems with the quality of the traffic count. Sometimes there would be no counts, sometimes the counts were doubled, sensors would get blocked, and it was a challenge."

Management saw the potential of traffic and conversion data, but they also realized that it would only be useful if it was reliable. To solve the data quality issue, ALDO management dedicated resources to focus on it. The operations team started reviewing the traffic data on a weekly basis to look for anomalies and conduct hygiene when needed. The effort paid off. Confidence in the data grew and management was able to start putting the insights to use.

## Conversion – A new KPI is born

As an organizational development expert, Eric knew that getting the field managers to truly buy-in wasn't going to be easy – even with executive support. "Getting buy-in from the field was critical and we had to work hard to make the case for this new KPI we were introducing." The task wasn't made any easier with all the data and technical issues they initially had to deal with.

But even with the data issues under control, there were a barrage of questions from the field management team: *How important is this? Should it take priority over other initiatives? How will managers be measured? How will we know if the data is right before we measure managers?* All good and fair questions.

For ALDO, an important part of the execution plan was education. Numerous training sessions, conference calls, and store visits, were conducted with not only the senior field management group, but also with individual store managers to help them understand the value and importance of traffic and conversion.

Over time, the message started to take hold and managers began to truly buy-in as they saw their own store's results improve. As one Store Manager said, "WOW...this is really powerful information; I'm using it more and my store's doing much better because of it."

*"Wow...this is really powerful information...my store's doing much better because of it."*

## Keeping the Conversion train rolling

When you have the president of the company looking at conversion rates on a regular basis, as is the case at the ALDO Group, it's easier to keep managers on track with it than otherwise. However, to keep managers really focused, you need to do even more.

Creating incentives around conversion was an important mechanism for maintaining momentum and keeping it top-of-mind among managers. To that end, the company's top-tier incentive program that gives managers the opportunity to earn prizes on an annual basis and financial bonuses on a monthly basis was modified to include conversion. In fact, the program today is heavily influenced by store-level conversion results.

Traffic and conversion have become part of what managers do on a day-to-day basis. For example, Store Managers have access to daily traffic reports that show traffic for the current week, the previous three weeks, along with various key sales stats including their "customer-to-staff ratio" – an important measure that all Store Managers must understand. ALDO management realized that when this ratio got too large, it resulted in lower conversion rates and missed sales.

Head office provides Store Managers with a scheduling tool; however they are encouraged to look at their store's traffic data and adjust staff schedules if warranted.

Conversion is a heavily emphasized message in the ALDO store manager training program today. Every new manager gets trained on key metrics and the factors that drive business results in the store. According to Eric, it's important to reinforce the conversion message when a new manager joins the team. "A new manager may be happy because his sales went up, but if his conversion rate went down, the store didn't do as well as it could have. We would say, 'congratulations, you had a great day, but you missed opportunities.'"

## Measuring potential

Although the company has been tracking traffic and measuring conversion for about nine years, it's been in the past four years in particular where conversion has become a core metric fundamental to how the company operates.

In fact, traffic and conversion have become key elements of the business modeling and planning process. The ALDO team looks at traffic, conversion rate, and average sale as underlying sales drivers and incorporates these variables in forecasts.

For business planning purposes, conversion is truly vital at ALDO. "Conversion is one of the true performance measures that indicate performance versus last year, last month and what the current potential is." In continuous improvement, conversion is an important area of focus. And after all these years, executive support hasn't waned; conversion rates are studied constantly.

> *"Conversion is one of the true measures of performance...and potential."*

## Do the math and be patient

For ALDO, seeing the value of traffic and conversion came quickly. "Conceptually it didn't take too long to understand the value of this information, but the organization as a whole really started to 'get it' in year two when year-over-year comparable traffic and conversion results were available."

The math also makes it very compelling: the impact of even a modest increase in conversion rate over 900 stores is staggering. So, notwithstanding the investment in time, money and energy to get their traffic and conversion program off-the-ground successfully, the upside from improving conversion rates and saving on payroll made it all worthwhile.[1]

> *"The impact of even a modest increase in conversion rate over 900 stores is staggering."*

But despite all the advantages ALDO has, like executive support, field manager buy-in, and a dedicated store operations team to keep the data clean and flowing to stakeholders, it still takes time and effort. "Introducing a new KPI like conversion and slipping it into the culture doesn't happen overnight – it's an ongoing process."

The ALDO team remains vigilant, not only in keeping these important metrics top-of-mind for their managers, but in their pursuit of continuous improvement and delivering better business results. Traffic and conversion metrics are important parts of the process.

## Advice for retailers

Given that so many retailers don't track traffic or measure conversion in their stores, I asked the ALDO team what they thought of the idea of running a retail operation without the benefit of traffic and conversion data. Their answer came in the form of the following questions:

- *How do you know how productive you are?*
- *How will you know if your staff resources are scheduled right?*
- *How will you know how your stores are performing compared to their opportunities?*

Good questions. I wonder the same.

For ALDO, traffic and conversion are now so solidly entrenched in their business, that it's hard for them to imagine doing without.

When asked what specific sage advice he could offer other retailers, Eric was concise: understand the data before you rush to conclusions. "Make sure you understand the data. Build up some history and then use these benchmarks to set realistic and achievable goals –and do it individually by store."

Finally, reflecting on the trials and tribulations of initial rollout and getting managers to accept the new conversion KPI, as someone who has obviously been-there-done-that, he says matter-of-factly, *"Get the bugs out...then get the buy-in."*

# HMV Canada

HMV Canada is part of the United Kingdom-based HMV Group that today operates some 400 entertainment stores and websites in the UK, Ireland, Canada, Hong Kong and Singapore.

With some 125 stores from coast to coast and over 2,000 Associates, HMV Canada is the leading entertainment retailer in the country.

Just as the music industry has been transformed by online music, so has HMV. Going far beyond selling music, today HMV carries a wide array of entertainment products, including music, video games, DVDs, books, iPods, accessories, and clothing. And their product offerings continue to expand and evolve.

# Diane Blois, Vice President, Human Resources, has been with the

company for 13 years, most of these as head of Human Resources. Diane has overall responsibility for all facets of the HR program — scheduling, payroll, benefits, employee relations, training, recruitment, and performance management.

Recently, customer service and in-store experience were added to her portfolio.

The decision to start tacking store traffic and measuring customer conversion was not the result of some grand strategic plan or an epiphany on the part of a visionary CEO; rather, it came about innocuously, as part of a regular senior manager's team meeting. The discussion turned to data – what they had, what they didn't have, and what they thought they might need to be able to better service customers, drive sales results, and, ultimately, get away from the decision making by "gut," which in 2004 was all too common. The collective wisdom of the senior team was that traffic and customer conversion were important, missing pieces of the puzzle.

In 2005 traffic counters were installed chain-wide, and the data started to flow – lots of it. At first, the senior team members were the primary recipients of the data. Collectively and individually they poked and prodded the voluminous streams of traffic and conversion data, trying to find ways to make sense of what they were seeing. Very early on in the process, they made the data available to all managers via the company's intranet, and staff members were encouraged to look at it for themselves.

At this stage, beyond the senior team at Head Office, no one was really talking much about traffic or conversion. And while all managers had access to the data and were encouraged to look at it, there was no formal training available to help managers use it. At least initially, senior management was content with letting the data ferment, allowing it to slowly sink in so managers could get used to it. Unfortunately, traffic and conversion became just more data that further complicated an already significant mass of metrics and data that managers had at their disposal. While there was a "community belief" in the value of traffic and conversion, they were far from being consumed in a meaningful way.

## Taking it to the next level

As Diane put it, "Data is just data. What's valuable is the story the data tells you....So early on it took a while to get used to this...to understand what it meant...to digest what it was saying and then get a grip on what the story being told from traffic and conversion was. We needed time to figure out the plot that the data story was trying to tell us. It takes time."

First Diane and her colleagues needed to look at the data; then they needed to understand it – no small task, given the amount of dense, numerical data that traffic and conversion analysis produces. Once you have a handle on what the data is, the next task — and in many ways the more important one — is to figure out what to do with it.

It's this figuring-out part that led Diane and HR to get more involved. Like her colleagues, Diane believed that traffic and conversion data were valuable, but she also knew that she needed to find a way to present the data in a way that would enable managers to put it to use; she needed to find a way to help managers connect the dots, to put traffic and conversion in a context, so that they could easily and practically process it.

"There's so much information vying for top spot in a manager's brain. I needed to find ways to help them sort it out, and I was concerned that just adding traffic and conversion to the mix wasn't going to help matters – a retail manager's job is already tough enough."

To get the process started, Diane and her team developed and conducted training programs around delivering value to shoppers and how traffic and conversion data could help do that. She also realized that traffic and conversion were clearly tied to financial results, so she smartly weaved a financial training element into the overall concept.

With the benefit of the training, managers now had a good handle on traffic and conversion, and HMV was able to start to move the performance needle by holding managers and Associates accountable for customer conversion in their stores. Over time, mystery shop scores were replaced by customer conversion rates as the critical performance measure, and over the last two years, conversion has been formally integrated into performance appraisals and bonus plans — which helps keep it relevant.

# Daily scorecard was a game-changer.

Even after all the significant accomplishments, Diane and her colleagues believed that there was still more that could be done. So in 2009 they launched a new program to help take traffic and conversion (and store performance) to a whole level – daily performance scorecards. The innovative daily scorecards were developed specifically for HMV and intended to improve the company in three key areas that Diane and her team identified: (1) simplicity, (2) timeliness, and (3) "actionability."

As Diane put it, "We needed to not only sustain interest, but also enable managers to action the insights. The daily scorecard made a huge difference for us because it turned data into real, practical, tangible insights that spoke to each of us in a way he/she could understand." The simple one-page reports were e-mailed to each store by nine every morning and used basic charts and arrows showing how the store did yesterday, in traffic, conversion, average ticket and overall sales; the scorecards also indicated what today's targets and traffic and conversion patterns were likely to be.

Beyond presenting the analytics, there was a place on the report where Store Managers were required to comment on conversion sags from the prior day and to identify specific actions the store team could take to try to improve conversion today. Customer conversion became a team sport at HMV. The daily scorecard became the cornerstone of the entire program.

The HR team provided some basic instructions on how to read and use the daily scorecards when they first launched the program, but getting bogged down with too many instructions would have missed the point. As Diane said, "If all the managers and Associates ever do is look at which direction the arrows are pointing (e.g. conversion rate pointing down)...that's OK with me – they get it; they see the cause and effect, and they become part of the process in making changes to improve outcomes."

There were two unintended but very positive side-effects of the daily scorecard program: (1) it brought store teams together and (2) it provided managers and Associates with a common language.

---

According to Diane, "Store staff started to talk about the results…'Traffic was strong, but conversion rates sagged between 7 PM and 9 PM I think we were short staffed on the till…so tonight we're going to make sure we have better coverage.' They got curious about the trends, and they began to self-diagnose and develop strategies and tactics based the reports — and then started seeing little wins. This brought store teams together more…than I ever realized it could."

Diane knew that the daily scorecard program was making a difference, but if there was any doubt, it completely evaporated one morning a couple of months into the program, when a data transmission glitch caused the daily scorecard to be late. "The daily scorecards usually arrive in a store's in-boxes by 8:46 every morning – but it didn't on this day. By 9 AM, I was inundated with calls and e-mails from store personnel wondering where their daily scorecard was – this is authentic engagement. These managers totally get it."

Programs are just programs unless store staff does something with them. As Diane rightly points out, "As a large retail organization, there's only so much we can do to get meaningful engagement down to the store level. You can create programs, launch them, provide training, and even nag managers to comply, but if they don't see the value, if they don't understand the story, they won't use it – and you can't force them to use it."

## Sustaining a culture of conversion

By any measure HMV's deployment and use of traffic and conversion analytics is a success: however, over time, even the most successful programs can lose their efficacy. The retailers who have achieved market leadership in the use of traffic and conversion have also accomplished something very difficult – conversion has become part of their corporate culture.

> *"Conversion has absolutely become part of the culture at HMV. It's allowed us to 'open the books' to our staff in a way that is understandable and digestible...it's become part of how they speak about and understand what's happening in their stores."*

According to Diane, "Conversion has absolutely become part of the culture at HMV. It's allowed us to open the books to our staff in a way that is understandable and digestible; it feeds into our managers' natural curiosity about the business of their stores and their need to achieve; it's become part of how they speak about and understand what's happening in their stores." At HMV, conversion is owned by everyone, and everyone on the team plays a role in serving customers and ultimately driving customer conversion. "Thinking about customer conversion has become as normal as putting on your staff T-shirt... it's just what we do here," says Diane.

## Advice to retailers who don't

As for retailers who don't track traffic or measure customer conversion in their stores, says Diane, "Why wouldn't you do it? There is such a pot of information and value sitting there for Store Managers, Marketing, Operations... I can't think of a single reason why a retailer wouldn't do this."

Driving store performance requires management to constantly look for new ways to improve, to find an edge. We didn't wake up one day and have an "a-ha" moment about traffic and conversion, thinking that it was some kind of silver bullet. There wasn't just one question or answer; there were many along the way...we were looking for more... [because] you can't do the same thing over and over...you need to do something different."

Diane and her team at HMV do many things right, but a key lesson she would pass along to other retailers is simply to remember that the process takes time to evolve and that the *single most important thing the senior management team did was to remain persistent.* They stuck with it, kept poking and prodding and trying new things, and eventually traffic/conversion data paid off in ways they hadn't even imagined – now they can't image being without it.[2]

# Black's Photo Corporation

Black's Photo Corporation is a leading retailer of digital imaging products and services, with 114 locations across Canada. With an 80-year history, this thriving operation, now part of TELUS Corporation, has maintained its "family business" feel, with a mission to be the industry's leader in helping customers establish a new routine to capture, print, share and store their images. And this ideal hasn't changed since Black's became part of TELUS Corporation, one of the country's leading wireless providers. In fact, it's a great fit. The advent of digital technology has transformed the photography industry in profound ways. Today, more wireless devices have embedded high quality photo and video capabilities, so connecting the imaging business with wireless technologies and services just makes sense. And that's the Black's Photo of today.

# Peter Scully, Senior Vice President, Sales and Operations, at Black's Photo Corporation

is no stranger to technology. He spent most of his career working in technology retailing. Pete had a 22-year career with Radio Shack Canada that saw him move through the ranks from Store Manager to Regional Vice President and finally to Senior Vice President of Sales and Operations, responsible for over 450 corporate stores nationwide. He brings to his current position considerable technology retailing experience and a strong belief in the power of customer conversion.

## Conversion: the third way to grow

Peter's affinity for the power and importance of customer conversion started with a challenge. The CEO challenged his executive team to come up with ways to grow the business. As they went around the table, one executive chimed in, "Sell to more people." Another followed with "Sell more to each person"...and after what seemed to be a long silence, the CEO said, "We're missing an important third way to grow: sell to more of the people who are already in the store." This was Peter's first exposure to the notion of customer conversion, and the concept resonated powerfully.

By 2000, about 140 of the 453 corporate Radio Shack stores had traffic counters, but despite the CEO's challenge, the company wasn't yet doing much with the data. Peter says, "We started to look more closely at the data and calculate conversion rates, and initially it was met with a lot of resistance – in fact, the initial reaction was visceral. "Thirteen percent conversion? Impossible!" said one Regional Manager. "I've been in that store many times, and that Store Manager is good – the data can't be right'!" According to Peter, the initial efforts of getting the field managers engaged with conversion were tough. "People were defensive and initially spent way too much time trying to disprove the accuracy of traffic counts – and too little trying to improve conversion rates."

## The $5 million "a-ha" moment

Despite the struggles, Peter persevered. Part of what kept him going wasn't just the CEO's challenge – it was the math. "I took out a calculator and actually calculated what a 200 basis-point improvement in customer conversion rate would mean to the bottom line, and that's when I had my 'a-ha' moment." Peter determined that a modest improvement in conversion rate would deliver $5 million of incremental net profit, and that was the moment conversion because his personal cause.

## The Conversion roadshow

As much as he believed, Peter knew that it was critical to get his field management team onboard if the company was going to realize the gains his math showed. Peter rightly understood that he couldn't just force this down the collective throats of field managers – they needed to see the light.

As a way to keep conversion top-of-mind for everyone, Peter printed up little pocket reminder cards for all managers that included the basic formula that showed how conversion rate improvement could deliver $5 million extra net profit. But for Peter that wasn't enough – he took his conversion message on the road.

*"I literally took out a calculator and calculated what a 200 basis point improvement in customer conversion rate would mean to the bottom line – that's when I had my "a-ha" moment."*

Traveling across the country, Peter delivered countless presentations and talked about the importance of conversion. As part of the sessions, he would ask each Store Manager to do the math and calculate what an increase in conversion rate could mean to his or her store. Says Peter, "Once we got managers focused on their own conversion rates, that's when they started to get jazzed about it."

Peter got his managers to forget about trying to justify their conversion rate and instead focus their attention on improving conversion. If a store had a 12% conversion rate, get it to 14%, if another store had a 20% conversion rate, get it to 22%. The field managers started to get it, and that's when the results really started to show.

## BIG Wins

"My goal was to improve conversion rates across the board by 200 basis points. In the first 18 months, conversion rates improved by 300 basis points! A as impressive as these bottom-line results of conversion rate improvement were, the expense savings from labor optimization was another, somewhat surprising win...You have no idea how overstaffed and understaffed your stores are until you see traffic data – it's about timing, getting the right people in the right place...We saved close to $2 million in payroll expense just by better aligning our staff to traffic – that was huge!"

*"We improved our conversion rate by 300 basis points in 18 months."*

## Even champions can struggle.

As much success as Peter has had with conversion, it hasn't always been easy. Peter brought his conversion evangelism to Black's Photo about three years ago. He found an organization that clearly "got" traffic and conversion, with counters installed in a large percentage of the stores. But as Peter looked at what was being done with the data compared to what he knew was possible, he knew just what to do.

Black's was a different kind of retail environment, so he had to think carefully about what conversion meant. For example, many of the Black's stores include a production lab that produces prints. This service element created a very different conversion profile in the stores than Peter was accustom to, and Peter had to get his head around the "how" of it before he could get his field team engaged.

The other challenge Peter had was traffic count accuracy. The counters that Black's had were not ideally suited for the store, so data quality and reliability began to dominate the executive meetings. Says Peter, "Between the traffic counter issues, store layout and product changes, I had a hard time convincing the leadership team to get behind conversion – they just didn't believe the data."

Over time the data issues slowly got resolved, but there was still more to do. As much as Peter didn't enjoy data analysis, he found himself spending hours and hours painstakingly going through data and trying to make it make sense. Peter needed a simple but impactful way to represent the data to help managers use it to drive business results. With the help of a crack Regional Director, he rolled up his sleeves and produced some new reporting that included traffic and conversion. Then — you guessed it — he took it on the road, just as he had done before.

According to Peter, "It's not about the data you have...what matters is what you do with the data." Getting field managers in particular onboard is what ultimately leads to better business results. Peter and his Regional Director created a new manager-training program that included a talk on conversion — and took his traveling conversion show nation-wide.

Today, traffic and customer conversion analytics are a big part of daily operations at Black's, thanks in no small part to Pete and an executive team who know a good thing when they see it.

## Why doesn't every retailer do this?

Peter is a true Conversion Champion, so it's hard for him to think about running a retail operation without it. Says Peter, "Every Retail Operations leader should be a Conversion Champion!" While he has no exact answers for why all retailers aren't, his own experiences provide some powerful clues: "Even as someone who truly believes in this like I do, I can tell you it's not hard for these programs to get off track and fall into disuse... sketchy data, changes to store layouts, new products, and even management changes can all contribute."[3]

Beyond this, Peter offers one final thought for other retailers to consider: "I think retailers have an innate tendency to compare: stores, people, themselves to other chains...it's all about comparisons. With conversion it's not about comparisons; it's about *driving individual performance relative to oneself* – an 8% conversion rate might be good for one store, and a 35% conversion rate may be bad for another. It's about moving your own needle, and I think some retail executives have a hard time getting their heads around that."[3]

In the introduction of this book I mentioned that the retail industry collectively – including experts, consultants, and academics – was generally ambivalent about traffic and conversion. Still, there are Conversion Champions among the ranks of industry supporters.

These folks don't have any vested interest in traffic and conversion analytics or in selling traffic counters, but they do understand the criticality of traffic and conversion data, and they are not afraid to speak out and say so.

So in addition to the compelling stories from the retailers you just read, I've also included a collection of stories from a stellar group of industry experts who will provide their unique perspectives on traffic and customer conversion.

First, Larry Leibach, an expert in workforce management; next, Kevin Graff, an internationally recognized retail training expert; then, Dr. Bernard LeFange, a leader in mystery shop and customer experience, and last, Dr. Jay Swaminathan, a leading academic researcher.

# Workforce Management

 **Larry Leibach** is a Principal with **Workforce Insight**, a leading provider of strategic workforce management and consulting services. At Workforce Insight, Larry helps some of the largest, most well-known retailers leverage solutions to improve customer service, labor productivity, compliance, and customer conversion.

Larry is a seasoned veteran of the retail trade. He started his career with a ten-year stint at Target Corporation, then went on to Payless Shoe Source for another 20 years. At Payless, Larry began as a District Manager and moved on to Regional Manager. In that position he oversaw several hundred stores. From there, he moved on to a Head Office role in corporate retail operations administration and ultimately became Profit Improvement Director, overseeing projects across the entire organization.

It was in this role that he supervised the enterprise-wide implementation of a workforce management system across some 4,000 stores.

## Seeing is believing.

Larry's first exposure to traffic and conversion began with Payless. When he took the Head Office position, the company was in the process of installing traffic counters in about 15% of its stores. The vision was to gain insights from the traffic and conversion data from this representative group of sample stores, then apply them chain-wide. Initially the areas of interest included the impact of marketing on store traffic and of inventory on customer conversion.

Duane L. Cantrell, the visionary President of Payless at that time, was the catalyst for installing traffic counters. Cantrell strongly believed that traffic and conversion data could be incredibly useful information, so Larry found himself knee-deep in traffic counters, taking on the role of "implementer" for the traffic counter project. Like many retailers, Larry was at first skeptical that traffic and conversion information could be specific enough to be useful. "I was your typical retailer," he says.

In the early days, Larry had plenty to be skeptical about. One of the first concerns was data accuracy and validity. Early counters weren't nearly as accurate as they are today, but as technology evolved, Larry and his team gained confidence in the data. "With the data accuracy issues under control, we started slicing and dicing the data with focus on identifying and extracting the key insights."

## Four key levers – three-pronged approach

Once the traffic data was available, it was decided to break down the business into four key levers: traffic, conversion rate, units per transaction (UPTs), and average unit retail. The Payless leadership started to focus on and manage their business by these four levers and according to Larry, it got them away from "small thinking."

Historically, with only sales transaction data available, the company focused on increasing UPTs as a way to drive sales growth, but management realized that this approach wasn't delivering what they needed. "We discovered that we could increase UPTs over time, but this really didn't deliver big sales gains. In our case, Associates were adding on shoe shine sponges to a sale, which did increase units per transaction but did very little in the way of delivering meaningful sales growth."

*"We shifted focus to driving up customer conversion... that's where the real money started to materialize."*

According to Larry, "We just weren't selling any better or sharpening our skills in the aisles where the bigger dollar purchases were. So instead of focusing on UPTs, we shifted our attention to driving up customer conversion. That's where the real money started to materialize. That's when I became a believer!"

Armed with traffic and conversion data, Larry and his team set out to improve customer conversion rates with a three-pronged approach: first, they developed "customer engagement programs" designed to guide Associates' interactions with prospects; second, they implemented a formal workforce management system; and third, they used traffic counts as a way to allocate labor – that is, they staffed to traffic instead of to transaction counts. The synergy of those three changes, along with fine tuning the employee mix, incentives, and training, had a phenomenal result.

The customer engagement program and workforce management initiatives helped deliver improved customer conversion rates, turning Larry into a disciple for the value of traffic and customer conversion analysis. "Over a four-to-five year period, we dramatically improved conversion through the implementation of these programs, while delivering a clear picture of our business drivers."

## Staffing to traffic

According to Larry, the majority of retailers today use transaction data to forecast labor demand and create staff schedules. "Annually, Workforce Insight performs a benchmarking study and hosts the Retail WFM Leadership Summit to evaluate maturity and adoption of retail systems and processes for labor budgeting, forecasting, scheduling and customer conversion. Even with leading technology in place, many retailers are barely scratching the surface in leveraging the powerful data at their disposal. Relying on transaction data to schedule staff is a mistake. Most transaction data has been influenced by past circumstances: merchandising in-stock, promo pricing, staff availability, staff performance...it's all factored into the historical transaction data – the good, bad and ugly. You may have had a great week, but many factors contribute to sales outcomes. Traffic data, on the other hand, has not been influenced by these factors, and that's why it gives you the best, most unbiased future forecast to base your staff scheduling on." That's what makes it especially useful as a leading indicator.

*"Relying on transaction data to schedule staff is a mistake... traffic data gives you the best, most unbiased future forecast to base your staff scheduling on."*

Staffing to traffic causes you to think about the opportunity created by each customer walking in the door. As Larry points out, "Without traffic data, how can you ensure you are ready for and staffed for a consistent level of customer engagement?" He goes on to say, "Not only do you need to know the traffic opportunity, but you also need to understand the customer service requirements to produce a great customer experience and ultimately a sale. Most retailers don't know if they are funding this service level appropriately."

## Combining workforce management with traffic and conversion

While traffic, customer conversion, and workforce management are a natural fit, most retailers are not taking advantage of the insights and leverage that come from combining these critical systems. In Larry's experience, most are still using transaction-based data and other traditional KPIs to manage their labor. "Using transaction counts as a proxy for traffic counts just isn't precise enough; it's just not as scientific as it can and should be today. Traffic data helps you understand how you are capitalizing on the opportunity to bring closure to customers who are coming to your store – transactions don't."

In Larry's experience, there's still a lot of educating that needs to be done with respect to workforce management and the use of traffic and conversion analysis. In his work with domestic and global retailers, Larry typically recommends that organizations start with a proof of concept and then evolve toward full implementation over time. "There are many moving parts: staffing, scheduling, forecasting, traffic, customer engagement, conversion and performance feedback – these are all important and integral pieces of the optimization process. It's a journey."

As a first step, Larry recommends that retailers engage in a thorough and objective evaluation of their current customer service situation to understand where they're starting from. How much service is available? What would be optimal? Can you afford it? Are you over- or under-staffing to the opportunity?

Once there is a clear understanding of the starting point, then the retailer needs to be specific about the goal, the "ideal" of customer service. From there, staffing levels and skill requirements are reviewed, gaps are identified, and programs can be developed to deliver the desired outcomes. This can all be put in place in a set of test stores, and the results can be compared to a set of comparable "control" stores and overall chain trends to understand outcomes.

As important as the initial testing and implementation are, once you have identified the actions and behaviors that lead to better conversion performance, you need a process to sustain the performance and keep it as a focus.

Larry notes that "people are responsive to performance indicators when they are specific to them personally." To this end, he and his team have developed an innovative "conversion by Associate" tracking system that quantifies a unique customer conversion rate to each Associate. Using traffic and conversion data, POS transaction data and time punch data, they can create a weekly conversion score for each Associate that takes into account different work schedules and tasks assigned. Once they have conversion rate by Associate, they layer on traffic counts per hour. They then compare each Associate's conversion score to the store and chain averages and look for variances.

Larry finds that "if the delta between top and bottom performers is small, it's an indication of good staffing levels, proper training and customer engagement, because regardless of who is working, conversion rates are similar. However, often there are large deltas between the top and bottom scores, which indicate that there are staff scheduling and or performance issues."

Conducting the analysis I outlined above puts results in an entirely new context. As retailers come to understand the levers, they can start to take actions to try to influence results — for example, putting their best Associates on during peak times to see what impact they can have on conversion. As Larry rightly puts it, "When you have actionable data and the desire to improve it, that's when the wheels really start to get turning."

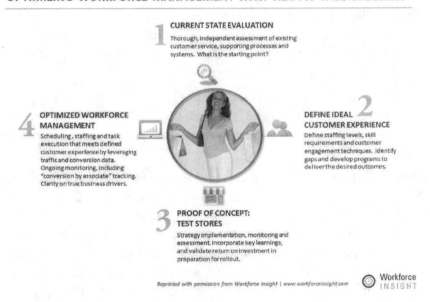

**OPTIMIZING WORKFORCE MANAGEMENT WITH TRAFFIC & CONVERSION**

**1 CURRENT STATE EVALUATION**
Thorough, independent assessment of existing customer service, supporting processes and systems. What is the starting point?

**4 OPTIMIZED WORKFORCE MANAGEMENT**
Scheduling, staffing and task execution that meets defined customer experience by leveraging traffic and conversion data. Ongoing monitoring, including "conversion by associate" tracking. Clarity on true business drivers.

**2 DEFINE IDEAL CUSTOMER EXPERIENCE**
Define staffing levels, skill requirements and customer engagement techniques. Identify gaps and develop programs to deliver the desired outcomes.

**3 PROOF OF CONCEPT: TEST STORES**
Strategy implementation, monitoring and assessment. Incorporate key learnings, and validate return on investment in preparation for rollout.

Reprinted with permission from Workforce Insight | www.workforceinsight.com

Workforce INSIGHT

## Why doesn't every retailer do this?

Good question, says Larry. "There is such huge leverage in conversion that sooner or later, every retailer is going to wake up to this, just as many of our customers have. For example, in a store with a 20% conversion rate, if they improve conversion by just one point (i.e., from 20% to 21%), it will result in a 5% improvement in comp-sales." In Larry's experience, a one-point improvement is not at all unusual and can often be achieved by simply focusing on staffing and engagement basics that have been proven to improve a retailer's conversion rate.

From Larry's perspective, there's a number of reasons why these practices aren't as pervasive as they should be: "There is a real lack of published results in the industry that prove the case for combining traffic and conversion data with workforce management."

Notwithstanding the still low penetration rates of workforce management systems and traffic counters, Larry believes that there is a real sense among retailers that traffic, conversion, and workforce management are important, and they are slowly making their way up the priority list.[4]

## Retail Training

**Kevin Graff** is the founder and president of **GRAFF RETAIL**, the creator of **GRAFF RETAIL TV Online Training for Retail**, and an international authority on retail training and development. With over 22 years of experience, Kevin specializes in helping retailers drive results through improving staff performance and works with some of the leading retailers in North America.

As a professional retail trainer and thought leader in business growth and development, he notes that traffic and customer conversion come up frequently in conversations. When retailers ask him how important traffic and customer conversion are Kevin doesn't mince words: "I wouldn't own a retail store without a traffic counter and customer conversion data. It's just absolutely fundamental to understand the traffic that comes in your door and then what you're doing with it."

According to Kevin, the old retailer equation of traffic x conversion rate x average sale = sales applies as much today as it ever did. If you don't understand traffic through the door and, more importantly, how many prospects you're turning into buyers, you have no idea of the effectiveness of your store. He says, "What conversion rate does that's really powerful, is that it enables you to manage the business to its potential."

## Sales results don't tell the whole story.

As much as driving positive, same-store sales is an important solve-for with sales training, it's not the only or even the most important measure of success. As Kevin puts it, "If you were completely ineffective last year and had lousy sales, what does it matter that your comp sales are up 5%...does that mean you're good? Not at all!"

According to Kevin, the focus on driving sales performance relative to potential is a far more productive than driving performance relative to some financial baseline (e.g., last year's sales), which may or may not have any relevance to how you are truly performing. Traffic and customer conversion data is the only way to measure your performance.

*"What conversion rate does that's really powerful, is that it enables you to manage the business to its potential."*

## Traffic, conversion and training

Kevin and his team have developed numerous retail training and development programs across a wide range of categories, and in his opinion, retailers who have traffic and conversion data have a distinct advantage over retailers who don't. "It's not that traffic and conversion data help me develop training programs *per se*, but what it helps with is in targeting training and coaching efforts to where they are most needed – it allows me to pinpoint."

As Kevin points out, traffic and conversion data won't tell him exactly what the training imperative needs to be: Is it the way Associates are greeting customers? Is it a lack of product knowledge? Are Associates too busy doing other tasks rather than serving customers? Is it a lack of basic selling skills? There's a myriad of potential issues that could be impacting sales performance, and a big part of what sales training is about is to determine what the problems are, and then to design training programs to improve outcomes. So while traffic and conversion can't help with the specifics of the training requirements, they do clearly reveal which stores have a problem or which stores have something really great going on. And that's an important advantage compared to retailers who don't have the benefit of these data.

Of course, for retailers who don't have traffic and conversion data, the only way to understand performance is to analyze the sales data. Says Kevin, "If you take conversion rate out of the equation, all I have is comp sales or sales versus plan or other sales KPIs. That's fine, and that's what a lot of retailers have, so that's what I work with."

"But if you look at sales results along with traffic and conversion data, you can reach completely different conclusions. For example, if comp sales are down 5% in a store, but traffic is down 15%, you're actually a rock star, not an under-performer, as your sales results would suggest."

Kevin sees a fundamental difference between the mindset of retailers who have conversion data versus those who do not. "In my experience, retailers who have traffic and conversion data seem to more effectively manage the selling culture inside their business – it's not that every retailer who has traffic and conversion data manages it well, but those who have it and manage it right... completely outpace everyone else."

## Conversion helps create accountability.

Beyond enabling Kevin to pinpoint where training is needed most, conversion data does something that is very important to sustain effort— it creates accountability. Says Kevin, "I can put a sales goal in place and measure people against it. I can provide Associates all the training in the world, but if there's no accountability, it's very difficult to get sustained performance improvements. It's human nature — when people are held accountable, they'll give better effort than if they're not held accountable."

As important as conversion rate is, Kevin cautions retailers to think carefully when using it as the basis for financial incentives or a bonus program. "I'm a big believer in balanced scorecards. Conversion rate is important, but performance measures should also include other factors vital to running a great store including: average sale, mystery shop scores, compliance, loss results, etc."

In Kevin's opinion, "sales staff effectiveness certainly does impact conversion rate, but it's not the only thing that does – conversion rates can go up for reasons that have nothing to do with sales staff, like if marketing launches a wildly effective advertising campaign, or the merchandising team creates a compelling display, or a lovely round of markdowns comes down from the Head Office."

## Why don't all retailers do this?

"I don't know the answer. It could be a lot of things or even a combination of things: a lack of understanding of the value; concerns about cost; concerns about exactly how the data will get used. In my experience, there's just not one simple answer." He goes on to say, "And while I think traffic counting and measuring customer conversion is not new – it's been around for ages – for many retailers, it is new. The idea is not new, but the application of traffic and conversion analytics is. It's kind of like the iPhone and Apps...traffic counters are like iPhones, no big deal. But what's really cool are the great Apps you can use on it – conversion rate is like a really cool App."

*"Retailers that have traffic and conversion data and use it effectively have the decided advantage over those who do not...that's the God's honest truth."*

It comes down to having an edge. "Retailers that have traffic and conversion data and use it effectively have the decided advantage over those who do not. They can drive productivity through their staff far better than those who don't – that's the God's honest truth."[5]

# Mystery Shopping & Customer Experience

 **Bernard E. Lefang, Ph.D.** is Vice President of Research and Analytics at **Market Force**, the leading global customer intelligence solutions company for business-to-consumer companies, including major retailers, restaurants, grocery and convenience stores, financial institutions, entertainment studios, and consumer packaged goods companies.

The company measures store-level operations and customer attitudes through mystery shopping, customer feedback, market audits and merchandising services, with analytics that drive targeted improvements. Bernard and his team are in charge of assembling and analyzing the multiple forms of customer data and turning them into actionable insights: How have things changed? Do I have a problem? If so, where is it, and what can I do to fix it?

## The connection between traffic, conversion and customer experience

While the benefits of conducting mystery shops and measuring customer satisfaction are well understood by retailers, combining these with traffic and conversion data can yield important additional insights. According to Bernard, "Mystery shopping allows us to objectively measure operational performance of stores alongside compliance; it provides an objective measure that enables retailers to better understand in-store experience and allows them to take specific actions in areas where sales performance does not meet expectations. But what mystery shop and customer satisfaction alone doesn't do is tell us the "why."

Bernard and his team are doing some innovative work around combining mystery shop and customer satisfaction data with traffic and conversion data. The results are compelling. "We already merge mystery shop and customer satisfaction data with financial data to model the impact of variations in operational performance and have a patent pending decision support solution, the MFI Loyalty Lift Calculator™, to allow decision makers to take action based on the models we create, but this only goes so far. We have discovered that traffic and conversion are important, missing explanatory variables – by including traffic and conversion in our analysis, we are better able to explain what's driving the operational performance of a store and what impact this is having on customer satisfaction, loyalty and overall financial performance."

We know from experience that operational performance is typically inversely proportional to traffic – that is, the higher the store traffic, all things being equal (staffing levels, for example), you would expect a lower mystery shop score. So without traffic and conversion data to help explain the "operational performance" variable, one would tend to draw incorrect conclusions. Bernard says, "I believe traffic and conversion are critical to help us better understand customer experience."

## Conversion and customer satisfaction – significantly correlated

It was their quest to find more reliable links between mystery shop and financial performance that led Bernard and his team to look more closely at traffic and conversion data. "The connection between great customer satisfaction scores and great financial performance should be direct and clear, but that's not always the case. Time and again, we found the link between customer satisfaction, loyalty and sales to be elusive."

Bernard goes on to say, "In some cases we actually saw a negative relationship between operational store performance and customer satisfaction scores – which is completely counter-intuitive."

According to Bernard, in statistical studies it is not uncommon for moderating or mediating variables to influence results, and in the case of customer satisfaction and sales performance, he believes that conversion acts as both a mediating and moderating variable. "Based on the analysis we have conducted, conversion rate definitely helps to moderate and mediate the relationship between store performance and customer satisfaction."

For Bernard, it's only when you deconstruct sales into traffic, conversion and average ticket, and then step back and think about which variables are impacting sales performance...do you realize how critical traffic and conversion are in explaining how in-store operational performance affects sales. Of course, operational performance and customer satisfaction do impact store traffic and average sale via their impact on a customer's likelihood to recommend and return to a store, but that impact is relatively small, says Bernard. He adds: "Based on our research of these underlying variables, the one which is most impacted by operational performance and customer satisfaction is conversion rate." As Bernard points out, when you consider that store performance happens within the four walls of the store, it's not hard to understand why conversion rate plays such an important role in moderating and mediating the relationship between performance and sales results.

Many factors, both internal and external, can impact a store's sales performance. Over the past few years, Bernard and his team have merged and analyzed many data sources, including demographics, economic indicators, site specific characteristics, and others, in order to help refine and make their models more robust. Says Bernard, "Of all the data sets we've analyzed, the ones that have had the most impact in our modeling have been traffic and conversion data." According to Bernard, the impact has been significant. "We have been able to make our sales performance model stronger, more robust and more significant. To give you an understanding of the magnitude of bringing traffic and conversion data into our models, we have increased the explanatory impact of the model by about 7-8 times!" Bernard's conclusion: "traffic and conversion are critical pieces of the puzzle."

## Misinterpreting customer satisfaction scores

Retailers invest in collecting and analyzing mystery shop and customer satisfaction results so that they can determine how to move the sales performance lever. They want to know how to improve their bottom line. Increasingly, to do that you have to target your mystery shops, as opposed to looking at these data at the brand or banner level and drawing general conclusions. It is critical for retailers to go down to site-level detail, and part of what they you need to look at when they get there is conversion rate.

Bernard offers the following example. A mystery shop is conducted at a store on a particular Monday, and the score was excellent – 90%. However, on a Tuesday another shop was conducted, and the score was significantly lower – only 70%. So the retailer compares sales on the Monday to sales on the Tuesday and discovers that sales were actually higher on the Tuesday when shop scores were lower than they were on Monday.

*"Without having traffic and customer conversion data at the store-level to put the shop scores in context, it's going to be very difficult to take any specific action with that data."*

This seems totally illogical. Of course, the obvious question is: why? According to Bernard, "Without having traffic and customer conversion data at the store level to put the shop scores in context, it's going to be very difficult to take any specific action with that data."

Sometimes high customer satisfaction scores can give managers a false sense of comfort. When a store manager sees a satisfaction score of, say, 83% for his store, this may seem like an impressively high score compared to other reference points such as school grades. This perception of having a good score can create complacency.

Bernard has seen it before, and in fact, he says it's quite common. "This is exactly why we present the customer satisfaction results in a way that declares that it's not OK to be just OK." Bernard's team typically presents customer satisfaction scores on a 7-point scale, so if a store gets a 5 or even a 6, there tends be less complacency.

But beyond the optics, there is a significant practical difference between the scores, in how they impact the bottom line, and in what they actually mean to the business. "We are able to show managers that the difference between a 7 score and a 6 score in terms of recommendation levels is usually between 2-3 pulls...that means that a customer who gave a 7 on the "how satisfied I am" question, is three times as likely to recommend your store as somebody who gives you a 6." The top store performance comes from delighting customers, not just serving them satisfactorily.

But even if you have customer satisfaction scores that appear high you, should still review traffic and conversion. For example, if you had two stores that both had 90% customer satisfaction ratings and similar sales volume, you might conclude that both stores were top performers. But if you knew that one store had a customer conversion rate of 30% and the other, 50%, it would completely change how you view their respective performance.

## Why don't all retailers do this?

Given that traffic and customer conversion are apparently such an important link to customer satisfaction, it's perplexing that it hasn't come up before. "Frankly, it had not come up much at all –I read a little about it, but it's not something that was on our radar screen," says Bernard. "When you think about all the work that has been done in the domain of customer experience, satisfaction, and mystery shopping, it's almost as if traffic and customer conversion are forgotten parts of the customer experience spectrum."

*"...conversion is one of the most important things a retailer can look at..."*

The more Bernard learns about traffic and conversion, the more he comes to appreciate just how valuable the insights are. "Knowing what I know now about traffic and conversion, in my opinion, it is one of the most important things a retailer can look at because it's so fundamentally tied to operational performance."

According to Bernard, part of the problem could be related to the pervasive use of transaction data by retailers as a pseudo-substitute for traffic conversion, but as Bernard rightly points out, "that won't get you to the level of accuracy you need in order to model and have actionable information. You cannot deny the evidence, traffic and conversion is something that retailers need to look at."[6]

## Retail Research

### Dr. Jayashankar (Jay) Swaminathan is Senior Associate Dean of Academic Affairs and Glaxo Distinguished Professor of Global Business and Operations, Technology and Innovation Management at the Kenan-Flagler Business School, University of North Carolina, Chapel Hill. He was the Chair of Operations faculty from 2001 to 2008. While more academic work is being done in the area of traffic and customer conversion all the time, Jay and his colleagues at UNC Chapel Hill are, in my estimation, leading the effort.

Over his 15-year career, Jay has conducted research work in many facets of business operations, from manufacturing and distribution to the impact of pricing and promotions. His earlier work focused on product variety as well as inventory and production planning; this work led to assortment planning and his first introduction to retail operations as a research stream. Over the last eight years, this worked on retail, collaboration with his colleagues at UNC Chapel Hill and his former doctoral students who are now faculty at Indiana University, Georgetown University, Texas A& M, and Penn State University.

"About seven or eight years ago I was studying the impact of pricing and promotions on retail performance, and through this research it occurred to me that traffic and customer conversion were key aspects that retailers were missing. This is where I really got interested in store-level operations."

Jay was particularly interested in the issue of how sales can be impacted by misplaced inventory and the role that technology could play in minimizing inventory misplacements. He discovered that inventory misplacements tended to be higher during promotional periods than during non-promotional periods – in fact, several times higher. So clearly inventory misplacement was playing a significant role in store sales performance, but it wasn't the only factor. Says Jay, "We looked at all the other variables that influence the successful conversion of a prospect to an actual buyer. We looked at staffing, technology, store ambience, information provided to customers and many other elements. Fundamentally, we were trying to answer the question: how do you turn more of the people walking into the store into buyers?"

Says Jay, "I discovered that most research stopped at advertising and pricing, but you can't fully understand the impact on sales outcomes without looking at the intermediate aspects of the process which can have a big role in the eventual outcomes." For example, even if inventory is not misplaced during a promotion, still, if there are not enough salespeople available to serve prospects visiting the store, the sale could be still be lost. Solving the misplacement problem alone doesn't guarantee positive sales outcomes.

## Traffic and conversion data for research

According to Jay, too little is known about what retailers are doing to manage prospects from the point they walk into the store to the moment they are converted into an actual sale. As he narrowed his work to understand customer conversion and how it could be optimized to enable retailers to get more from this walk-in traffic, he made a curious discovery: "We started our work in this important area of retail operations by first analyzing what work had already been done. Much to our surprise, we learned that not much formal research had been conducted."

Jay believes that a big factor in the dearth of research was related to the lack of traffic and conversion data: "Many retailers simply didn't have traffic counters in their stores, and so there was no data to analyze." As traffic counter technology became more accurate and reliable and as traffic counter penetration levels slowly climbed, the availability of traffic and conversion data for research increased.

In 2007, Jay and his team identified several key research issues related to traffic and conversion and set out to establish relationships with a number of chain retailers who were willing to share their data with him for research purposes. "Several retailers were interested in what we could learn by analyzing their data and were quite willing to share large data sets with us." Essentially they said, "You take the data and tell us what you can make of it.'"

Jay's reaction to seeing traffic and conversion data for the first time is telling: "My first impression of seeing the actual data was 'WOW – this is amazing data!' We were immediately able to slice and dice the data at a very granular level, which was critical in order to understand aspects of performance variability we were looking for."

> *"My first impression of seeing the actual data was 'WOW'—this is amazing data."*

With a good supply of well understood data, Jay and his team started to explore several areas of interest, including understanding the impact of labor on overall sales and conversion rates; determining the impact of conversion rate on future sales; and dealing with issues related to understanding traffic patterns and weather in order to better plan and execute at store level. As Jay and his team discovered, traffic and conversion data turned out to be even more fertile than they expected, and they were able to pursue new avenues of research that were not available before.

## Research frontiers in traffic and conversion

According to Jay, we're just scratching the surface of what we can learn, not only with traffic and conversion data, but also with data from other in-store technologies, such as queue management. "I see the analysis of in-store data becoming a central theme for academic researchers, as retailers move away from relying upon the art of operating their stores to more of the science." According to Jay, a minority of retailers are doing this today, but he predicts that many more will in the future: "I see this coming in a big way."

There are so many questions and areas to explore that it's almost as if the field suffers from an abundance of research opportunities. For example, the whole area of store format and presentation – what aspects encourage or facilitate higher conversion than others? How does this vary by category? Another significant area is labor planning. Is there a set of heterogeneous principles that can be applied across different retail segments? How should one be customizing operations based on the segment? What are the key success factors?

On a broader, macro level, Jay and his team are interested in developing a framework that can be used to inform retail practice to advance the science. He says, "Our goal is to come up with guiding principles...that will identify success factors based on the retailer's operating paradigm."

The other side of the puzzle is to take a single retailer and see how you can help them optimize performance by looking at dynamic changes within the store. "The objective here would be to come up with a 'what-if' tool that enables retail managers to channel resources in a way that delivers better sales results. Today this is largely being accomplished through the manager's own experience based heuristics – there is very little data or intelligence."

## Using the research insights

While having traffic and conversion data for research purposes is proving to be extremely valuable, the availability of too much data, particularly at store-level, may not necessarily be a good thing. Says Jay, "With so much data available, managers run the risk of being overwhelmed. Because people tend to overreact to data, one of our research objectives is to create guiding principles for how managers can best put the data to use."

Another potentially significant benefit to retailers lies in research related to traffic-based decision support and forecasting. To a large extent, labor planning today is driven by sales results. The problem, according to Jay, is that traffic into the store is mediated by the sales force results, and when you take the sales number and feed it back into the forecast, you are often not getting the right number of people because of this mediation. Jay says that "with traffic data, labor forecasting will be far better and accurate."

### Impact of traffic and conversion data on future research

As a leading researcher who has the opportunity to study virtually anything he wants, it's worth noting that Jay chooses to include traffic and conversion data as a critical element of his work: "This is an extremely important area of research. I could be researching anything, and I picked this."

There are two key reasons. First, there's the significant potential impact this research could have on the retail industry: "The areas we are exploring are problems almost every retailer is struggling with today." Second, the availability of deep, rich data sets. While traffic counter penetration rates are still relatively low, more retailers have access to traffic and conversion data than ever before. This type of research was simply not possible before.

Jay is enthusiastic about the possibilities. "Traffic and conversion data help create a wonderful test bed for all these cool ideas and research topics around retail operations – I believe the area will be hot for many years."[7]

# What makes a Conversion Champion?

Every story is different. There is no single success formula or path by which these retailers discovered traffic and customer conversion and made it a meaningful and critical part of their operations. The barriers they faced and overcame, the tenacity and conviction to carry on, the realization that this was not a project but rather a process, a journey, and ultimately the success they achieved – each Champion's experience is unique.

As I reflect on these stories and on the others who chose not to contribute to this book, there are some common themes and prerequisites:

- visionary executive leadership as the initial catalyst;
- evolutionary process and ongoing journey of discovery;
- trials, tribulations and perseverance; and finally...
- transformational results.

It's curious that this list does not include technological superiority, analytical prowess, or deep financial resources that can be unleashed to solve any problem. It occurred to me then, and it is my strong belief now, that the ability to achieve Conversion Champion status is well within the reach of any retailer – large or small.

## You too can be a Conversion Champion.

So what's your story? Never tried? Don't believe? Tried, but struggled and quit? Regardless of where you are today, embracing traffic and customer conversion will profoundly change the way you run your retail operation, and the remainder of the book will lay out the argument for why you should.

Now, let's begin with our old friend and nemesis – same-store-sales. It's the one metric that virtually all retailers live and die by, and I'll show you how traffic and conversion can fundamentally change the way you think about it.

# Chapter 1.3

## Living and Dying by Same-Store Sales

I met a retail executive who confidently summarized the criticality of same-store sales as follows: "The only thing that I worry about is same-store sales...if my comps are up, then the rest will take care of itself." I can safely say that every retailer intuitively understands the importance of same-store sales as a performance metric. In fact, it's so pervasive and deeply internalized that its interpretation can be distilled to just six words: positive comps, good; negative comps, bad.

The terms "same-store sales'" or "comparable store sales" (often referred to simply as "comp-sales") are used interchangeably. Comp-store sales are *the* measure of retail performance. No single metric defines the retail category as much as comp-store sales do – retailers live and die by this one simple measure. And while I wouldn't disagree with its importance as a measure of overall performance, evaluating comp-store sales in the context of traffic and customer conversion can dramatically alter how you interpret it.

Simply put, comp-store sales are defined as: *A measurement of productivity in revenue which  compares sales of retail stores that have been open for a year or more.*[1]

Measuring comp-store sales is so useful partly because it enables us to understand how much of a chain's sales growth is generated from existing stores rather than from new ones. The implication is that growing sales from existing stores means that the chain is performing well, selling more stuff to people coming into those stores. You can easily generate more overall sales revenue by adding new stores; however, declining sales at existing stores (i.e., negative comp-store sales) is an ominous sign because you can't keep adding stores indefinitely.

The comp-store sales metric nicely takes these new stores out of the performance equation.

Comp-store sales is obviously not the only metric used to evaluate retail performance – crack open any first-year college textbook on retail management and you'll find literally dozens of them – it is by far the one most relied upon by retailers and the industry in general to assess individual store and overall chain performance. In fact, according to one analyst, retail stocks tend to trade on same store sales performance more than on any other metric. [2]

OK, we all agree, same-store sales is not only a great metric, it's probably the greatest retail metric. A Google search on "same-store sales" will deliver over 2.7 million hits., but a search of "retail conversion rate" will generate only 4,200 hits. And, if you read these hits carefully, you'll discover that most are related to Web store conversion, which is not what I'm talking about here.

Frankly, if I could pick just one retail metric to live and die by, I would pick same-store sales. Really, I would. But the beauty is that we don't have to just pick one.

## What same-store sales data tells you – and what it doesn't

As a metric, same-store sales does two very important things: it eliminates any incremental sales generated by new stores, and it accounts for seasonality. Obviously, for most retailers, December is a huge sales month, so it would be meaningless to compare December sales to October sales. Comp sales are calculated by simply comparing sales results from stores that have been open for at least one full year and comparing them to only these same stores for a specific, comparable period of time (e.g., December sales this year versus December sales last year).

The problem with relying so heavily on comp sales is that it eliminates only new-store incremental sales and seasonality — and nothing more. Given the "greatness" that has been bestowed upon this metric, you might think that it tells us more, but it doesn't. The underlying assumption about comp sales that grates on me is that, beyond new stores and the time of year, everything else is the same or comparable. I would argue that other than these two items, <u>almost nothing</u> is truly comparable.

Think about it: Was the competitive landscape the same? Was your staff the same? Was the product offering the same? Was your advertising the same? Was the weather the same? Were economic conditions the same? You get the picture. It's not a tremendous leap of logic to realize that virtually NOTHING was the same this year as it was last year.

Sales performance is relative. How can you know what "good" or "great" or even "bad" performance is, without a comparison to what was possible? You can't. And so, as great as comp-sales is as a performance metric, it tells us nothing about what the true opportunity was or what drove the performance. While it's good if comp sales are up, you can't look at this one metric in isolation or without the context that other powerful metrics like traffic and customer conversion offer.

In fact, looking at comp sales in context of traffic and customer conversion can dramatically change the way you interpret the result, as you'll see in the following hypothetical example.

# Comps are up – comps are down: how do you feel?

Let's say that in May your top performing store was up 10% on a comp-store sales basis, and average ticket values and gross margins remained unchanged from a year ago. How do you feel? Comps are up 10%; life is good. Most retailers would consider this to be pretty solid performance.

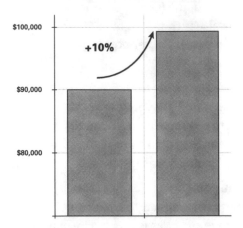

In order to better understand what drove the strong  performance, the Operations team pulled the monthly management report using their slick business analytics tool, and the summary results are displayed in the table below.

| MAY | Last Year | This Year | % Change |
|---|---|---|---|
| Sales | $90,000 | $99,000 | 10% |
| | | | |
| Transaction Count | 1,800 | 1,980 | 10% |
| | | | |
| Average Sale | $50.00 | $50.00 | 0% |

The data tell us what happened in May. Comp sales are up 10%, average sale values didn't change, but the number of sales transactions grew by 10%. Obviously, store traffic was up 10%, and that's what drove the 10% comp sales increase. No-brainer. Good job, Marketing, for getting more people into the store!

Just as the warmth of the sunny May sales results starts to subside, the June numbers are in – and it's not pretty. In June, this same store had comp sales of -10%. As with May, average ticket value and gross margins remained unchanged from a year ago. These are very disappointing results – what happened?

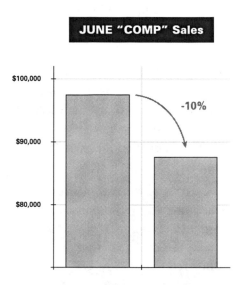

**JUNE "COMP" Sales**

Once again, the Operations team pulls the monthly management report, this time with the exactitude of a crime scene investigation. Sales tanked, and we need to explain why. The summary results are shown in the table below.

| JUNE | Last Year | This Year | % Change |
|---|---|---|---|
| Sales | $96,000 | $86,400 | -10% |
| Transaction Count | 1,920 | 1,728 | -10% |
| Average Sale | $50.00 | $50.00 | 0% |

These data tell us why June was such a disaster. Comp sales were down 10%, average sale values didn't change, but *the number of sales transactions* decreased by a whopping 10%. Obviously, store traffic was down 10%, and that's what drove comp sales down. The real question is: *Why was traffic down 10%?* Marketing...over to you. The Operations team slowly backs away from the executive boardroom table, the Marketing team takes their place on the witness stand, and the grilling begins.

For most retailers, these are the only logical conclusions you can draw from the data — that is, from the *available* data. Comp-sales don't lie. There's not much more to say about what drove the numbers, is there? No matter how far you dig in your mountain of transaction data, you're not going to find any more insights to help you explain the results. However, with store traffic counts and customer conversion added to the analytics mix, there's more to say, a lot more.

Let's start with May. Store traffic wasn't up 10%, as the transaction counts suggested. In fact, it was  up a whopping +22% compared to May of last year,  based on actual prospect traffic counts. If you think of prospect traffic in terms of opportunity size, you could say that the sales opportunity got 22% bigger this May compared to last May. OK, great, but if the opportunity got 22% bigger, why are comp-sales only up 10%? The answer is **conversion rate**.

You can drive all the prospect traffic you want into a store, and believe me, traffic is a good thing: however, it doesn't do you much good if you don't convert this prospect traffic into paying customers. Remember that sales are a function of TRAFFIC x CONVERSION RATE % x AVERAGE SALE, so during the month of May, traffic skyrocketed, but the percentage of visitors who made a purchase (i.e., the customer conversion rate) dropped by 10% — more people in the store, but fewer buying. Average sale values stayed constant, so the net result was that comp-sales were up only 10%.

Yes, *only 10%*.

I know — we agreed that a 10% comp-sale increase was an impressive result. But that was before we knew that the sales opportunity, as measured by prospect traffic in the store, actually grew by 22%. Without any context, 10% looks good; in the context of what the potential was, 10% doesn't look quite as impressive. Ten percent is good, but 22% is even better. So in this case, the question is really: *What happened to conversion rates in the store?* Over to you, Store Operations.

Without viewing the comp-sales results in the context of traffic and conversion, it's impossible to know and to fully understand whether the result were good or great.

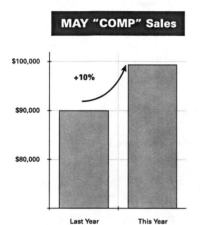

| MAY | Last Year | This Year | % Change |
|---|---|---|---|
| Sales | $90,000 | $99,000 | 10% |
| Transaction Count | 1,800 | 1,980 | 10% |
| Average Sale | $50.00 | $50.00 | 0% |
| Store Traffic | 9,000 | 11,000 | 22% |
| Conversion Rate | 20% | 18% | -10% |

**This Year:** 11,000 x 18% x $50 = $99,000
**Last Year:** 9,000 x 20% x $50 = $90,000

Now on to June. Transaction accounts, used here as a proxy for store traffic, showed that store traffic was down 10%, but in fact, it was actually down 20% — a huge decline from the previous June. In terms of sales opportunity size, it got 20% smaller. Not good at all. But comp-sales were down only 10%. Customer conversion rate fills in the missing piece. Store traffic was down 20%, but the customer conversion rate went from 16% to 18% — that's a two-point or 13% increase.

Customer conversion is a measure of how well the store did at converting prospects into customers — of how, despite the dramatically lower traffic, it was able to sell to more of the people who did visit the store. A drop of 10% in comp sales is bad, but the situation could have been a lot worse: If the store had maintained its 16% customer conversion rate, comp sales would have been down exactly 20%.

As bad as the comps look, I would argue that the store actually performed better against a shrinking opportunity! Clearly Marketing needs to further investigate the traffic drop, because it's a lot more serious than the transaction counts suggested. All the numbers are contained in the table below.

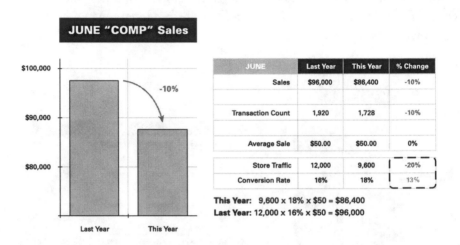

| JUNE | Last Year | This Year | % Change |
|---|---|---|---|
| Sales | $96,000 | $86,400 | -10% |
| Transaction Count | 1,920 | 1,728 | -10% |
| Average Sale | $50.00 | $50.00 | 0% |
| Store Traffic | 12,000 | 9,600 | -20% |
| Conversion Rate | 16% | 18% | 13% |

**This Year:** 9,600 x 18% x $50 = $86,400
**Last Year:** 12,000 x 16% x $50 = $96,000

As this very rudimentary example illustrates, putting comp sales results in context can make a big difference in the way you interpret results and in the actions you take. Without the context of store traffic counts and customer conversion, describing store performance using comp sales only is incomplete at best and potentially misleading. Putting comp sales results in context is vital if retailers hope to truly understand what was possible and how their stores are actually performing.

# Transaction counts vs. traffic counts

There seems to be a tremendous amount of confusion about the simple concept of traffic. To be clear, by "traffic" I mean prospect visits to the store, including buyers as well as non-buyers. When you ask retailers about their traffic – was it up or down? – they will almost always have an answer. However, more often than not, they mean "transaction count," not "prospect count."

Of course, transaction count is not the same as traffic count and as we see in the following chart of a sample of stores from an actual housewares retailer, the difference between the two can be dramatic.

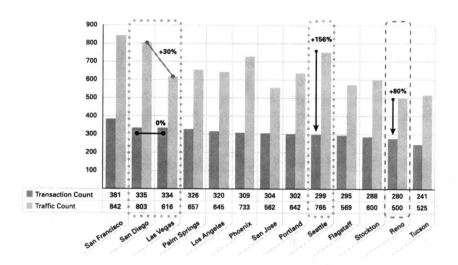

| | San Francisco | San Diego | Las Vegas | Palm Springs | Los Angeles | Phoenix | San Jose | Portland | Seattle | Flagstaff | Stockton | Reno | Tucson |
|---|---|---|---|---|---|---|---|---|---|---|---|---|---|
| Transaction Count | 381 | 335 | 334 | 326 | 320 | 309 | 304 | 302 | 299 | 295 | 288 | 280 | 241 |
| Traffic Count | 842 | 803 | 616 | 657 | 645 | 733 | 562 | 642 | 765 | 569 | 600 | 500 | 525 |

Across this 13-store sample, average daily transaction counts were 310, and the average daily traffic counts were 650. Traffic counts were a little more than twice the transaction counts. The difference between the traffic count and the transaction count represents potential prospects that entered the store but didn't buy. Of course, a traffic count will include people who are not true prospects (e.g., family members shopping together in a group), but many of the individuals really are potential buyers, and collectively they represent the lost sales opportunity.

Not only is there a big difference between transaction counts and traffic counts generally, but these differences vary by store. In its Seattle store, the average daily traffic was 765, while transaction counts were only 299 – that's a 156% difference and the largest of all the stores. Reno had the smallest delta between traffic counts and transaction counts, but it was still significant at 80%.

Conclusion: If you're scheduling staff based on transaction counts, you'll be way off the mark. And, if you simply apply some general "load" factor to the transaction counts to try to estimate store traffic, you'll be wrong because the stores are different.

Another point of interest is the comparison between San Diego and Las Vegas. Based on transaction counts, these stores had virtually the exact same amount of traffic. Again, if you used transaction counts as your guide, you would erroneously conclude that these two stores were substantially similar. But, again, traffic tells the real story. In fact, the San Diego store was getting 30% more prospect traffic than Las Vegas.

## Transactions are NOT a reliable proxy for traffic.

I have had many heated discussions with retailers on this point. They argue that a transaction count represents the number of actual "buyers" the store had, and therefore it's a legitimate and meaningful "customer count," which they then conveniently use as a proxy for "traffic." The fundamental flaw in this calculation is that it accounts only for the buyers.

What about the people who came into the store, wandered around, didn't get served, and left? I ask the retailer, "Aren't you even mildly interested in how many potential sales were lost?" Blank stare.

Beyond talking to retail executives directly, I have also monitored countless quarterly earnings calls where retailer after retailer, when asked by Wall Street analysts whether their comp-sales performance was driven by average ticket or traffic, will respond by saying traffic was down – *even when I know the retailer in question doesn't track prospect traffic in his stores*. It's clear (to me at least) that he's referring to transaction counts, not traffic counts, but no one seems to care about the distinction.

*So the term "traffic" remains ambiguous, and the retail industry collectively tolerates and perpetuates the confusion to this day.*

If a retailer doesn't have traffic count data, instead of exploiting the ambiguity, he should simply say, for example, that he doesn't have traffic counts, but he does know that transaction counts are down. But I have <u>never</u> once heard a Wall Street analyst ask a retailer for clarification on what was meant by "traffic."

Without the benefit of traffic and conversion data to put results in context, retailers are left with having to make do with what they do have – transaction data. I know that, deep down, all retail executives want to know traffic counts in their stores. But instead of investing in traffic counters to get actual traffic counts, they dig deeper into their mountain of POS data and come up with all kinds of creative ways to interpret transaction data.

*You may say that transactions are a proxy for traffic, but that doesn't mean they actually are.* Here's an excerpt from a recent Q10 filing from PetSmart, the largest specialty retailer of pet supplies and services.[3]

> *"Comparable store transactions, which we use as a proxy for traffic, represented 3.6% of the comparable store sales growth..."*

I see that statement, and I ask, "Did sales increase because there were actually more customers visiting the stores, or was it that more of the existing visitors made a purchase?"

This may seem like a subtle difference, but it's not. Transactions are a function of traffic multiplied by customer conversion rate and so, while it may very well be that 3.6% more people visited PetSmart stores and this increase is indeed what generated the increase in sales, it may also be that traffic was actually flat or even down, but the customer conversion rate increased, and <u>that's</u> why transactions increased. It may have had nothing to do with traffic at all!

If market-leading, brilliant retailers like PetSmart can be led astray by transaction counts, then it's not hard to understand why the same is true for so many other retailers. Without traffic and customer conversion data, there's no way to know for certain what drove the comp-sales growth,  so the best I could say about PetSmart's assertion is that it's inconclusive. But at least the company is absolutely clear about its definition of traffic – even if I disagree with it.

## Comparative store performance

For all you transaction data junkies, I have a couple of real-world examples to illustrate how relying on transactions as a proxy for traffic can lead you down the garden path to serious misconceptions about your business. As you'll see, the world looks very different through the prism of traffic and customer conversion.

My company was working with a specialty-cosmetics retailer who was interested in the comparative performance of two stores in particular. Management wanted to understand why there was such a difference between them.

The Vancouver store had 15% higher sales than the Toronto store did. Digging into the transaction data showed that the Vancouver store had 38% more transactions, but its average sale values were 17% lower than Toronto. The retailer therefore assumed that the Vancouver store had 38% higher "traffic" than the Toronto store and, despite the fact that average sale was lower, still generated 15% higher sales. Management concluded that the Vancouver store needed more staff to deal with the extra traffic and that the Toronto store needed more traffic.

Before they took any action, we analyzed the traffic and customer conversion data for the stores, and here's what we found.

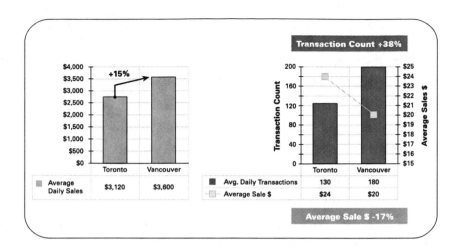

Traffic was actually <u>lower</u> in Vancouver despite having <u>higher</u> sales. This was a very surprising discovery in light of the 38% higher transaction count. Of course, transactions are a function of TRAFFIC x CUSTOMER CONVERSION RATE%, so, given that store traffic volume was lower, the answer had to be conversion rate.

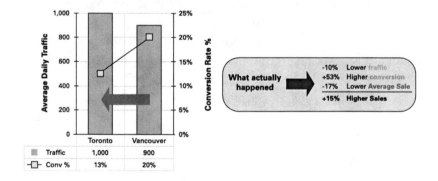

To be precise, store traffic at the Vancouver store was 10% lower than the Toronto store, but its customer conversion rate was 53% higher. So, despite having a 17% lower average ticket, the Vancouver store generated 15% higher sales.

This was a game changing insight for management. If they'd relied upon transactions and sales data to guide their decisions, they would have staffed up at the Vancouver store for what they believed was higher traffic, and they would invested in advertising to try to drive more traffic into Toronto store – both bad decisions.

The Toronto store already had a low customer conversion rate – clearly, it was not converting the traffic it was getting. Investing in advertising to drive more traffic into the store would have exacerbated the problem. What they needed to do is focus on staffing levels and selling skills.

The Vancouver was already doing a great job at converting the traffic they were getting; increasing staff expense isn't the answer. However, it made a lot of sense to brush up on cross-selling and up-selling to get the average sale values up. It all seems so obvious when you have the right data.

## Transaction trends vs. traffic trends

As I said earlier, sales transactions are outcomes. A sale is what happens if you are successful at converting a shopper into a buyer. While traffic and transactions are obviously related, relying on transaction counts as a proxy for store traffic can obfuscate what really happened in-store. The chart below shows actual sales transaction counts for a big-box specialty retailer over a three-week period. From the transaction count trend, it's obvious that there's not a whole lot going on. This is rather unfortunate, because the retailer actually ran a promotion during week #2. Ouch.

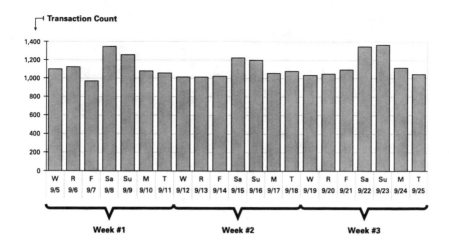

If you tallied up all the transactions and grouped them by week as I did on the following chart, you would find that week #2 actually had 5% fewer transactions than week #1 and 6% fewer than week #3. In this case, average ticket values were substantially similar across all three weeks, so overall sales trends correlated perfectly to transactions. *If average sale values don't change, sales will always mirror transactions.*

Management was dumbfounded. How can you run a promotion and have transactions and sales go down? It doesn't make any sense. As it turns out, it makes perfect sense when you look at the traffic and customer conversion data.

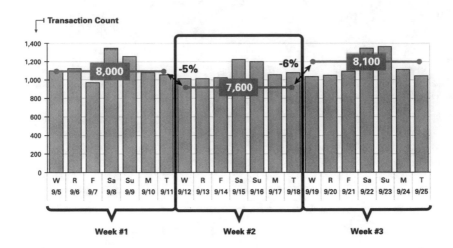

When we look at the same three-week period in the context of store traffic and customer conversion, we draw a very different conclusion. The sales results don't change, but how we interpret them most certainly does. Let's start with store traffic.

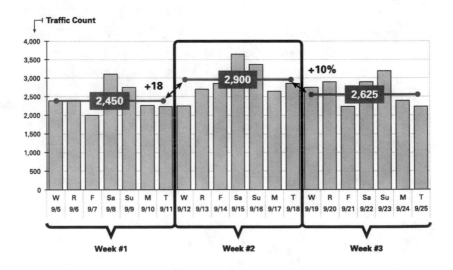

As shown in the chart above, store traffic during week #2 was actually up compared to weeks #1 and #3. In fact, store traffic was up significantly

– by 18% compared to week #1 and 10% compared to week #3. If store traffic defines the sales opportunity, this means the opportunity got bigger – yet sales went down.

Please note: Traffic and conversion tend to be inversely related, so as traffic rises, often, customer conversion rates sag: shoppers don't get served, line-ups get long, and other in-store factors related to conversion come into play. This dynamic became painfully clear when we overlaid customer conversion rate onto traffic, as in the chart below.

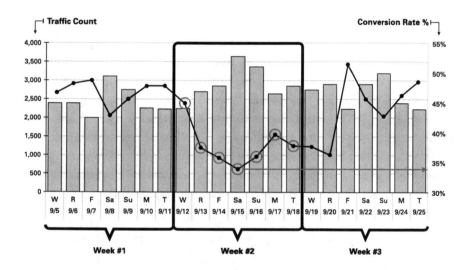

Traffic went up, but customer conversion rates fell significantly. During week #2, average customer conversion rates were a whopping 20% lower than in week #1 and 15% lower compared to week #3. With traffic and conversion data, the impact is clear – there was a significant increase in store traffic during week #2, but the store seriously failed to convert these shoppers into buyers. If the store could have maintained a 45% customer conversion rate (i.e., the rate it averaged for week# 1 and week #3), the increase in store traffic would, in week#2, have generated 9,000 sales transactions – 12.5% more than week #1 and 11% more than week #3.

By breaking out store traffic and customer conversion rate, we can clearly see what drove results. From the transaction counts alone, it would have been very easy to simply conclude that there was a slight drop-off in traffic during week #2, but overall it was not material. Move on.

With traffic and conversion data, the picture is clear; we drove more traffic into the store, but we failed to capitalize on it. And we can now ask: What really went wrong? In this case the culprit turned out to be a stock-out situation on a number of high-demand SKUs. Did this retailer already know that he'd stocked-out on hot items? Yes. Did management know that the stock-outs probably impacted sales results? Sure.

But could they quantify the carnage? Nope. Not without traffic and conversion data.

As you can easily imagine, the reverse can also happen. There could be fewer shoppers coming into the store, but because conversion rates go up (perhaps because the staff does a better job of converting the shoppers into buyers), transaction counts will increase. If transaction counts increase, and if the retailer believes that transactions are a proxy for traffic, he might be inclined to staff-up to serve the increased number of customers. It's an understandable mistake when all you have to rely on is transaction data. This type of "transaction misdirection" can't occur when retailers measure store traffic and customer conversion rate.

## Traffic vs. transactions: even Wall Street seems confused.

At first I thought that the lack of appreciation for traffic and especially customer conversion was mostly a "small" retailer issue. Surely all the big chains must get this stuff, right? So as a way to better understand what the big guys were thinking, I started to monitor quarterly earnings calls and webcasts where most publicly traded retailers provide an overview of business results and then let Wall Street analysts take pot-shots at them during a question–and-answer segment.

These analysts are paid to understand the retail chains intimately. They need to look beyond the financial results and dig deeper into what's driving performance and what the chain's prospects are, so that they can advise their clients to buy, hold or sell the retailer's stock.

If you've ever followed publicly traded companies, you'll appreciate just how important these analysts' reports can be. An unflattering report – e.g., the analyst suggests the purchase rating on stock in question should be lowered from a "buy" to a "hold" – can have a significantly negative impact on the company's stock price, as the market is flooded with "sell" orders.

In conjunction with the "earnings call," the presenting company will typically release a wave of detailed support information including press releases, presentations and financial reports – some formal, mandatory filings and some less formal – that provide additional "color" or context for the results.

The point is, if these retailers, who represent some of the biggest and most sophisticated, are going to talk about traffic and customer conversion, then I should see some reference in these important disclosures and during these earnings calls. So I started monitoring the calls. First one – nothing. No reference to traffic or customer conversion. OK, no problem.

Then another – nothing. Then another and another and another – still nothing! Why aren't these retailers talking about traffic and customer conversion? Then finally, a retailer mentioned that "traffic" was down. As the call continued, it was clear he meant "transaction counts," not store traffic.

I was so surprised by this that I decided to dig even deeper. In late 2007, I analyzed the public disclosures of over 140 (See Appendix A) major brick-and-mortar retailers traded on the New York Stock Exchange, NASDAQ and the Toronto Stock Exchange, to see if I could find any references to either traffic and or customer conversion, and here's what I found.

I started with traffic. Clearly, retailers understand that "traffic" is one of the great metrics, as it was cited by 61% of these retailers in their disclosures. Given the importance of traffic to retailing, it's almost a little surprising that it was mentioned by only 61%. As I noted above, many retailers still use transactions as a proxy for traffic, so of the 61% who cited "traffic," it's impossible to tell which ones were referring to transactions.

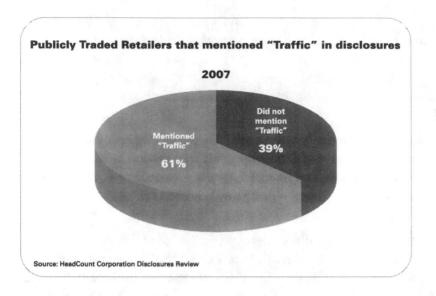

**Publicly Traded Retailers that mentioned "Traffic" in disclosures**

**2007**

Did not mention "Traffic" 39%

Mentioned "Traffic" 61%

Source: HeadCount Corporation Disclosures Review

The more telling — and in many ways more disturbing — finding had to do with conversion. Here we had to exercise some caution, as the word "conversion" is frequently found in these financial reports. We weeded out "store conversion," "stock conversion," "debt conversion," and every other "conversion" that had nothing to do with customer conversion. In the final analysis, only 6% of retailers mentioned "customer conversion" – a measly 6%.

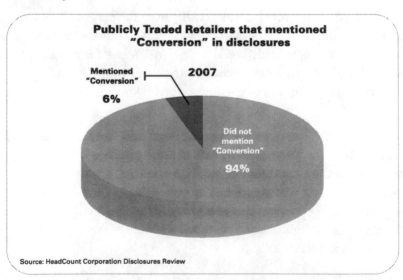

**Publicly Traded Retailers that mentioned "Conversion" in disclosures**

Mentioned "Conversion"     2007

6%

Did not mention "Conversion" 94%

Source: HeadCount Corporation Disclosures Review

So how is it that most retailers talk about traffic, yet almost none of them mention customer conversion? As I thought about it, I concluded that there were three possible reasons for this: (1) customer conversion is a meaningless metric that's not worth mentioning; (2) top executives do know their customer conversion rate but are disinclined to disclose this important data; or (3) the retailer doesn't track traffic and therefore is incapable of calculating its customer conversion rate.

Obviously it wasn't widely regarded as a high priority. But beyond my own personal experience as a retailer, I had spoken with far too many retailers who were rabid users of traffic and customer conversion data and were adamant that these were vital metrics. The importance of traffic and customer conversion is not a figment of my imagination.

So on to point two; perhaps these retailers had the data, but just didn't want to share the results. Unfortunately, traffic counter penetration rates just didn't support this theory. I was aware of some retailers who did have traffic counters installed but didn't reference customer conversion rate in their public disclosures. But according to our best estimates of traffic counter penetration rates at that time, only about 30% of these retailers actually had traffic counters in all their stores. So, I don't think that retailers had the data and just weren't sharing it.

The only reasonable conclusion was point three: retailers simply didn't have the data. You can't calculate conversion rates without store traffic counts, and most retailers didn't have traffic counters. That's why they didn't talk about customer conversion. Interestingly, that didn't stop 61% of them from mentioning "traffic."

I was so intrigued by the findings that I set out to talk to a Wall Street analyst to get some additional explanation. My first attempts at finding an analyst willing to talk didn't pan out, but then I got a nibble. This particular retail stock analyst agreed to speak with me but only "off the record." I quickly agreed, and a call was scheduled.

In particular, there were three questions to which I wanted answers: (1) Why does the industry tolerate transactions as a proxy for traffic, when they are not at all the same? (2) Why don't more retailers track store traffic and customer conversion in their stores? And (3) for an analyst trying to understand a retail chain's performance, wouldn't traffic and customer conversion data be especially helpful?

To respect confidentiality I won't name names, but the call went substantially as follows:

**Me:** I see that you track the retailer XYZ Inc....you probably noticed that they just sent out an earnings guidance press release about Q4 sales...they said that "due to lower traffic in [their] stores," they expect sales to be down. Did you see it?

**Wall Street Analyst:** Yes, of course I saw it, I cover the stock.

Doing my best 60 Minutes, smoking-gun interviewer impression, I asked:

**Me:** Well, I happen to know that this chain doesn't actually track store traffic, so what do you think they meant by "traffic?"

**Wall Street Analyst:** Clearly they're using sales transactions as a proxy for traffic.

**Me:** Yes, I agree. They are using transactions as a proxy for traffic, so really all they are saying here is that because the number of sales are down, they expect sales to be down... as a stock analyst, what does this tell you about their performance? Is this a meaningful insight?

After what seemed to be an uncomfortably long, awkward silence (I was almost expecting to hear the 'click' of the receiver hanging up), the analyst finally spoke.

**Wall Street Analyst:** Yes, I see your point.

I'll spare you all the gory detail, but suffice it to say what I discovered on this call was that retailers were indeed missing the boat on customer conversion because they just weren't measuring it. And it seems the industry, including stock analysts, had become so accustomed to retailers using transactions as a proxy for traffic, they just accepted it.

You can't ask retailers to talk about data that they don't have, the analyst told me. To which I responded: And they won't ever be inclined to, if you in the analyst community continue to tolerate the "don't ask, don't tell" mentality. After some discussion and a couple of examples, the analyst agreed that store traffic and customer conversion would indeed provide valuable insight into store performance.

We first conducted this investigation back in late 2007, and obviously the world has changed a lot since then. So we decided to re-run our analysis of the public disclosures of the same 140 publicly traded retailers, and here's what we found.

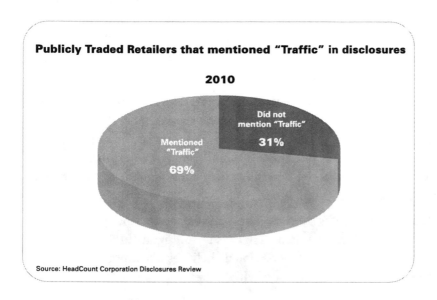

**Publicly Traded Retailers that mentioned "Traffic" in disclosures**

**2010**

Did not mention "Traffic" **31%**

Mentioned "Traffic" **69%**

Source: HeadCount Corporation Disclosures Review

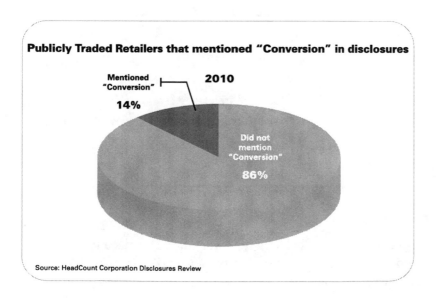

**Publicly Traded Retailers that mentioned "Conversion" in disclosures**

Mentioned "Conversion" **2010**

**14%**

Did not mention "Conversion" **86%**

Source: HeadCount Corporation Disclosures Review

The percentage of retailers who mentioned "traffic" as of the end of 2010 was 69% — that's an eight-point or 13% increase over 2007. Even more retailers were talking about traffic in their financial disclosures. It still boggles my mind that the number isn't closer to 100%.

The big change between 2010 and 2007 was in the mentions of "customer conversion." From a measly 6% in 2007, the number of companies mentioning customer conversion jumped to a whopping 14% in 2010. Think about it – mentions of "conversion" more than doubled. In fact, it was a 122% increase over 2007.

Despite the still low overall percentage of retailers mentioning customer conversion, the more important trend is the growth trajectory. What caused these retailers to start mentioning customer conversion? It's important to remember that these publicly traded retailers are among the biggest and most successful – perhaps they know something that the rest of the market has yet to figure out.

The following excerpt is from the latest annual report from Coldwater Creek, a women's apparel chain. There is no ambiguity in their disclosures. Management here obviously believes it's important to fully describe the results and the underlying drivers.

*"The decrease in our comparable store sales of 1.4 percent reflects a decrease in comparable retail store traffic of 5.3 percent and a 4.4 percent decline in the average transaction values, partially offset by an increase in comparable retail conversion rate of 2.8 percentage points."*[4]

OK, comp sales are down, but we know what drove the decline – lower store traffic and a softer average transaction value. We also know that customer conversion rates increased – the stores sold to more of the traffic that visited the stores (a tell-tale sign of great store-level execution), and this helped offset the decreases in traffic and average ticket. Maybe it's just me, but I have a lot more confidence in a retailer who presents results like Coldwater Creek does.

While the retail industry has a long way to go, I'm encouraged to see statements like the one below, from the annual report of apparel retailer dELiA*s.

*"During 2009, we installed traffic counters and related software in our retail locations in order to evaluate store by store customer conversion rates. We expect this will be helpful in evaluating and managing store performance, establishing effective staffing models and focusing our training efforts."[5]*

# Don't be fooled by positive same-store results.

In terms of putting same-store sales in context, I think the bright folks at the financial website Motley Fool said it best: "The most important thing to remember about comps is that, just like any other metric or number, they are a part of the picture, not the entire tableau. Just because comps are rising, that doesn't necessarily mean the company is a good investment. And likewise, falling comps do not always mean it's a bad one. The trends that you see and the reasons for those trends matter."[6]

Obviously same-store sales is a critically important and probably the most important indicator of the overall health of any retail operation. However, same-store sales results cannot be fully understood without the context that traffic and customer conversion data provide. When same-store sales are positive, everyone is happy, there is dancing in the executive suite. The underlying drivers that helped deliver the positive results may seem less important – but don't be fooled. <u>How</u> you delivered the results matters. Here's why:

- Even though same-store sales are up, they could have been even better. With traffic and customer conversion data, you'll know by how much – customer conversion enables you to quantify the potential.

- If you want to continue to deliver positive same-store results, you need to understand what drove the results: was it traffic, customer conversion, average sale or some combination of all three? Transaction data and sales results don't provide the answer.

- Inevitably you will experience negative same-store sales. You need to understand what drove the results and, more importantly, what you have to do to turn the situation around. Traffic and customer conversion analysis will provide you with the context you need to make the right decisions. If your comp sales are dropping because your customer conversion rates are dropping (i.e., your store personnel aren't converting the traffic they are getting), driving more traffic into the stores won't effectively — or at least not efficiently — improve sales results. When things go bad, you need to understand what lever to pull. Traffic and customer conversion help you do that.

Now that we've put comparable sales results in context, let's turn our attention to another  important area: customer experience.

# Chapter 1.4

## Conversion takes the mystery out of mystery shopping

It's estimated that retailers in North America spend over a billion[1] dollars annually on mystery shopping. When we add to that the cost of all the other ways retailers measure customer experience in their stores, we're looking at a very substantial investment. But retailers often find it difficult to turn their customer-experience data and insights into action that delivers better sales performance.

Pursuing the ultimate "customer experience" has become an obsession with retailers today, and there is no shortage of clever ways to try to measure it. From online surveys and social media monitoring to good old-fashioned customer satisfaction surveys, focus groups and mystery shopping, retailers will go to great lengths to hear the "voice of the customer."

It doesn't matter that many retailers struggle with extracting actionable insights – or that often they derive few tangible benefits from their investments. Measuring customer experience is just the right thing to do, isn't it? To suggest otherwise is borderline heresy.

Retailers instinctively understand that prospects that visit their stores and have a positive experience are more likely to make a purchase, return to the store in the future, and recommend the store to others – all highly desirable outcomes.

So, if this is indeed the case, great customer experience should translate directly into great sales results. The problem is that it often doesn't. And no matter how hard retailers try to measure and improve customer experience, they're often left scratching their heads when these efforts don't translate into better results.

---

From the many discussions I've had with retail executives about mystery shop and measuring customer experience, I can tell that there's a lot of frustration. Obviously cost is part of the issue, but it's not the primary one; the key issue is actionability.

*"We had mystery shop for a number of year...it served a purpose but we hit a point where it just lost the value that it once had."*

Here's what one retail executive told me when I asked her about what her chain did for mystery shop. "We had mystery shop for a number of years, and it served a purpose. However, we seemed to hit a point with it where it just lost the value that it once had. We just couldn't find a meaningful way to make better decisions with the data. We had consistently high scores in all our stores – so one store got 85% and another got 82%. Well, so what? What does it mean? When a store manager sees an 82% score, she's happy with the number. After all, compared to things she can relate to — test scores in school, for example — 82% seems pretty good. There's not a lot of motivation to drive the score up to 100%. Conversion rate is a whole different story. If a store has a 35% conversion rate – which was pretty high for our stores – it leaves an important question unanswered: What about the 65% who didn't buy? To me, conversion data fills in more pieces of the puzzle than mystery shop data does."

That's why I want to discuss the measurement of customer experience. I'll explain why it so often seems confounding – and how traffic and customer conversion insights can help you make sense out of it and help you get more value from your investment.

# Why customer experience doesn't always correlate to sales

If we were to plot customer experience scores against sales performance, the outcomes should be obvious and intuitive: as customer experience scores increase (however they may be measured), sales performance should also increase. And when customer experience scores decrease, sales performance should also suffer.

In the first chart below, stores in quadrant 1, with high customer experience scores, deliver higher sales performance, and the stores in quadrant 3, with lower customer experience scores deliver lower sales performance. This all squares nicely with logic and common sense until, of course, you realize that some of your stores fall into quadrants 2 and 4.

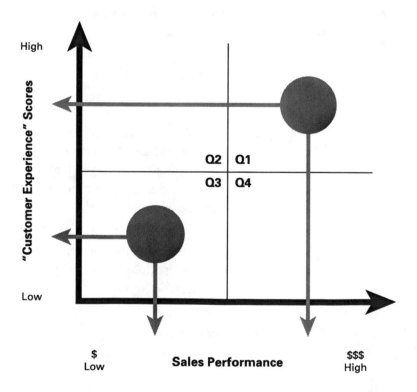

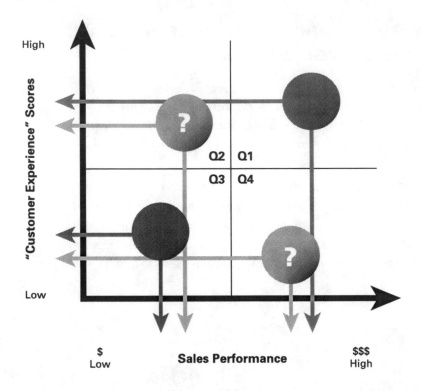

As intuitive and sensible as the results from stores in quadrant 1 and 3 are, stores in quadrants 2 and 4 make no sense at all. These are the Bermuda Triangle quadrants that defy management comprehension. How can it be possible that stores could have high customer experience scores but low sales performance (quadrant 2)or low customer experience scores, but high sales performance (quadrant 4)?

The explanation lies in a simple truth: *the relationship between customer experience scores and sales performance doesn't always hold. In fact, very often customer experience scores don't correlate with sales performance at all.*

So how do you reconcile the fact that customer experience scores and sales performance don't always relate? And how do you act on this information?

Sadly, if you're like some retailers, you just simply go along continuing to do what you've always done, investing huge sums in measuring customer experience without fully understanding what to do with the results. If this all sounds futile and hopeless, don't despair. With traffic and conversion data, it all makes sense – even the enigmatic quadrants 2 and 4.

## Store traffic impacts customer experience.

Imagine what the customer experience would be like in the two stores below. In Store A, the check-out line is clogged, it's hard to find a Sales Associate, and by any measure, I'm sure we would agree that this store does not deliver the best customer experience. If we had a mystery shopper visit the store or if we conducted an exit survey of customers when it looked like this, the scores would likely not be stellar.

Store B is a very different case. It's very quiet; there's hardly anyone in the store. There are no lines at the check-out, it would be easy to find an Associate for help, and in short, the store experience, from the customer's perspective, would be great. If we conducted a mystery shop or surveyed customers, without doubt the scores would be positive – especially compared to Store A.

**Store A**

Here's the problem: Store A delivered significantly higher sales than store B <u>despite the poorer customer experience</u>. Store A had an abundance of traffic, and even though customer conversion rates likely sagged, as some prospects left the store because they couldn't find what they were looking for or gave up on the long lines at the check-out, the store still generated more sales than Store B, which had an exceptional store experience, but due to the lack of prospects in the store, generated only modest sales.

**Store B**

In this case, conversion rates were very high, but without sufficient traffic, the store was unable to generate significant sales.

Every retailer who has ever measured customer experience has likely seen conflicting results similar to these. So from management's perspective, a "great" customer experience is one that strikes the right balance between serving customers and maximizing sales. To do this, retailers need to understand that a great store experience is not an isolated phenomenon; it must be understood in context. Solving for "customer experience" without understanding the context will lead to sub-optimal results.

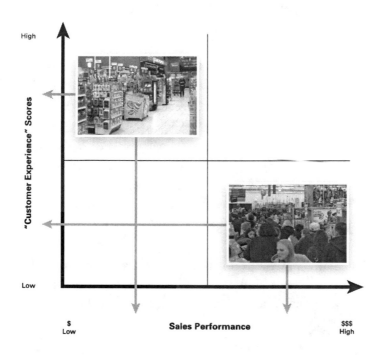

When we plot Store A and Store B on the customer experience and sales performance axes, it's not hard to see how stores with higher customer experience scores can generate low sales, and stores low customer experience scores can generate high sales. In fact, it makes perfect sense when we view customer experience scores in light of traffic and customer conversion data.

Without knowing the stores' traffic volume and customer conversion rates, there's no way for management to understand what may be driving sales results and, in this case, the customer experience data just add to the confusion because they indicate that the store with the lower customer experience scores is producing better sales results than the store that has a better store experience!

# Filling the gaps in customer experience measures

Customer experience is continuous. It changes with the seasons, product launches, staff changes, and the multitude of other factors that impact the customer's in-store experience. On any given day, any store can deliver a brilliant or poor customer experience.

Customer experience depends not only on what's happening in the store and the other factors the store controls, but also on variables the store doesn't control, such as the perceptions of the customers themselves. What may be a "great" store experience for one customer may be a "poor" experience for another. So customer experience and the ways retailers try to measure are subjective.

Two of the most common methods for measuring customer experience are post-purchase surveying and mystery shopping. Both methods have merit and can provide useful insights into store experience; however, both have limitations.

- **Customer Satisfaction surveys:** As a way to increase the amount of data collected and reduce the cost of data collection, more and more customer surveys are conducted online. Typically, check-out staff will invite the customer to participate in an online survey, with details for the website address and store coordinates printed on the sales receipt. Incentives and other tactics are often used to encourage responses.

  Surveying in this way does provide the retailer with a perspective on what some customers think, but it doesn't go far enough. For example, if customers are asked to complete a survey whose details are printed on their sales receipt, the survey will poll only those customers who actually made a purchase. What about the prospects who came into the store and didn't make a purchase? In many ways these non-buyers may have the more important opinions and insights; after all, despite the retailer's best efforts, they didn't buy. Unfortunately, while many retailers do have general customer feedback capabilities on their websites, the number of non-buyers who actually make the effort to go and complete a survey or complain is small. It's hard to find any evidence that these surveys are delivering the insights retailers truly need. Customer satisfaction surveys do have a place, but retailers need to seriously ask themselves what this information means and how they should interpret it.

- **Mystery Shopping:** The advantages of mystery shopping are that it enables the retailer to better control when the sampling is happening, where it's happening, and what data is to be collected.

Because the mystery shops are being conducted by "professional" shoppers, the data collected should be more complete and reliable. Still, there are two key challenges: cost and objectivity. According to the Mystery Shopping Providers Association, the average shop costs $65.[2] For a 200 store chain that conducts three shops a month that would translate into $468,000 per year – load in some upfront set-up and reporting fees, and you could easily get to half a million dollars – quite a substantial sum of money.

Because of the cost, many retailers simply don't do mystery shop or don't do it frequently enough. Also, just as with inviting buyers to fill out a survey, there is an inherent and well-understood sampling error: mystery shoppers aren't real customers. They're not spending their own hard earned dollars, and this fact must, to some extent, influence the way they interpret and score the "customer" experience in the stores they are paid to visit.

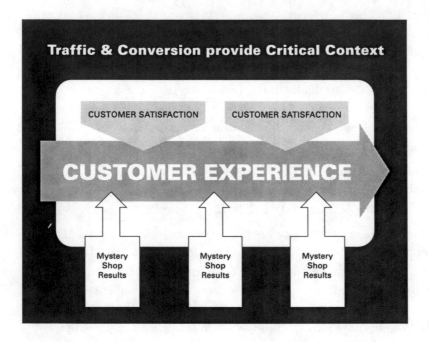

While I'm not suggesting that retailers should stop investing in customer surveys and mystery shopping, I do believe that looking at these data in isolation offers limited value.[3] Customer experience is a continuous process that is in effect every hour of every day the store is open, so it shouldn't be surprising that infrequent sampling of subjective experience (i.e., buyers in customer surveys and paid professional shoppers) produces customer experience results that often don't correlate to store sales performance.

Given all this, is it any wonder that retailers are confounded by measuring customer experience or that they question the value that they're getting for their investments? They seem to be caught in a damned-if-you–do-damned-if-you-don't conundrum. If you don't try to measure customer experience, it appears that you don't care about customers – retail blasphemy. If you do invest in customer experience measures, you squander precious financial resources on activities that often don't directly tie to sales outcomes and are difficult if not impossible to act upon.

So if customer satisfaction surveys and mystery shop data are too subjective and too infrequent, how can retailers truly understand customer experience in their stores? The answer: *look at customer experience measures in the context of traffic and customer conversion.*

Traffic and customer conversion data make customer experience measures more meaningful and more actionable by providing critical context that is otherwise missed. Customer surveys provide ongoing insights, but the results are tainted by the sample error; mystery shop potentially provides very deep and rich insights, but the data is collected very infrequently, and since the shoppers are not true customers, their opinions won't be quite what the retailer needs.

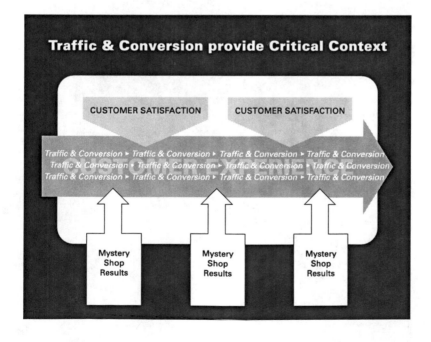

But traffic and customer conversion data are captured every hour of every day, so they effectively provide the insights that are unattainable with customer surveys and mystery shopping.

Why is this? Like the customer experience itself, traffic and conversion data are continuously collected. Furthermore, traffic and customer conversion data are pure measures of actual prospect behavior versus opinion – they are thus completely objective. Traffic and customer conversion fill in the "insight gaps" and help reconcile customer experience measures with sales results.

Now back to Store A and Store B. If instead of comparing customer experience scores to sales results, we compared customer experience scores to customer conversion rates, we would understand that Store A has low customer conversion, which is consistent with the low customer experience scores. Furthermore, we know that the store's high sales results are being generated by the high traffic volume in the store. This is a store that is underperforming versus its traffic opportunity.

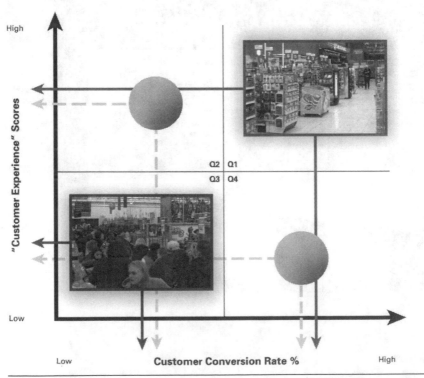

Store A is missing sales opportunities, as evidenced by the low customer conversion rates, and these missed opportunities are clearly reflected in its customer experience scores. The high sales volume has no bearing on the in-store experience, which needs to be improved.

With traffic and conversion data, we would understand that Store B has high customer experience scores and is effectively converting the traffic it receives – it's performing well. However, it would also now be clear that the lack of sales results is a function of the low prospect traffic in the store; it has nothing to do with the in-store experience. Trying to improve the customer experience will not impact the poor sales results – this store needs more traffic, and that's a challenge for Marketing.

*Sales results are not a reliable proxy for customer experience, but customer conversion rate is.* In fact, conversion rate is an excellent proxy for customer experience. You would be very hard pressed to find a scenario where customer experience scores are high and customer conversion rates are low, as in quadrant 2 in the top left corner of the graph. In effect, this would mean that people loved the store experience, but just didn't buy. That's not very likely. Also, results like those in quadrant 4, while more plausible, would also be unlikely or a result of extenuating circumstances — for example, long lines at the Apple store as people wait for the release of the latest iPhone.

# Customer experience measures "conversion-ability."

Sales are a function of traffic, customer conversion rate, and average sale value. We know that customer experience doesn't directly correlate to sales — so what <u>does</u> it correlate to? The answer is **customer conversion**. Prospects are converted into customers when they have a good customer experience. Customer conversion is a function of all those things that make a great customer experience in-store and that ultimately lead to a sale. To a great extent, mystery shop and customer surveys are research techniques meant to provide retail management with an understanding of the factors that create a store environment conducive to prospects making a purchase – conducive to prospects being <u>converted</u> into buyers.

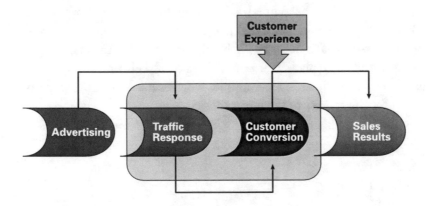

In fact, we could easily replace the "Customer Conversion" label in the fundamental framework with "Customer Experience," as shown below. Customer conversion is a simple measure of visit versus purchase, and while the measure is simple, the factors that create customer conversion are many and complex. Think of everything that makes up the customer experience in your store. Staff, merchandising, product mix, pricing, inventory, plus store atmospherics and intangibles that make a store's unique customer experience truly unique – they're all part of the alchemy.

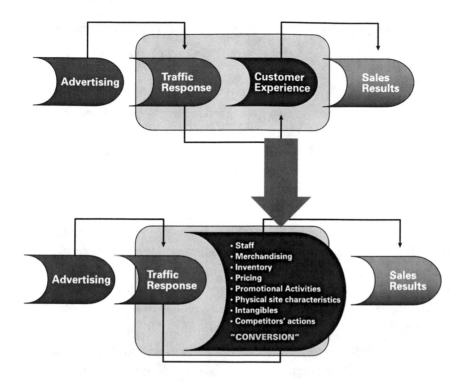

Customer conversion rate is an important indicator of areas where there may be customer experience issues. Uninformed staff, long lines at check-out, poorly merchandised displays, and stock-outs are just a few of the many issues that create bad customer experiences, and they also happen to drive down conversion rates.

# Customer experience and customer conversion – why you need to measure both

Traffic and customer conversion data provide insight into where and when you may have customer experience issues. If conversion rates are sagging in a store and overall traffic levels aren't increasing, then one can reasonably conclude that the issues are related to what's going on in the store — in other words, there's something wrong with the customer experience.

On the other hand, if conversion rates are sagging but traffic volume is up significantly, then the drop in conversion rate (and likely poorer customer experience scores) may simply indicate that store staff is overwhelmed and just not able to manage the traffic volume. While this is still a problem, it's a different problem, and management can understand the difference.

Also, because traffic and customer conversion are typically measured every hour of every day, management gets a virtual non-stop stream of in-store experience measurement. Compared to the flaws, challenges and cost of conducting customer satisfaction surveys and doing mystery shopping, it's not entirely unreasonable to wonder if traffic and conversion analysis could completely replace these customer experience measurement programs. After all, if customer conversion is a good proxy for customer experience, and you get a constant stream of insights, why bother measuring customer experience at all?

The simple fact is that the greatest insight is achieved when both data sets are combined. Traffic and customer conversion provide answers about "when" and "where" in-store customer experience issues may be occurring, while customer satisfaction surveys and mystery shop data can help management understand and answer the "why" and the "how." For example, traffic and customer conversion analysis might tell you that customer conversion rates are consistently sagging in a particular store and that these sags are not a result of more traffic in the store. OK, so far so good, we know that there's a problem in-store, but what do we do next?

This is where customer satisfaction data and mystery shop play a vital role in helping management understand the circumstances and specifics about what may be causing conversion rates to sag. Perhaps it's a problem with staff scheduling that's causing bottlenecks at the cash-out, or poor merchandising that's making products hard to find, or poorly trained staff that are slow to serve or lack product knowledge. Traffic and customer conversion data alone can't answer these questions.

However, these are exactly the kinds of answers that customer satisfaction and mystery shop in particular can help answer. If a mystery shopper is dispatched to a store with a low conversion rate and upon arriving finds the store well merchandised and stocked but can't find an Associate and sees the check-out line extending halfway around the store, it's not hard for management to solve the problem.

Traffic and customer conversion analytics should be constantly monitored to identify customer experience issues, and customer experience measures should be used to help formulate theories about what's driving the conversion rate sags and to decide on the steps needed to resolve the problem.

# Optimize mystery shopping costs by "smart" shopping.

Combining traffic and customer conversion insights with customer satisfaction and mystery shop data not only provides management with better, more complete insights, but as they do so, they can also help retailers save money.

Without the benefit of traffic and customer conversion data to pinpoint where and when customer experience issues may be occurring, retailers are forced to continually visit all their stores.

Think about it: even if you had a very robust mystery shop program and each of your stores were shopped three times per month, the chances of these three spot-checks actually observing something meaningful is slim. If your store is open seven days a week, averaging 10 hours per day and operating 363 days of the year, that's a whopping 3,630 operating hours a year. A three-visit-per month mystery shop program would produce a paltry 36 hours of data – covering only about 1% of the total operating hours.[4]

Instead of shot-gunning all stores with mystery shop, retailers can save money and get better results by focusing their mystery shop efforts on where they are most needed – stores that have customer conversion rate sags, as the following example will show.

The chart below shows the year-over-year change in traffic and customer conversion rates by store for a  group of stores in the Los Angeles area. As the chart shows, each store has one of four potential traffic and conversion profiles: (1) traffic up/conversion rate up; (2) traffic up/conversion rate down; (3) traffic down/conversion rate up; and (4) traffic down/conversion rate down. By seeing the results in this way, we can focus on the stores that have issues.

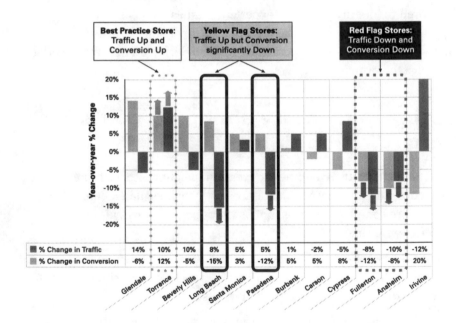

Year-over-year conversion rate declines are a tell-tale sign that a store has customer experience issues. Let's first focus on the stores that are most troubling. Stores that have decreases in year-over-year traffic and conversion rate should be considered "red flag" stores. Traffic volume and conversion rate tend to be inversely related, so when traffic levels go down, customer conversion rate should go up – not down, as they did at the Fullerton and Anaheim stores in the example above.

Our next priority should be the stores that had large decreases in year-over-year conversion rate but only modest increases in year-over-year traffic. Yes, it's true, traffic and conversion tend to be inversely related, so given that these stores did receive more traffic, it's not completely unexpected that the conversion rates would sag. However, in the case of Long Beach and Pasadena, stores I'll call "yellow flag" stores, the decrease in conversion rate was significantly disproportionate to the increase in traffic. This needs to be investigated.

While it's only natural for management to want to focus attention on the stores with sags in customer conversion rate, some mystery shop resources should also be devoted to the best-performing stores – in this case Torrance .

At the Torrance store, both year-over-year traffic and conversion rate have materially increased. Clearly, something good is going on at this store, and it's worth management's time to understand what it is. Here's where the mystery shop should be dispatched, not to look for problems, but rather to look for best practices that could potentially be shared with other stores.

Using traffic and conversion analysis, you can focus your mystery shop effort on the stores that need it most. Stores that have consistent year-over-year conversion could be shopped less frequently or skipped altogether, as there's no evidence to suggest that there are any issues. Perhaps these stores can get shopped once per month instead of three times, while the problematic stores get shopped more than three times. The point of the exercise is simple: save money by optimizing where and how frequently you deploy your mystery shoppers and significantly improve your odds of identifying the in-store issues that require action.

In addition to helping you tell which stores need to be mystery shopped, knowing the prevailing traffic and customer conversion trends for those stores can help define what the mystery shop should focus on. Beyond some number of standard observations that the mystery shoppers might collect in order to provide chain-wide comparative scores, the shoppers' scripts can be tailored to the conditions of the stores.

The table below provides some examples of what mystery shoppers might be directed to look for, given the traffic and customer conversion profiles for any given store.

| | |
|---|---|
| • Traffic UP/Conversion UP<br>• Traffic UP/Conversion DOWN | • Stores are busier, expect reduction in service levels. Watch for good triage practices or opportunities to improve triage. |
| • Traffic FLAT/Conversion UP<br>• Traffic FLAT/Conversion DOWN | • Expect higher conversion and serivce levels. Decreases in conversion could indicate scheduling, training, or staff issues. |
| • Traffic DOWN/Conversion UP<br>• Traffic DOWN/Conversion DOWN | • Reduced traffic should enable staff to provide higher service levels—conversion should increase. Store personnel should be delivering top service, focusing on conversion and average sale. |

# Precision targeting mystery shop

Traffic and customer conversion data are typically captured by hour, so mystery shops can be even more precisely targeted. They can be scheduled on the specific days and even specific hours when customer conversion sags are persistent.

The chart below shows the year-over-year customer conversion rates by day-of-week for a particular store. In this case, year-over-year traffic was virtually flat every day of the week. On Mondays and Tuesdays, conversion rates were actually up year-over-year, while Wednesday through Friday, rates were flat. It's not hard to see where the problems are.

Average conversion rates on Sundays are down, but the real culprit is Saturdays. Average conversion rate on Saturdays dropped from 18% last year to only 10% this year – that's a huge decrease. In this case, traffic was way up on Saturdays, so the year-over-year sales results did not indicate a problem.

So if you were planning a mystery shop for this store, it's not hard to figure out which day to schedule it on. Clearly, the mystery shop should be conducted on a Saturday.

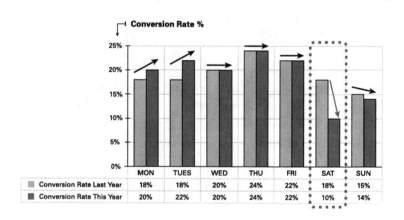

| | MON | TUES | WED | THU | FRI | SAT | SUN |
|---|---|---|---|---|---|---|---|
| Conversion Rate Last Year | 18% | 18% | 20% | 24% | 22% | 18% | 15% |
| Conversion Rate This Year | 20% | 22% | 20% | 24% | 22% | 10% | 14% |

With hourly traffic and conversion data, we can narrow the results even further. The chart below shows the traffic and conversion trend for the average Saturday for the store in question. It's clear that while conversion rates remain high and consistent between 10 AM and 3 PM, things change dramatically at 4 PM – conversion drops like a rock and stays low, right through to closing.

Perhaps this store is not effectively scheduling staff around these last three hours of the day. Perhaps the Associates working these hours are doing a poor job of serving customers. Whatever the issue may be, with traffic and conversion data, you can see exactly where issues are occurring – right down to the hour of day.

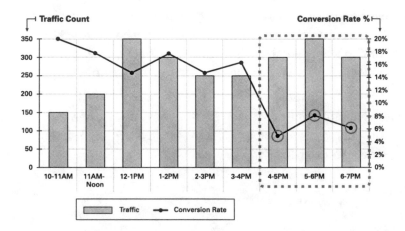

Obviously, precisely scheduling mystery shops by day and even to the hour does not guarantee that the mystery shopper will find what he or she was looking for. However, I would argue that the shopper has a significantly better chance at uncovering an important insight than in a random visit without a clue as to what to look for or when.

Yes, some mystery shop firms do charge more for visits at specific times. But I would argue that with all the money wasted on random shops, the incremental scheduling premium would be more than covered by optimizing the mystery shops to where they are needed most. Not only can you conduct fewer visits overall, but you'll also have a better chance of uncovering meaningful insights.

Targeting mystery shops in this way can dramatically improve the odds that the mystery shopper will observe the behaviors that may be driving the customer conversion sags and resultant customer experience issues.

# A fusion of in-store insights

Traffic and conversion data, properly combined with mystery shop and customer experience data, create a fusion of store-level insight that can result in lower costs and deeper insights that help deliver better store sales performance. Not only will you understand the "where" and the "when" of customer experience issues, but you will also understand the "how" and the "why."

If you think the ideas presented here seem blatantly self-evident, I would enthusiastically agree. *It's all so obvious when you have the data. Without traffic and customer conversion data, none of these insights would be possible.* And most readers of this book don't track traffic or measure conversion in all their stores.

Speaking of traffic counters...while it is not my intention to delve into technological minutiae, given the confusion I hear from retailers, a brief overview of how traffic counters work and what they cost is in order, and that's where we turn next.

No traffic counter, no traffic data; no traffic data, no conversion metric.

# Chapter 1.5

## Why traffic counters can be a pain

There's no way to sugar-coat this: collecting traffic counts accurately and consistently can be a real pain, and the financial investment required to install traffic counters in your stores might cause apoplexy among those who write the checks. But compared to other enterprise systems like CRM, ERP, workforce management or POS, the cost is very reasonable, and the potential benefits are significant.

While it's not my intention to get into the technical nitty-gritty of how traffic counters work, the confusion I see among retailers requires that I provide at least a brief discussion of traffic counting systems and what they cost.

Traffic counters aren't cheap, especially if you have a lot of stores to put them into. And, beyond the cost of the buying the counters, the cost of having them properly installed, along with ongoing maintenance really adds up. Then, once you have traffic counters installed, there is a cost to dedicating resources to extracting the insights and putting these insights to use. The choice of which traffic data capture system to use should not simply be delegated to the IT department. Executives should have a least a rudimentary understanding of the traffic counting systems available and of the relative strengths and weaknesses of the main types. That's what I'll provide in this chapter.

# Traffic counters – how they work

While the specifics of traffic counting systems may vary, the basics of practically all systems are the same. Sensors are installed at the front entrance of the store. Every time a prospect enters the store, a count is logged and stored in a data collection device. The data collector is either directly connected to an Internet connection (or to a PC that is connected to the Internet), where the traffic counts are transmitted to a central server, either at the retailer's Head Office or the service provider's office.

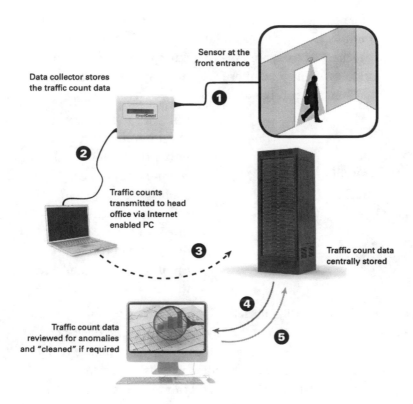

Sensor at the front entrance

Data collector stores the traffic count data

**1**

**2**

Traffic counts transmitted to head office via Internet enabled PC

**3**

Traffic count data centrally stored

**4**

Traffic count data reviewed for anomalies and "cleaned" if required

**5**

# Prevailing traffic counting systems

There are several major types of traffic counting systems. They vary in the way traffic counts are captured, the degree of accuracy and, naturally, cost. Choosing a traffic counter is not just about cost: an inexpensive, basic infrared beam sensor can provide perfectly adequate and accurate counts for the right retail environment; however, in the wrong environment, it's virtually useless.

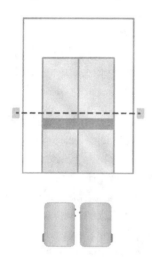

- **Infrared Beam Sensors:** These simple sensors have been available since the 1970s and are still commonly used today. These small sensors shoot an infrared beam across the doorway of the store. Every time a person passes through the entrance, the beam is broken and a count is logged. It's not a very sophisticated data capture system, but it can work well, depending upon the physical characteristics of the store entrance.

One of the major shortcomings of these sensors is that they cannot detect directionality, so total counts must be divided in half in order to estimate incoming traffic (i.e., a person gets counted when entering and leaving the store). Sometimes these beam sensors are installed as double beams, which make it possible to sense direction, but if directionality is important, I recommend using a different sensor type.

Beam sensors offer a low cost, basic traffic count capture solution that, notwithstanding its lack of cool technological sophistication, can do the job. For example, if your stores have a simple entrance where customers come into the store through the entrance but leave through a separate exit door, you don't need to worry about directionality.

Beam sensors can start at about $200 a set and go up from there. While the low cost makes these sensors attractive, there are limitations beyond lack of directionality. First, beam sensors are less effective in stores with wide openings or entrances. For example, the mall entrance to a department store may be 60 feet wide or even wider. If a single beam is transmitted across a span of this length, you can image how inaccurate the counts would be on a busy Saturday afternoon with countless people walking in and out of the department store.

Sensor beam blockages are another huge potential downside. For example, if the store places product displays near the front entrance such that the beam is blocked, then it functionally stops counting. Also, customers sometimes loiter near the front entrance looking at merchandising and blocking the sensor – in either case, counts will not be logged and the integrity of the data becomes compromised.

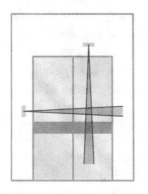

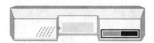

- **Overhead motion detectors:** Overhead motion detectors are basic sensors that trigger a count when anything passes under them. Thus, unfortunately, they count objects like shopping carts or anything else that creates movement. Like beam sensors, overhead motion detectors are not directional, so total counts need to be divided in half to account for the in and out movements. Because these sensors are typically mounted above the door, blockages are not an issue; however, if they're not very carefully installed and calibrated, any incidental movement (e.g., customers milling about at the front of the store looking at merchandise) will trigger superfluous counts. Inordinately high counts generated by these types of superfluous triggerings create data integrity issues that can seriously compromise your ability to use the traffic data. These sensors are inexpensive and widely available; however, they do not offer directional counts and are susceptible to miscounts. Additionally, in my experience, these sensors can malfunction when they are placed in vestibules (as in a freestanding store) and are subjected to more extreme changes in temperature.

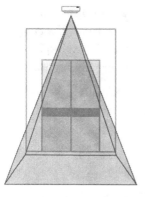

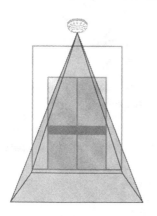

- **Overhead video sensors:** Unlike motion detectors, video-based sensors capture images and then use complex software to extract the traffic counts. These sensors provide directional counting capabilities and are more precise than beams or motion detectors. They're typically found in mall store locations, where capturing counts around high traffic entrances is important. Video-based sensors are significantly more expensive than beam or motion sensors but provide a far higher level of accuracy. That said, care must be exercised in how these sensors are installed and calibrated. In my experience, when video-based sensors are used in environments where light conditions change frequently or are extreme, count accuracy can be affected.

- **Overhead thermal sensors:** The advanced technology of these sensors provides a high level of count precision and directional counts. Because these sensors capture counts based on changes in emissions from moving targets rather than visual impressions, they are not influenced by light conditions; they are thus more versatile than video-based systems. Thermal sensors will actually lock on to the prospect that enters the count zone, and they're smart enough not to double-count these people. So, for example, if your store has a display at the front, as prospects enter the store and walk around it, the sensor, if set up and calibrated properly, will not count these prospects multiple times. This is a significant advantage over other types of sensors. Of course, with precision and sophistication comes price. These sensors cost about the same as video-based sensors, which can run as much as 10 times the cost of a basic beam or motion detectors. I've used thermal sensors in many different environments, and I find them to be an excellent choice.

Sensors are a big part of the overall cost, and it's important to keep in mind that you may need more than one — or even many — sensors for each of your stores. One major department store client of mine needed no fewer than 22 sensors – for one store!

# Installation and maintenance cost

Beyond the cost of the sensors, you'll likely need data collectors and other hardware. The additional components are typically quoted as part of the traffic counting package. However, one area that is often overlooked is the cost of installation. Installation alone can cost anywhere from a few hundred dollars to many thousands of dollars per store.

The key cost drivers for installation include:

- **number of sensors:** more sensors, more cost;
- **type of sensors:** thermal and video sensors typically require more time for setup and calibration than basic beam sensors;
- **length of the cable runs:** in general, the longer the run from the door sensors to the data collector, the higher the cost;
- **ceiling height and type:** ceiling heights above 16 feet often require a man-lift, which can add significant additional cost; also, if the store has a fixed ceiling (as opposed to an open beam ceiling) and the cabling needs to be fished from the entrance door to the back office, installation can take significantly more time;
- **travel costs:** stores located in major markets typically cost less than stores located in secondary or tertiary markets, where technicians need to include travel time in the project cost;
- **installation restrictions:** as a matter of policy, some retailers will not allow installations to be completed during store hours; when installations need to be completed either before or after store hours, additional fees might be charged.

Of course, as with any electronic system, some form of ongoing maintenance will also be required. As reliable as traffic counters are, they can, like any device, malfunction and require repair or replacement. Maintenance costs are generally offered as part of a system package and vary by supplier.

# Traffic count accuracy: the Holy Grail?

The traffic count industry is fixated on the pursuit of precision. The technology used in some traffic counters is extremely sophisticated, delivering very impressive levels of accuracy. The "Statement of Accuracy" below from industry leading thermal sensor manufacturer IRISYS gives you a good idea of just how good the technology has become.

As impressive as 95%-98% accuracy is, the reality is that all traffic data contains some "noise." As I noted above, beam and motion detector type sensors are susceptible to blockages or over-counts. There can be significant issues with data analysis when either zero counts or wildly high traffic counts show up in the data logs. It's the bane of any traffic analyst's existence.

Red Hot Intelligence

Reprinted with permission from IRISYS

While it is true that the use of video and thermal sensors with directional count capabilities do provide a more accurate count, even the most advanced technology can't differentiate a staff member or a delivery person from a real prospective customer.

The other issue that confounds traffic counters is buying groups. There is no foolproof way for a traffic counter to distinguish between individual prospects and a family shopping together. Though it should be noted that some traffic counter manufacturers claim that they can identify buying groups, I remain skeptical.

Another problem is naturally occurring superfluous counts, as when kids run in and out of the store numerous times as their parents shop – these are technically legitimate counts. The electronic counter accurately counted the number of times there was movement through the door. The problem, of course, is that these counts did not represent true prospects.

While these technology focused companies struggle with trying to deliver on the traffic counter Holy Grail of delivering perfectly precise counts, the fact is that it is virtually impossible to do so. Traffic data has natural impurities, and instead of trying to chase theoretically better (and more expensive) traffic technologies, retailers should focus on getting good reliable, consistent counts. Traffic data inconsistencies tend to happen consistently (e.g., staff movements and buying groups), so beyond the wild movements like from a child inordinately running in and out of a store or a blockage, retailers should focus on the trends and be slightly less concerned with perfect accuracy. It's impossible to achieve, regardless of the claims made by some traffic counter manufacturers.

Over the years, I have used all kinds of different traffic counting technologies, and we continue to experiment with the latest and greatest ones. In our experience, regardless of how sophisticated the technology gets, the only way to be absolutely certain the data are right is to have a traffic analyst with a trained eye periodically review the traffic counts to make sure they are right. I know it seems a little old fashioned, but it works.

In the early years at HeadCount, we spent an incredible amount of time scrutinizing traffic data, looking for strange patterns, weird spikes, data anomalies, and wacky counts. Remember, we don't just sell traffic counters. It's our responsibility to deliver reliable, actionable analytics, so collecting valid traffic count data is critical. In fact it's so critical, we've become downright obsessive about it. Validating traffic counts – painstakingly reviewing the quality of the data — is still a big part of what we do today. *Traffic data can be quirky. You have to stay vigilant, looking for anomalies and conducting manual traffic audits if need be. Your Managers will never action the data if they don't believe it.*

# A few unkind words about manual counting systems

Believe it or not, some retailers try to capture traffic counts manually or with very primitive traffic counters that require staff to read the traffic count from the LCD display on the counter regularly. These are only modestly better than counting by hand.

While in some sad, strange way I admire retailers who believe enough in traffic counting that they are willing to subject their staff to the pain and agony of trying to do this manually, in the 21st century, that's just nuts.

Manual counting is often done by sales staff — an in-store administration or reception person — and while I understand that these retailers are trying to save a few bucks on buying a proper traffic counter, you have to wonder if these employees might have better things to do — like serving customers.

When counts are collected manually by staff, the one small advantage is that instead of counting all traffic movements like electronic counters do, staff will often only count "ups" or individual prospects, thus weeding out buying groups, kids or other superfluous counts; however, the negatives of collecting data manually far outweigh any positives. Here are some of the reasons why:

- **subjective counts:** Was that really a prospect or just a "tire-kicker"? In manual counting situations, particularly when sales staff is tasked with counting, subjective judgments about what actually constitutes a "legitimate" prospect count are made. The obvious problem here is that staff shouldn't be making judgments about whether a customer is a prospect or not. For example, if the sales person is not particularly capable and engages the prospect but is unable to close the sale, the counter might not include this person as a prospect because "they weren't a serious buyer." Furthermore, across multiple locations (and even within the same store), different people will count differently; therefore, count consistency is a significant problem.

- **missed counts:** Unless staff is standing guard 100% of the time, counts will be missed. If Sales Associates are tasked with counting but they're all engaged with prospects, it's likely that they will miss additional prospects that enter the store.

- **manual capture errors:** When manual counts are captured, they are then usually transcribed on a log sheet and/or entered in a basic spreadsheet. Every time data are transcribed or re-entered, there is an opportunity for a mistake.

- **lack of hourly precision:** Given how painstaking manual traffic counting is, it's completely impractical to capture counts any more granularly than daily totals. But hourly level data are critical to scheduling staff and measuring conversion. Thus, much of the value in collecting the data in the first place is lost when it's done manually.

Given the pitfalls of capturing traffic data manually, it is incredible that some retailers still try to do it. Even in a low-traffic retail environment, it could hardly make sense. I have yet to see a manual traffic counting system work effectively, and anyone considering this approach should think twice – if you can't afford a real traffic counter, save your money.

# Loss prevention and traffic counting

Loss prevention and surveillance technology continues to advance, and while the benefits of a robust LP program are undeniable, what is often lost on executives is just how valuable the data captured by their surveillance systems is, beyond the obvious loss prevention benefits. Retail executives need to stop viewing surveillance technology as a necessary evil and start to look at how these sophisticated data capture systems can be leveraged to measure results, drive performance, and better manage costs in their stores.

While the idea of capturing traffic counts with loss prevention equipment is not necessarily new – basic counters built into security gates have been around for many years – the sophistication of the technology has gotten much better and continues to improve dramatically.

The loss prevention industry is fast moving away from CCTV (closed caption television) systems with unruly and inadequate videotape systems — and turning to high quality digital cameras with sophisticated recording and retrieval software that can not only offer numerous loss-prevention benefits but can also capture traffic counts.

 According to Vy Hoang, Executive Vice President of i3 International, a leading manufacturer of loss prevention and video analytic systems, "Traffic counting is very much becoming a standard part of our loss prevention systems." With over two decades of experience in the field, Vy has seen a significant evolution in the sophistication and capabilities of loss prevention technology, which continues to evolve at an ever-accelerating pace.

Says Vy, "When we started talking about this just a few years ago, we could barely get retailers to listen to us; today most of our meetings begin with traffic counting – it's not just a discussion with the loss prevention team anymore."

According to Vy, the evolution from video tape surveillance recording to digital recording transformed the industry. Instead of painstakingly poring over stacks of sketchy video tapes to find an incident, digital recording made it possible to easily search and find incidents anywhere across the chain. The time, effort, and cost of conducting investigations are thus significantly reduced. However, as much as this was a significant benefit, there has been a downside: data overload and cost.

Says Vy, "We work with some retailers who have amassed four to five terabytes of data per store – in a 1,500 store chain, this amounts to literally a mountain of data. And as inexpensive as hard drives and storage have become, you still need to manage the data, maintain the systems and provide tools for staff to access the data. This is not inconsequential." But despite the significant investment in these great new technologies, according to Vy, most retailers only use only about 1% of the video they collect over the life of the equipment. As important as loss prevention is, using these advanced systems for loss prevention alone represents a significant underutilization of the technology.

About three years ago, it occurred to Vy that retailers were missing out on a huge part of the value from these sophisticated surveillance systems. Beyond spotting shoplifters, these systems could count traffic into the store, as well as in-store movements, dwell times, and much more. As Vy points out, "The data is really a gold mine for retailers. Compared to the complex movements and behaviors we need to capture for loss prevention purposes, counting prospect traffic is very basic."

Vy goes on to say, "The loss prevention industry definitely sees the value of offering traffic counting as part of the overall package – the problem is that many loss prevention directors and managers have had a hard time convincing senior management of the importance of traffic counting."

For some retailers, using your loss prevention system for traffic counting may be a good option. Given the investment required to outfit stores with dedicated traffic counting systems that do nothing but count traffic, retailers should consider the idea of upgrading their loss prevention surveillance equipment to systems that have traffic counting already built in. Not only does this represent a potential savings in the hardware, software (including the typical annual maintenance fees) and cabling, but there are also potential savings for the IT department as well. Think about it: how much time and effort does it take IT to support one system instead of two entirely separate systems?

According to Vy, "Providing traffic counting as part of a loss prevention solution just makes sense – the loss prevention departments can easily and cost effectively deliver traffic count data to other stakeholders in the organization."

While advances in loss prevention surveillance technology offer great opportunities in capturing and storing traffic data, Vy cautions that capturing data is only part of the objective: "Without some kind of intelligence or mining ability, at the end of the day, you'll just have a big hunk of data, and this in and of itself won't help you deliver better business results."[1]

**Video count captured by surveillance camera -**
Reprinted with permission from i3 International

# Turing traffic counts into insights

OK, so you made the financial plunge and installed traffic counters in your stores. The data are starting to flow, and you're eager to see results. A lot of retailers get to this stage, but it's about at this point that the wheels start to wobble.

What's the big deal – compare traffic to transactions, throw the data into a table or, if you want to get fancy, produce a few bar charts, and we're done. How hard can it be? Most traffic systems come with some form of reporting software, but retailers still need to combine it with other data.

This is a lot harder that it may first appear. While a skilled data analyst is capable of conducting this type of procedure, some retailers delegate the task to a general administrative resource or some other person who is not dedicated to working — or even trained to work — with the data (or even worse, an executive!)

I met with a VP of Sales for a large furniture retailer who was quite proud of the fact that he was doing his own traffic and conversion analysis in a spreadsheet. Frankly, he was pretty good – he had the skills of a solid junior analyst, in my estimation. To all the executives who are currently "dabbling" with traffic and conversion analysis, my simple question is: don't you have better things to do with your time?

Furthermore, because of their lack of time and skill, whether it's an executive or some other poor manager who has to compile traffic and conversion data as an additional task piled on top of an already full plate, most often the analysis is far from robust.

Getting traffic data is only the first part. Once the data is collected and validated,  it needs to be married with other types of data – notably, transaction counts. Remember that customer conversion rate is calculated by dividing sales transactions by gross traffic counts.

In addition to sales transactions, many other types of data should be analyzed alongside traffic and conversion: labor hours, staff schedules, advertising and promotional calendars, merchandising initiatives, training programs, grand openings, competitive activities, inventory data, weather data, and any other mitigating factors.

As you bring data together for analysis, here are some challenges you may face at the outset:

- **missing or erroneous data:** Traffic and transaction data can be hard to manage. Missing or erroneous data is not uncommon. The anomalies need to be tracked down. These can occur because of traffic counter technical failures, or, in the case of transactions, they can result from erroneous data pulls from your POS system. If a store usually converts in the 20% range, and for one day the conversion rate comes in at 80%, there's a good chance that the data is bad somewhere. But not only does this hinder the analysis for the store in question, but depending upon the discrepancy, it can throw off the averages for the region or even the chain.

- **disparate data sources:** One of the significant issues in conducting analysis is pulling in other data to compare to traffic and conversion data. Let's take marketing plans and staff schedules – two key inputs. Obviously, these both come from different departments and will likely require the involvement of several people, who provide inputs on a regular basis. In addition to internal sources, external sources may also need to be sourced and acquired, as with weather data.

- **disparate data formats:** Associated with the disparate data sources is the practical issue of disparate data formats. The more types of data you bring into the analysis, the more insights you get. Because the data comes from a variety of sources, there's a very good chance that the data will also come in a variety of formats and structures – fitting these disparate data formats with your traffic and conversion data can be problematic.

- **massive data volume:** Think about it — if you have 200 stores and you're analyzing traffic and conversion data at the hourly granularity (and if you're not, you're significantly underutilizing your data), in a typical 10 operating hours per day at 363 selling days per year, there are over 725,000 traffic data points. As you marry the traffic counts with sales transactions and other data inputs, the sheer amount of data that needs to be managed is enormous.

## Traffic counting in complex retail formats

Retail stores come in all sizes, shapes and formats. In some stores it's easier to capture traffic counts than in others. Some are virtually impossible. For example, retail kiosks are as much a part of the retail landscape as any format, but given their physical characteristics, capturing traffic counts using typical traffic counters is virtually impossible. But kiosk operators also need to know how many prospects are visiting their "store" and what their conversion rate is.

Unfortunately, today there are no practical traffic counting alternatives for these retailers; however, some of the work being done with loss prevention video surveillance equipment may ultimately provide a solution.

Department stores or large-format retailers have an additional challenge in traffic counting. While capturing total traffic coming into the store may be relatively straightforward, some of these retailers also want to know how many prospects visited specific departments. This is a far more difficult problem to solve.

Traditional traffic counters are not designed to practically capture these types of traffic movements. But there's at least one system on the market that claims to be able to "map" an entire large-footprint store and provide accurate counts and movements throughout the whole store. According to the provider of this camera-based counting system, in order to cover a 50,000- square-foot electronics retailer, some 200 cameras were required. With the cost of the cameras, the cabling, software, calibration, and ongoing maintenance, this type of solution is far beyond the investment tolerance of most retailers – even the biggest.

Large format retailers shouldn't get too discouraged. Just as with kiosk retailers, I believe that loss prevention surveillance providers will also ultimately provide a cost effective and practical solution to the problem. In the meantime, capturing traffic counts at the entrances is still well worth the time, cost, and effort. The departmental data will be a bonus when they're available.

## RFID and mobile for traffic counting and privacy

As other technologies emerge, there very well may be other ways to collect traffic counts. Radio Frequency ID tagging is potentially one of these. RFID is commonly used to track inventory and make product easier to locate in the store.

Some in the industry have wondered if RFID could also provide customer counts. The challenge, of course, is that you would need to get the prospect to be "tagged" in some way. For example, an RFID tag could be embedded in a loyalty card, in a shopping cart, or in a discount card given out to every prospect that enters the store. While these are all possibilities, they seem somewhat onerous compared to how traffic data is captured today, even by basic beam counters. I'm not convinced that RFID is the most suitable way of collecting traffic count data.

Another idea that has recently surfaced is the idea of using cellular phones to track customer counts. Cell phones have built-in transmitters that can be enabled so that the person holding the phone can be tracked and therefore counted. Notwithstanding the obvious problem that not everyone has a cell phone, there is a potential concern with privacy. Not every shopper will be agreeable to being tracked in this way,  so you will never have complete data.

In this increasingly digital age, personal privacy is becoming a serious concern for many consumers. From credit card breaches to overly invasive surveillance systems, watchdog organizations and the media are starting to take notice.[2] Putting in a system that counts prospects but alienates shoppers to the extent that they are reluctant to visit your store defeats the purpose.

# A final word on traffic counting technology

If you think you can simply install a couple of sensors at your front door, string out some Cat5 cable and start improving your customer conversion rate, I'll save you some time and money: it's just not that simple.

Traffic counter system manufacturers continue to push the bounds of technology with ever more accurate and sophisticated systems, but I think we're seeing only the tip of the iceberg. No doubt, developing more accurate sensors is admirable; however, increasingly accurate counts won't in and of themselves make a difference in your business. Yes, technology is a part of the traffic and conversion story, but it's really just a means to an end.

As noted, traffic count data can include some amount of "noise" and no traffic counting system is perfect. Whether you use basic infrared beam counters or sophisticated thermal sensors, or you leverage your loss prevention system to get traffic counts, *the technology is less important than what you do with the data to make decisions and drive performance.*

Collecting data is the easy part; turning it into meaningful insights that make a difference in your business, not so easy. It's like owning a piano and making beautiful music; these are two very different propositions, and so is having traffic counters and driving conversion.

Now that we have the technology discussion out of the way, let's turn our attention to the exciting stuff: finding and extracting insights from traffic and conversion data.

# Part 2

## Extracting Insights from Traffic and Conversion Data

# Chapter 2.1

## Conversion Calculation Fundamentals

Before we start exploring the wonderful world of conversion analysis – and show you how you can drive performance in your stores — we need to clear up a few basics about how you calculate conversion rate.

The basic calculation for conversion rate is simple enough (see figure below); however, issues can sometimes arise with the traffic counts, transaction counts, or both. In this chapter I'll look at how the definition of a transaction and timing of transactions can impact conversion calculations. I'll also examine conversion rate benchmarks and discuss the impact a single point improvement of conversion can have on top-line sales.

## Calculating conversion

As I mentioned in Chapter 1.1, conversion rate is calculated by simply dividing discrete sales transactions by gross traffic counts.

$$\text{Conversion Rate} = \frac{\text{Sales Transactions}}{\text{Gross Traffic Count}}$$

$$20\% = \frac{200}{1{,}000} \quad \frac{\text{(Transactions)}}{\text{(Traffic Count)}}$$

To calculate conversion rate, simply extract your discrete sales transaction counts from your POS system and divide them by the traffic counts you get from your traffic data capture system, and you've got it — conversion rate. For many retailers, it will be just this simple, but for others, there are nuances to their transaction data, traffic data, or both; these must be carefully considered.

## Defining traffic – not every count is a prospect.

Not every count logged by a traffic counter is a legitimate prospect. I noted in Chapter 1.5 that as sophisticated as traffic counting technology has become, there is no foolproof way to eliminate extraneous, non-prospect counts from the count data. Traffic counters will count everything that comes through the door including actual prospects, children, staff, and non-prospects (e.g., deliveries, friends, or family of staff). The net effect of these extraneous counts is that prospect traffic is overstated and conversion rate is understated.

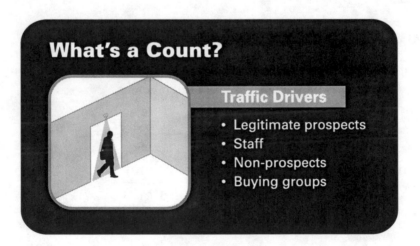

**What's a Count?**

**Traffic Drivers**
- Legitimate prospects
- Staff
- Non-prospects
- Buying groups

# Buying-group impact on results

As anyone who has worked in retail knows, not every buyer is represented by a single person. People often shop together in a group – a buying group. As illustrated below, buying group size can have a significant impact on conversion rates.

For example, if I visit your store on a Wednesday and make a purchase, I represent one count and one sales transaction. If I were the only person that came into the store that day, the conversion rate would be 100%. If I came to your store on a Saturday with my wife and two children, we would generate four traffic counts. Even if we each went to different areas of the store to shop, there's a good chance we would consolidate all our purchases into one basket (always mine!), which would result in a single sales transaction. Again, if we were the only visitors that day, you would have four traffic counts and one sales transaction, which would result in a conversion rate of only 25%.

| | Traffic Count | Transaction Count | Conversion Rate |
|---|---|---|---|
|  | 1 | 1 | 100% |
|  | 2 | 1 | 50% |
|  | 4 | 1 | 25% |

Could it have been any better? Not unless we each decided to check out separately — but this is unlikely. There is no way the store could have improved its conversion rate in this case. This is why we often see conversion rates lower on weekends compared to weekdays, as people tend to shop together in a group on weekends. The point is, absolute conversion rates are less important than the trends.

# When to adjust the traffic count

Generally, I recommend that retailers not adjust the traffic counts and just accept that there are some impurities in the count data which will understate conversion rates. You want to get as accurate a prospect count as possible, so that you can implement changes in-store — for example, having staff use a rear entrance when they leave for breaks.

Part of the decision about adjusting traffic count data comes down to materiality. In high traffic retail environments (e.g., a big-box general merchandiser), the total traffic volume of prospects compared to the extraneous counts will be modest. Adjusting traffic counts down will not materially change the insights at all, and in this case, there is no value in adjusting the counts.

There are cases where the traffic data can be inordinately "noisy," and in these cases applying an adjustment factor to the traffic counts makes the insights more meaningful and ultimately more actionable. Auto dealers are a good example of the most extreme case.

We started working with a dealer and soon realized that the majority of traffic counts logged were staff movements and prospects coming in and going out of the showroom numerous times as they test drove vehicles. The data was just too noisy. So, as a way to measure the noise factor, we conducted a series of in-store audits — we actually watched everyone who came in and out of the door. We conducted the audits over several days, including weekdays and weekends, so that we could understand what a traffic adjustment factor should be at different times of the week. In the end, we discovered that only about 5% of the total traffic counts logged represented actual prospects, and the rest was noise.

Using these audit results, we adjusted the auto dealer's traffic counts down accordingly to calculate what we call the "estimated prospect count." Using our estimated prospect count number yielded conversion rates in the 30% range.

As I said, the absolute values are less important than following the trends; however, when the traffic counts are so noisy that the conversion metric is hard for staff to comprehend or believe, then adjusting the numbers is the right thing to do. Traffic adjustments should be avoided if at all possible. All traffic data has impurities, but despite these, the real prospects counts are in the data.

The less tampering you do with the data, the better. That said, if you do feel compelled to adjust the traffic counts, realize that whatever adjustment you apply will never be 100% perfect, so don't get too hung up on it. The more important aspect is consistency. If you're going to make adjustments, do it once, do it consistently, then leave it alone. The insights come from the trends.

## Defining "transactions" – not all "transactions" should count.

Conversion is calculated by dividing sales transactions by traffic. Simple enough. But unfortunately, POS systems capture lots of different "transactions," and some care needs to be taken when you're pulling transaction data for your conversion calculations. Not all transaction types should be included.

Let's start with defining a sales transaction. For a clothing retailer or any other cash-and carry environment, it's simple. It's the number of discrete sales transactions divided by traffic that gives you the conversion rate.

In a furniture store, it's more complicated. A customer comes into the store, engages a salesperson, and finds the perfect new coffee table at just the right price. The salesperson takes the order, with a deposit, but the coffee table actually needs to be ordered in, and consequently, the final sale won't actually be made until the table is delivered. In this case you need to give some additional thought to which transaction should be included in your conversion calculation.

*Conversion should measure the moment when the shopper was converted into a buyer.* So the transaction we're interested in counting is *the transaction that first captures the sale.* In the case of the furniture store, it's not the final sale when the table is delivered, but rather at the point at which the order was taken. This is the transaction from which we want to derive our conversion rate metric, because it most closely represents the moment the sale occurred. The final, financial transaction is not necessarily when the conversion occurred.

# Dealing with exchanges and returns

Product returns are negative sales transactions that occur virtually every day for most retailers. Because we're trying to measure the conversion of prospects into sales, product return transactions should be excluded from sales transaction data used to calculate conversion rate.

Product exchanges are a little trickier. When a customer returns a product to exchange the item for another product, there's both a negative and a positive transaction. If we counted the exchange as a positive transaction (because merchandise left the store), we would be overstating conversion. The customer would have been recorded as a conversion the day he/she first bought the item and then again, on the day the product was exchanged.

If your POS system can do it, you should exclude the exchange transactions from the conversion calculation by netting out the positive and negative transaction counts. If your POS system can't practically exclude these transactions, then don't worry about them. Exclude the negative transactions (i.e., returns), and leave all the positive transactions in the total transaction count. Yes, you'll be overstating conversion slightly, but unless you have a significant amount of exchange behavior, it won't materially influence overall results and conclusions. Again, the trends are what really matters.

We did some work with a retailer who was including returns or negative sales transactions in the total transaction counts used to calculate conversion rates. Of course, we recommend that these should be excluded, but given that returns usually represent a small number of total transactions, we didn't think it was too big a deal, until we discovered that this retailer had return rates that could reach 30% of total transactions! In this case, by including negative transactions in the conversion rate calculation, it was so overstated, it was difficult to make any sense of it.

This retailer's conversion rate improved from customers returning products to the store! This is <u>not</u> what conversion rate is intended to measure.

The table below is an example of what this retailer's data looked like in two stores. Because both positive and negative transactions were included in the conversion calculation, it appeared that both stores had the same customer conversion rate – 50%. The problem, of course, is that a large portion of Store B's transactions were returns. If these negative transactions are included in the conversion calculation, Store B's conversion rate is grossly overstated – and Store A's rate was modestly overstated. Not good in either case.

### Store A

| Traffic | | 100 |
|---|---|---|
| New Sales | 40 | |
| Returns | 10 | |
| Total Transactions | | 50 |
| Conversion Rate | | 50% |
| Average Sale | | $100 |
| Total Net Sales | | $3,000 |

### Store B

| Traffic | | 100 |
|---|---|---|
| New Sales | 30 | |
| Returns | 20 | |
| Total Transactions | | 50 |
| Conversion Rate | | 50% |
| Average Sale | | $100 |
| Total Net Sales | | $1,000 |

A far better approach is to eliminate the return transactions altogether and base conversion rate on positive sales only, as in the table below. When we base conversion on positive transactions only, we get a clearer picture of how the stores are performing. Store A is converting 40% of its traffic, while Store B is converting only 30%.

## Store A

| Traffic | | 100 |
|---|---|---|
| New Sales | 40 | |
| Total Transactions | | 40 |
| Conversion Rate | | 40% |
| Total New Sales | | $4,000 |
| Average Sale | | $100 |
| Returns | 10 | -$1,000 |
| Total Net Sales | | $3,000 |

## Store B

| Traffic | | 100 |
|---|---|---|
| New Sales | 30 | |
| Total Transactions | | 30 |
| Conversion Rate | | 30% |
| Total New Sales | | $3,000 |
| Average Sale | | $100 |
| Returns | 20 | -$2,000 |
| Total Net Sales | | $1,000 |

This is a very different and far more meaningful conclusion that senior executives can now focus on to help managers improve performance. Presenting the traffic and conversion for Store A and Store B graphically, as in the charts below, makes it even more compelling.

Store A and Store B received the same amount of traffic – 100 counts each. However, Store A converted 40% of the traffic into sales, whereas Store B converted only 30% of its traffic into sales. What was different about the stores? Management now has something to work with.

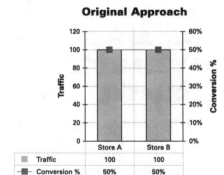

### Original Approach

| | Store A | Store B |
|---|---|---|
| Traffic | 100 | 100 |
| Conversion % | 50% | 50% |

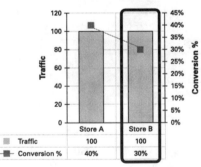

### Revised Approach

| | Store A | Store B |
|---|---|---|
| Traffic | 100 | 100 |
| Conversion % | 40% | 30% |

# Transaction timing is critical.

Getting the timing right when calculating conversion is critical. I met with the VP of Stores for a major consumer electronics retailer; he was an avid user of traffic and conversion analysis. In fact, the company had been tracking traffic and customer conversion in its stores for over five years. As we explored how they were using the insights, we discovered a huge problem with how they were calculating conversion.

As in the above example, conversion rates were being calculated on the basis of when the customer actually made final payment for his or her purchase instead of when he/she actually bought the item. For example, if a customer came in and purchased a set of headphones, this cash-and-carry transaction would count as a sale transaction for the day. However, if the customer came in and bought a flat-screen TV, typically an order would be entered into the system and a deposit taken from the customer. Because of the limited storage space, larger items were brought in as needed. In a week or so, when the item came in, the customer was contacted, and he would come back to the store, make final payment, and take his new TV home. This final payment transaction was captured in the POS as a sale for the day.

This may seem a subtle point, but it's an important one: you drive your conversion measure by starting with the transaction that occurred when the shopper was actually converted into a sale, not when the financial transaction was finalized. Timing is key. In the case of the electronics retailer, the company was capturing sales transactions to calculate its conversion rate, but management was measuring conversion when the financial payment was being made, which is not at all the same time as when the actual sale was made.

The table below shows what the traffic and sales transactions looked like for the store by day. Over a two-week period, 2,000 traffic counts were logged in the store, and the number of final payment transactions was 400. This retailer used these final payment transactions as the basis for conversion, so the overall conversion rate for the two week period was 20%.

| Day | Traffic Counts | Number of Orders, Deposits, and Cash & Carry Sales | Number of Final Payment Transactions | Conversion Rate |
|---|---|---|---|---|
| Mon | 100 | 15 | 20 | 20% |
| Tue | 100 | 35 | 20 | 20% |
| Wed | 100 | 20 | 30 | 30% |
| Thr | 130 | 25 | 55 | 42% |
| Fri | 200 | 45 | 20 | 10% |
| Sat | 250 | 75 | 30 | 12% |
| Sun | 120 | 10 | 15 | 13% |
| Mon | 100 | 10 | 20 | 20% |
| Tue | 100 | 35 | 20 | 20% |
| Wed | 100 | 20 | 30 | 30% |
| Thr | 130 | 30 | 55 | 42% |
| Fri | 200 | 35 | 20 | 10% |
| Sat | 250 | 30 | 40 | 16% |
| Sun | 120 | 15 | 25 | 21% |
| TOTAL | 2,000 | 400 | 400 | 20% |

$$\frac{\textbf{400 Completed Final Transactions}}{\textbf{2,000 Traffic Counts}} = \textbf{20\% Conversion Rate}$$

If we plotted traffic and conversion by day using the retailer's data, the result would look like the chart below. From these data, it's clear that the best conversion days are Thursdays – conversion rates on both Thursdays were well above the 20% average. The problem days were Friday and Saturday, when conversion rates appear anemic compared to the 20% average of the other days of the week.

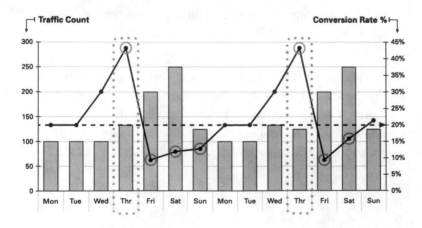

In order to improve conversion rates, management needs to understand what's driving high conversion as well as low conversion. Unfortunately, the real conversion activity in this case is being obscured by the way this retailer is calculating conversion rate.

In this case, deliveries usually happened on Thursdays. Because conversion was driven by final payment transactions, conversion rates were high on Thursdays – it didn't have much to do with how effective the salespeople were that day at all. The high conversion was merely a function of customers coming in, picking up their purchase, and making the final payment. So if this timing was causing the high conversion, what was driving the low converting days? And, more generally, what was management to make of the insights, and how could they be actioned?

The fact is, the way this retailer was calculating conversion didn't have a whole lot to do with sales staff effectiveness or much to do with converting shoppers into buyers.

It's no wonder this retailer struggled with operationalizing customer conversion in their stores.

In this example, the transactions that should be counted as part of the conversion calculation are (1) orders, (2) deposits and (3) all cash-and-carry purchases.

A prospect coming into the store to shop for a flat screen TV had to engage with a salesperson. The salesperson had to show different models, understand the customer's needs, make a recommendation and ultimately close the sale. If the TV wasn't in stock and the customer had to come back to make final payment, it doesn't change the fact that the sale happened on the day the customer made the decision, placed an order, and paid a deposit,

*This is the behavior we want to measure.* This is when the conversion happened.

Let's re-run the conversion calculations for the electronics retailer, this time using the orders, deposits, and cash-and-carry transactions as a basis for conversion. As the table below shows, for the two-week period, overall conversion didn't change – it's the same 20%. As it turns out, this retailer is very good at logistics, and typically customers who place orders are usually able to pick up their purchases the following week, so over a two-week period, payments caught up with the original sale, and that's why the overall conversion rate didn't change.

| Day | Traffic Counts | Number of Orders, Deposits, and Cash & Carry Sales | Number of Final Payment Transactions | Conversion Rate |
|---|---|---|---|---|
| Mon | 100 | 15 | 20 | 20% |
| Tue | 100 | 35 | 20 | 20% |
| Wed | 100 | 20 | 30 | 30% |
| Thr | 130 | 25 | 55 | 42% |
| Fri | 200 | 45 | 20 | 10% |
| Sat | 250 | 75 | 30 | 12% |
| Sun | 120 | 10 | 15 | 13% |
| Mon | 100 | 10 | 20 | 20% |
| Tue | 100 | 35 | 20 | 20% |
| Wed | 100 | 20 | 30 | 30% |
| Thr | 130 | 30 | 55 | 42% |
| Fri | 200 | 35 | 20 | 10% |
| Sat | 250 | 30 | 40 | 16% |
| Sun | 120 | 15 | 25 | 21% |
| TOTAL | 2,000 | 400 | 400 | 20% |

$$\frac{\textbf{400 Orders, Deposits and Cash \& Carry Sales}}{\textbf{2,000 Traffic Counts}} = \textbf{20\% Conversion Rate}$$

However, the conversion timing changed, and that's important. The chart below shows the traffic and conversion rate trends by day, but this time using the orders, deposits and cash-and-carry sales, instead of final sale transactions, to calculate conversion.

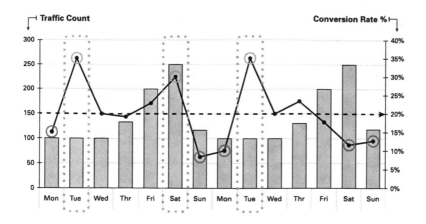

As is clear from the chart, the highest converting days were actually Tuesdays; Saturday during the first week was also a strong conversion day. These high-converting days are when the real sales performance happened – when the sales were actually made. The fact that customers came in and made a final payment later is irrelevant.

The moral of the story: *timing is important when we're calculating conversion.* If you match the prospect visit to the sale or sale proxy (i.e., order or deposit), you will have an accurate measurement of conversion performance. You will understand where the conversion highs and lows are and be able to explore drivers of this performance, replicating what's going on in the high conversion stores and improving the low conversion performers.

If, however, you calculate conversion based on final sale payments, the results become meaningless and impossible to action. Part of the challenge was in the way sales transactions were captured and then extracted from their POS system. The Store Operations team wanted "transactions," so IT extracted "transactions;" no one said anything about which transactions should be pulled. This particular retailer had been calculating conversion rates incorrectly for five years!

Conversion rate is a very simple metric, but you need to exercise some care in how it's actually calculated, interpreted and ultimately communicated to stakeholders. Because there are impurities in traffic counts, and because transaction data can sometimes be difficult to extract exactly the way you would like, the conversion metric sometimes gets miscalculated. Take the time upfront to think this through and get it right, or as right as you can. Always keep in mind that *conversion should measure the moment when the prospect was converted into a customer*. Be consistent in how you measure conversion. And follow the trends – the insights are in the trends.

# Conversion rate benchmarks

## Industry averages

Discussions about conversion rates often begin with the notion of an industry or category average. I'm frequently asked: "What's the standard conversion rate for my category?" Or, in some cases, the retailer informs me: "The standard conversion rate for my category is X%."

There are no industry averages. They don't exist. I wish they did, but they don't.

Because traffic counter penetration is so low generally, most retailers simply don't have a clue as to what their conversion rate is. And because there are so few retailers measuring conversion, let alone providing it to some industry group for compilation in an index or category average, it doesn't exist and probably won't for a long time, if ever.

I find it amusing and ironic that when I inform executives that formal industry averages don't exist, they are often surprised and incredulous: "What do you mean industry averages don't exist? That can't be!" When I point out that they don't measure conversion rates in their own stores, just like the majority of retailers, and that's partly why an industry average doesn't exist, I get blank stares and after a brief, awkward silence, the topic changes.

Conversion rates can vary significantly across categories, within categories and even across stores in the same chain. When you start to map conversion rates across a large number of retailers as I have, it becomes apparent why precise "industry averages" don't exist. The table below shows conversion rate ranges across a number of retail categories.

These are not formal averages or firm industry or category indices, but rather general guidelines based on retailers I have worked with.

| Retail Category | Conversion Rate Range |
| --- | --- |
| General Mass Merchandise | 40%–80% |
| Home Improvement | 40%–80% |
| Specialty/Gift/Hobby | 20%–50% |
| Department Store | 10%–40% |
| Electronics | 10%–30% |
| Apparel | 5%–25% |
| Furniture/Home Furnishings | 5%–20% |
| Shoes & Accessories | 3%–20% |
| Jewelry | 3%–15% |

Deloitte published a white paper a few years back on customer conversion; the paper reported ranges that were substantially similar to these.[1]

The general category ranges can provide at least a basic idea of conversion rate ranges. When I share this with retailers, some are underwhelmed. "Kind of broad, isn't it?" I'm not sure what these retailers expected the category ranges would be, but I think at least some of them expected me to say, "The average conversion rate for your category is precisely 25%." Unfortunately, it doesn't work that way.

It is not useful to represent the averages by category, because there can be significant variances among retailers in any given category. In women's apparel, we have tracked conversion rates anywhere from 5% or less to over 25%. To say the average is 15% would be misleading.

When you consider the wide spectrum of women's apparel retailers, it's not hard to understand the variations in conversion rate. Take two women's apparel stores in the same mall. One store sells high-end, exclusive designer labels, and the other sells trendy, affordable and highly promoted apparel.

The traffic and conversion rate profiles for these two stores would be very different merely by virtue of their offerings. The high-end store likely has a significantly lower conversion rate than the trendy store, as prospects visit the store looking to see the latest fashion — but ultimately are not in a position to pay the price.

The trendy store probably has much higher traffic and higher conversion, as women stream into the store to look and buy. It's irrelevant to compare the conversion rates of these two stores – they're too different; they're incomparable.

But what about stores in the same chain?

## Chain averages

While it is entirely reasonable to expect that conversion rates across chains, even chains in the same category, might have a wide range of customer conversion rates, it would seem quite reasonable to expect the conversion rates of stores within the same chain to be relatively consistent. Here we would expect to see fairly narrow gaps between low and high conversion rates.

The table below shows the actual conversion rate ranges for a number of retail chains. As you can see, the conversion rate ranges can be significant, even for stores in the same chain.[2] In a specialty electronics chain, we observed a seven-point variance from highest converting store to lowest, with an average for the chain of 14%. The biggest variance was in a home improvement retailer, where there was a whopping 34-point delta in conversion rate from highest to lowest store. If there can be so much conversion variance within a single chain, I question how useful it is to have a category average.

What drives conversion rates? Generally, there are two kinds of conversion influences: (1) external factors that the stores don't control and (2) internal factors that the stores do control.

# Conversion Rate Ranges
## for stores in the same chain

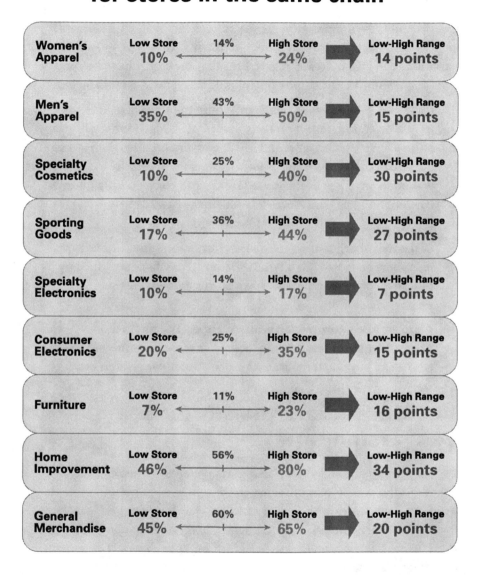

| | Low Store | | High Store | | Low-High Range |
|---|---|---|---|---|---|
| **Women's Apparel** | Low Store 10% | 14% | High Store 24% | ➡ | Low-High Range 14 points |
| **Men's Apparel** | Low Store 35% | 43% | High Store 50% | ➡ | Low-High Range 15 points |
| **Specialty Cosmetics** | Low Store 10% | 25% | High Store 40% | ➡ | Low-High Range 30 points |
| **Sporting Goods** | Low Store 17% | 36% | High Store 44% | ➡ | Low-High Range 27 points |
| **Specialty Electronics** | Low Store 10% | 14% | High Store 17% | ➡ | Low-High Range 7 points |
| **Consumer Electronics** | Low Store 20% | 25% | High Store 35% | ➡ | Low-High Range 15 points |
| **Furniture** | Low Store 7% | 11% | High Store 23% | ➡ | Low-High Range 16 points |
| **Home Improvement** | Low Store 46% | 56% | High Store 80% | ➡ | Low-High Range 34 points |
| **General Merchandise** | Low Store 45% | 60% | High Store 65% | ➡ | Low-High Range 20 points |

# External factors that can influence conversion rate

Conversion rate variations are greatly influenced by in-store factors such as staffing, inventory, and merchandising. However, in some cases, variations can be a function of variables that the stores have no control over at all. Some of these non-controllable conversion factors include:

- **physical site characteristics:** Where the store is situated can have a profound impact on conversion rates. Mall stores will almost always have higher traffic and lower conversion rates than stores outside of malls. Also, stores located in close proximity to food courts will often have higher incidental traffic and consequently lower conversion rates than stores located farther away.

- **trading area market demographics:** The demographic profile of the neighborhood can influence conversion rates. Stores in neighborhoods with high family incomes may have significantly different conversion profiles from stores in lower income neighborhoods.

- **trading area competitive landscape:** The number and aggressiveness of competitors located in close proximity to your stores can have material impact on customer conversion rates.

# In-store factors that influence conversion rate

Beyond these external factors, customer conversion rates can vary dramatically, even within the same chain selling substantially similar products from stores with similar physical characteristics and staffing levels. *Customer conversion is a function of all the variables that in total define the "customer experience" in any given store.* The customer experience is truly unique to each location. That's why conversion rates can vary so much, even among store s in the same chain.

Customer conversion is influenced by all those things that happen within the four walls of your stores.[3] There are no surprises or revelations here. Conversion doesn't happen magically or serendipitously; it happens because customers can find what they're looking for, get the assistance they need, and ultimately make a purchase. Some of the key conversion influences are summarized in the illustration below.

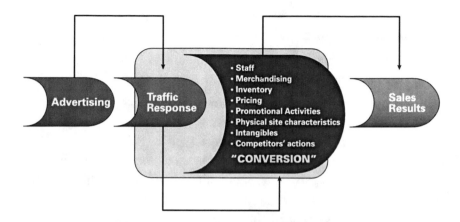

There are literally hundreds of little things that can happen in-store that make or break a sale, but for the majority of retail categories, the most critical are staff, inventory and merchandising.

Staff and staffing related issues have the greatest impact on conversion — by far. There are several dimensions:

- **staffing level:** having the right amount of staff available to deliver the service levels required to maximize customer conversion;

- **staff scheduling:** allocating staff resources to match traffic patterns in the store, to ensure that peak traffic periods are sufficiently covered;

- **staff effectiveness:** ensuring that staff have been adequately trained on systems and product and are ready, willing, and able to assist customers in a professional and courteous manner;

- **transaction processing and till availability:** ensuring that customers are processed efficiently at check-out and basket abandonment is minimized.

Inventory is another key conversion influencer. You can effectively drive prospects into your store looking to buy the hot new feature item, but if you don't have enough stock to meet demand, conversion rates will be negatively impacted. Conversion rate will be affected by:

- **product availability:** ensuring you have sufficient inventory levels to minimize stock-outs;
- **product mix:** ensuring you have the right mix of SKUs for the prospects visiting your store.

Effective merchandising is all about making products easy to find and buy. The more effective your merchandising, the more easily prospects will find what they're looking for. If they can't, or if products are displayed in an unappealing way, conversion rates can be negatively affected. The opposite is also true: compelling displays can help increase conversion rates.

None of what I described is revolutionary. Most retailers already have an intuitive sense of what drives conversion in their stores. But having an intuitive sense and actually measuring it is what makes all the difference. If you know where conversion rates are sagging, you can start to formulate strategies to resolve the issue(s). Without measuring conversion, you have no way of knowing. And, as you'll see, even a one-point improvement in conversion can have a significant impact on overall sales results.

## What's a one-point improvement in conversion worth?

The real-world examples below show the impact on top-line sales of a single-point improvement in customer conversion rate. In all cases, it's assumed that total traffic volume and average ticket values remain flat.

As you can see, the incremental top-line sales generated from a single point of conversion is impressive. But it's even more impressive when you consider that *this sales lift was achieved without having to drive any more prospects into these stores or increase average ticket values. The sales lift was achieved merely by selling to more of the people who were already in the store.*

## Furniture—50 Stores
### Average Daily Traffic = 250 per store

**Traffic x Conversion x Average Sale $ = SALES**

| | | | | | |
|---|---|---|---|---|---|
| Annual Results | 4.5 M x | 10% ↓ | x | $200 | = $90 M |
| Annual Results | 4.5 M x | 11% | x | $200 | = $100 M |

With 1-point lift in Conversion Rate

**Incremental Sales = $10 M**

## Specialty Cosmetics—300 Stores
### Average Daily Traffic = 110 per store

**Traffic x Conversion x Average Sale $ = SALES**

| | | | | | |
|---|---|---|---|---|---|
| Annual Results | 12 M x | 25% ↓ | x | $60 | = $180 M |
| Annual Results | 12 M x | 26% | x | $60 | = $187 M |

With 1-point lift in Conversion Rate

**Incremental Sales = $7 M**

## General Merchandiser—500 Stores
### Average Daily Traffic = 1,500 per store

**Traffic x Conversion x Average Sale $ = SALES**

| | | | | | |
|---|---|---|---|---|---|
| Annual Results | 272 M x | 60% ↓ | x | $20 | = $3.26 B |
| Annual Results | 272 M x | 61% | x | $20 | = $3.31 B |

With 1-point lift in Conversion Rate

**Incremental Sales = $54 M**

## Ladies' Apparel—200 Stores
### Average Daily Traffic = 600 per store

**Traffic x Conversion x Average Sale $ = SALES**

| | | | | | |
|---|---|---|---|---|---|
| Annual Results | 43 M x | 12% ↓ | x | $80 | = $413 M |
| Annual Results | 43 M x | 13% | x | $80 | = $447 M |

With 1-point lift in Conversion Rate

**Incremental Sales = $34 M**

# Sporting goods retailer – detailed example

Let's walk through another example in a little more detail. In this case, it's a specialty sporting goods retailer that logs 600 traffic counts per store per day. With 100 stores in the chain, operating 362 days a year, the chain, over the course of the year, will log 21 million counts.

The average conversion rate was 30%, and average ticket was $100. A one-point improvement in customer conversion rate, to 31%, based on the same traffic volume and average ticket, would generate an additional $21 million in top-line sales revenue.

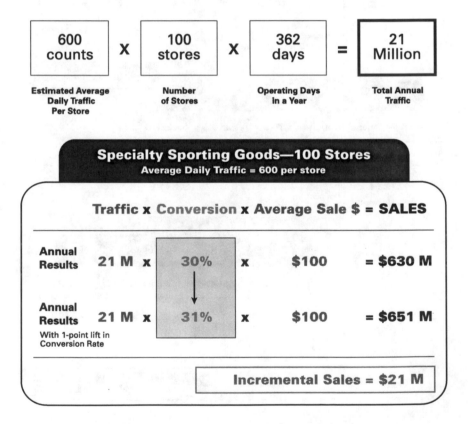

| | 600 counts | X | 100 stores | X | 362 days | = | 21 Million |
| Estimated Average Daily Traffic Per Store | | | Number of Stores | | Operating Days in a Year | | Total Annual Traffic |

**Specialty Sporting Goods—100 Stores**
Average Daily Traffic = 600 per store

**Traffic x Conversion x Average Sale $ = SALES**

| | | | | | |
| Annual Results | 21 M x | 30% | x | $100 | = $630 M |
| Annual Results (With 1-point lift in Conversion Rate) | 21 M x | 31% | x | $100 | = $651 M |

Incremental Sales = $21 M

# What's a one-point improvement in conversion worth to you?

For those who don't track traffic in your stores, we'll start with a quick exercise on estimating your annual traffic. Almost without fail, when I show a retailer how much traffic the stores receive, the person is dumbfounded: "Are you kidding me? There can't be that much traffic in my stores!" Of course, so many retailers are so accustomed to using sales transaction counts (i.e., "customer counts") as a proxy for traffic that gross prospect traffic seem unbelievably high.

To help with your traffic estimate, review the samples from the list below and find the store type that best matches your own. Once you've identified the daily traffic count estimate, plug in the actual number of stores in your chain and the number of operating days per year, and complete the calculation to determine your estimated annual traffic count. Don't be too surprised if it's significantly higher than you expect – that's perfectly normal.

## Store types

- small specialty off-mall store: 30 to 50 counts per day
- moderate sized specialty mall store: 200 to 500 counts per day
- large specialty store: 500 to 1,000 counts per day
- big-box retailer: 800 to 2,500 counts per day
- department store: 2,500 to 10,000 counts per day

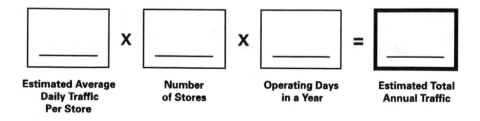

|  | Estimated Average Daily Traffic Per Store | X | Number of Stores | X | Operating Days in a Year | = | Estimated Total Annual Traffic |

Now plug your annual traffic count estimate into the table below. For conversion rate, review the list of sample chains from the previous pages to find the retail category that most closely matches your own. Now enter in your actual average ticket value, and calculate out your annual sales. If the sales figure does not match your actual sales, adjust the traffic and/or the conversion rate until the annual sales number matches your actual sales.

Now increase the customer conversion rate by one point, while holding all the other variables constant, and recalculate your total sales for the year, including incremental revenue produced from the conversion rate increase. Impressed?

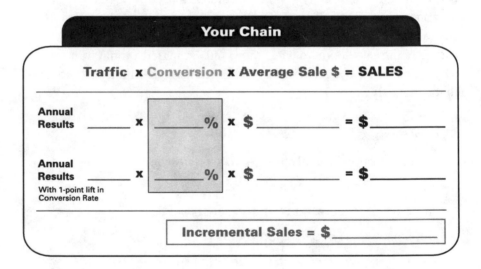

OK, so that's how the math works – at least when you can plug whatever numbers you like into the formula. But the real question is: how do you actually find conversion improvement opportunities? That's where we next turn our attention.

# Chapter 2.2

## Drilling Down — Finding the Opportunities

Every store can perform better than it does today. The trick, of course, is to figure out where to look and what to look for. As I mentioned earlier, performance issues can be masked by positive comparative sales results (and good performance can be masked by negative comps), so just looking at sales alone is not enough.

Recall that traffic counts measure the sales opportunity in the store, and customer conversion represents how well the store is performing relative to the opportunity.

A store that has low traffic volume, by definition, has a small opportunity. If this store has high conversion rates and average ticket values, then the store is performing well. Unfortunately, because the store has low traffic, overall sales volume will be modest, and the store may appear to be underperforming.

The opposite also holds. A store that has an abundance of traffic volume, even with low customer conversion rates and a below-par average sale, may indeed appear to be an overachieving store. However, in reality, this store is underperforming, and the higher sales mask this fact.

Putting sales results in the traffic and conversion context provides the only way to truly understand how stores are performing compared to their unique sales opportunity. Without traffic and conversion, you can never truly understand what "good" or "bad" performance is.

In this chapter we'll explore exactly how you can separate the top from the bottom performers. We'll start to drill down to understand what's driving performance and what you need to do to improve it.

# Putting results in context

We know that sales results are a function of traffic volume, the customer conversion rate and average ticket value. By looking at stores in the context of these three variables, we get a clear perspective of what's driving (or not driving) results in every store. As the examples will show, analyzing the three variables can fundamentally change the way you view a store's performance and can show you how to separate the top from the bottom performers. *You will begin to truly understand your sales results.*

The basis for understanding sales results is captured in what is sometimes referred to as the "retail sales equation," shown below. When we're looking for performance opportunities, a great place to start is by putting store sales results in the context of this formula. Breaking out results in this way will reveal what the true performance drivers are; you simply cannot identify them with sales results alone.

**Traffic** x **Conversion Rate %** x **Average Sale $** = **Sales**

Before we deconstruct results into the underlying drivers, let's start with sales results. After all, this is how most retailers measure performance. If a store has comparatively high store sales relative to other stores, great, it ain't broke, so don't try to fix it; if a store has comparatively low store sales to compared to other stores, focus your attention there, clearly the store isn't performing. As you will see, store performance and sales performance look very different

# Store rank by sales

Let's start with sales. Most retailers compare sales results across stores. Stores with the highest sales results are the top performing stores, and the stores with the lowest sales results are the underperforming stores, right? In this case, I'm simplifying by assuming that the stores have similar gross margins and profitability; of course, differences, if any, would be considered in the calculation.

The chart below shows a sample of ten stores from a region of a chain, ranked from highest to lowest average daily sales. The top store generates about $17,000 in sales daily, while the bottom store generates under $5,000 a day on average – that's a 276% difference from the top performing store to the bottom.

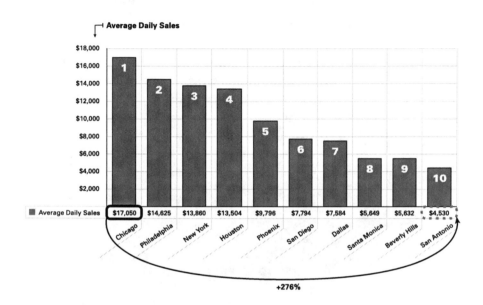

The results are unequivocal. If I'm the Regional Manager, it's clear that I need to focus on my underperforming stores, which in this case are obviously the stores ranked #5 through #10. These stores generate less than $10,000 per day in average daily sales, and in the case of the stores ranked #8, #9 and #10, these big-time laggards were generating less than $6,000 in average daily sales.

Traffic and conversion analysis alone will not change these results, but it will put the results in a context that can fundamentally change the way this Regional Manager thinks about performance and ultimately influence what steps he/she takes to improve performance in that region. Let's start with traffic.

---

# Store performance rank by traffic

We'll look at the same ten stores, but this time I'll rank them by average daily traffic volume – highest traffic to lowest traffic, as in the chart below. Additionally, so that we don't lose sight of the sales results, the sales rank for each store is indicated by the number embedded in the bar.

Remember, traffic defines the sales opportunity, so another way to think about it is that we are ranking stores from largest sales opportunity to smallest. Opportunity size should correlate to sales results, shouldn't it? As you can see below, traffic opportunity clearly plays a big role in store's sales performance. Stores with high traffic volume have better sales ranks than the stores with lower traffic.

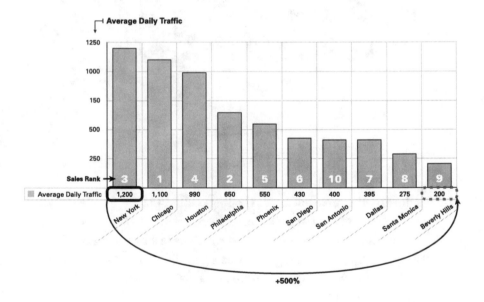

As the chart above shows, the store with the most traffic, New York, had 500% more traffic than the Beverly Hills, the lowest traffic store. That's a significant difference in opportunity size, so it isn't particularly remarkable that New York generated significantly higher sales.

But if you look at the chart closely, a number of interesting insights emerge. For example, Philadelphia, ranked second in sales, had only the fourth most traffic. In fact, it had considerably less traffic than the top three stores, yet it still delivered more sales than all but the Chicago store.

How did this happen? How was it able to achieve such sales results, given how modest its traffic was?

Curiously, New York had the most traffic but was able to achieve only a third-place sales rank. And the San Antonio store was ranked dead last in sales but had the seventh-most traffic – this is where the plot starts to thicken!

Traffic opportunity and sales should correlate — and often do. But when you see stores achieve higher sales ranks than their traffic ranks, it suggests that these stores are doing something particularly right – they are, in essence, delivering results above their traffic "weight-class." The opposite also holds: stores that have higher traffic ranks than their sales rank might be missing opportunities.

Traffic defines the sales opportunity size. Good or bad performance has to be looked at in light of the traffic opportunity. Generally, stores don't control traffic, but they do control what they do with the traffic, and so let's now turn our attention to customer conversion to see what conversion rate can tell us about store performance relative to the traffic opportunity.

# Store performance rank by conversion rate

The chart below shows the ten stores ranked from highest to lowest conversion rate, and again, the store's sales rank is embedded in the bar, so that we can compare the conversion rank to the sales ranking.

Beverly Hills had the highest conversion rate, an impressive 32%. Yet the store achieved only a ninth-place sales ranking. Philadelphia had the second-highest conversion rate (30%) and a matching sales ranking.

At the other end of the chart, we find New York and San Antonio. Both stores had low conversion rates, only 21% and 15% respectively, but the sales rankings weren't consistent either. Despite the low conversion rate, New York still ranked third in sales, while San Antonio's abysmal conversion rate perfectly suited its tenth-place sales rank.

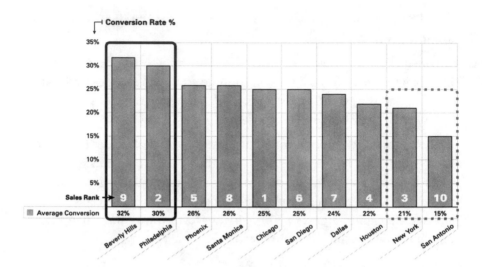

Given that conversion rate does not appear to correlate to overall sales results...does conversion rate even matter? As long as a store has high sales results, why should management care if the conversion rate is low? The short answer is: because the store can perform even better, and understanding the underlying drivers helps you understand specifically in what ways.

Before we dig into this any further, let's look at the last driver – average ticket.

# Store performance rank by average ticket

The last piece of the puzzle is average ticket. The chart below shows the ten stores ranked from highest average ticket to lowest, again with overall sales rank embedded in the bars, so that we can compare average ticket value rank to overall sales rank. Given that retailers pay so much attention to driving average ticket values, surely high average ticket must correlate to sales results, right?

As the chart shows, the stores with the highest average ticket values — Beverly Hills, Dallas, Santa Monica, and San Antonio — were ranked only 9th, 7th, 8th and 10th in sales, respectively – the stores with the highest average sale values actually had the lowest overall sales results! And, interestingly, the stores with some of the highest overall sales results — Chicago, Houston and New York — had the lowest average ticket values.

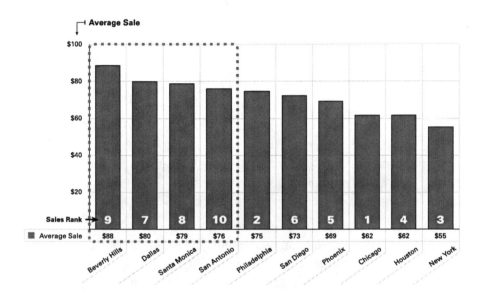

| Average Sale | | | | | | | | | | |
| --- | --- | --- | --- | --- | --- | --- | --- | --- | --- | --- |
| **Sales Rank** | 9 | 7 | 8 | 10 | 2 | 6 | 5 | 1 | 4 | 3 |
| **Average Sale** | $88 | $80 | $79 | $76 | $75 | $73 | $69 | $62 | $62 | $55 |
| | Beverly Hills | Dallas | Santa Monica | San Antonio | Philadelphia | San Diego | Phoenix | Chicago | Houston | New York |

Clearly, average ticket is not the key driver to overall sales results. In fact, based on this real-world data set, you would conclude that average ticket values and sales rank are actually inversely correlated! Which, I know, sounds insane.

Put yourself in the shoes of the Regional Manager and the Store Managers. You have a bunch of stores with high average ticket values, but the overall sales results are poor. How do you drive better sales results? What do you say to these Store Managers – you're all doing a great job of cross-selling and up-selling, but we need to get overall sales up. How do you propose we do that, asks the Store Manager?

Given how much attention and focus retailers pay to improving average ticket values (or items per transaction, which is just another way of saying "average ticket value") as a way to drive store performance, it seems that the results from this example run counter to the strategy.

As the above example clearly shows, average ticket alone is not the answer. And I can tell you that in analyzing results from hundreds of data sets like this, the above example is not merely an outlier. In virtually every chain I've analyzed, we have discovered that average ticket value is an important contributor to results, but it's not the key driver. I'll dig deeper into this topic in Chapter 3.1 *Driving Sales Results with Conversion.*

## Putting the pieces together: traffic and conversion

Sales performance is relative. How does anyone know what good or great performance is without a comparison to what was possible? You can't. But every day, retailers ask, "How are sales today?" How are sales compared to what? The answer: opportunity.

Putting traffic and customer conversion together enables us to understand performance relative to opportunity. The chart below shows the ten stores ranked from highest traffic to lowest, with the corresponding conversion rate for that store indicated by the dot above the bar corresponding to the conversion rate indicated on the secondary vertical axis on the right. Again, the sales rank is embedded in the bar, so we have a clear view of opportunity, performance versus the opportunity, and sales rank.

One of the first things you notice is that traffic and conversion rate tend to be inversely related. The higher-traffic stores tend to have lower customer conversion rates, and the lower-traffic stores tend to have higher customer conversion rates.

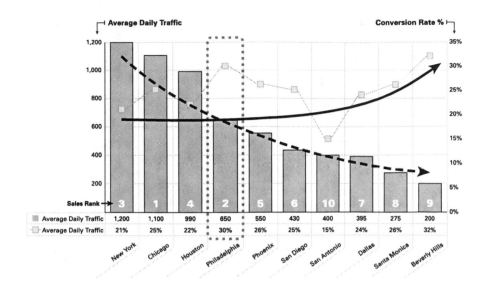

| | | | | | | | | | |
|---|---|---|---|---|---|---|---|---|---|
| Average Daily Traffic | 1,200 | 1,100 | 990 | 650 | 550 | 430 | 400 | 395 | 275 | 200 |
| Average Daily Traffic | 21% | 25% | 22% | 30% | 26% | 25% | 15% | 24% | 26% | 32% |

As I explained in Chapter 1.4, if you think about it, it makes perfect sense. When stores get busy, customers don't get served, line-ups get long, and prospects leave without making a purchase. In low-traffic stores, there's a better chance for prospects to be successfully converted into buyers, and the conversion rates reflect this.

By representing the data in this way, you can understand what's behind the sales ranks. Take the Philadelphia store, which ranked second in overall sales, despite having only the fourth most traffic. But it had the second-highest conversion rate, and it's this combination of traffic and conversion rate that explains the high sales rank.

Now let's compare results from sets of stores. As the chart below shows, Chicago ranked first in sales, but it didn't have the most traffic; New York did, but it managed only a third-place sales rank. In fact, if we compare these two stores, we learn that Chicago generated 23% higher overall sales, but it achieved this with 9% <u>less</u> traffic. Chicago had a higher average ticket, which helped, but the bigger driver was conversion rate – Chicago had a 19% higher conversion rate than New York.

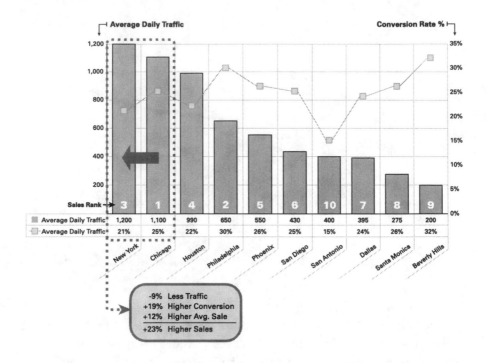

| | | | | | | | | | | |
|---|---|---|---|---|---|---|---|---|---|---|
| Sales Rank → | 3 | 1 | 4 | 2 | 5 | 6 | 10 | 7 | 8 | 9 |
| Average Daily Traffic | 1,200 | 1,100 | 990 | 650 | 550 | 430 | 400 | 395 | 275 | 200 |
| Average Daily Traffic | 21% | 25% | 22% | 30% | 26% | 25% | 15% | 24% | 26% | 32% |

| | New York | Chicago | Houston | Philadelphia | Phoenix | San Diego | San Antonio | Dallas | Santa Monica | Beverly Hills |

-9%  Less Traffic
+19%  Higher Conversion
+12%  Higher Avg. Sale
+23%  Higher Sales

Here's another interesting set in the chart below. Philadelphia is ranked second in sales, while Houston ranks fourth. Philadelphia generated 5% more sales than Houston, but what's remarkable is that it did so with 35% <u>less</u> traffic than Houston. Based on sales transaction data and sales results, these stores looked evenly matched.

But traffic and conversion completely change how we feel about the stores' performance. Philadelphia does an excellent job with the traffic it gets; Houston is underperforming versus a bigger traffic opportunity. Without traffic and conversion data, this retailer could never understand these differences.

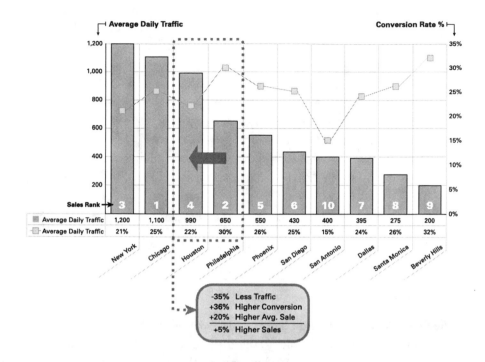

Each store in a chain is unique. Think about what I said earlier: each store is located in a unique geography. It has different staff, different demographics of the customers in its immediate market, different competitors, different climate, and different microeconomic conditions.

In the final analysis *it's less important how stores compare to other stores as it is to how it performs versus itself*; however, comparing stores does serve a purpose: it helps us more precisely target resource requirements and gain insight into what's possible. How does Philadelphia deliver these results? What's the staffing level? Who's the manager? Is he/she doing something that other stores should be emulating?

Let's look at another example of comparative store performance, first with sales results and transaction data, then again with traffic and conversion added into the mix.

The chart below shows a district of twelve stores from a different chain, ranked from highest average daily sales to lowest.

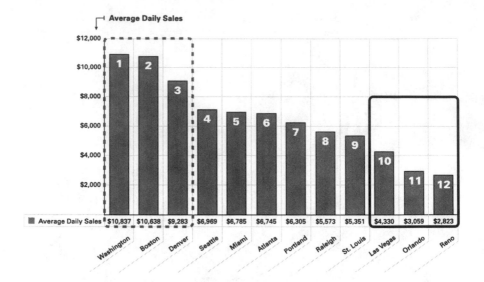

When we take the stores that had the highest and lowest average daily sales and compare these results to the number of sales transactions each produced, as in the chart below, we see that the transaction rank correlates to sales results fairly closely. The top three sales stores also had the top three transaction counts, and the lowest selling stores had the lowest number of transactions.

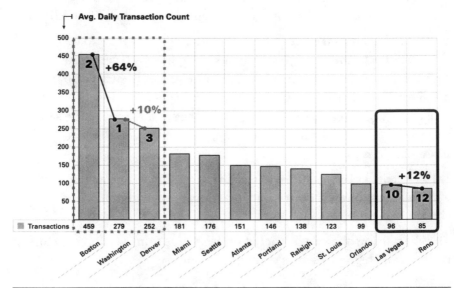

Given that so many retailers rely on transaction count data as a proxy for traffic, it's worth exploring these data further.

While the sales results and transaction count results are directionally consistent, they don't match perfectly. Washington ranked first in sales but trailed Boston in transaction counts by 64%. If we think of transaction counts as a proxy for traffic, we would conclude that Boston had 64% higher traffic than Washington, and that Denver had 10% less.

At the other end of the scale, the bottom three stores' transaction counts correlate very highly to overall sales results. The Reno store had the lowest number of transactions and the lowest sales rank. Using transactions as a proxy for traffic, we would conclude that Las Vegas had 12% more customer traffic than Reno.

Before we get too carried away with thinking that transactions are a good proxy for traffic, I want to dispel that idea right now: *transactions are not a good proxy for traffic*. The chart below shows average daily traffic compared to average daily transaction count by store. As you can see, the variances between transaction counts and traffic counts are very significant.

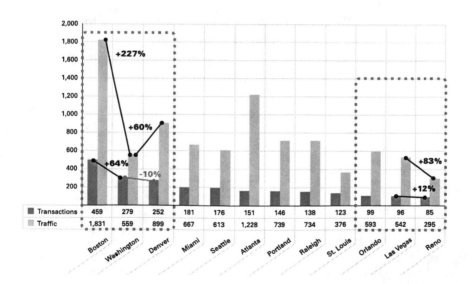

Let's look at the top three stores first. Boston had 64% more transactions than Washington, but it actually had 227% <u>more</u> prospect traffic. And on a transaction count basis, Denver had 10% fewer counts than Washington — but 60% more prospect traffic. At the low end of the scale, we see the same thing. Las Vegas didn't have 12% more traffic than Reno, as the transaction count implied; it had <u>83% more</u> prospect traffic.

These are not small variances. They're significant differences that have wide-ranging consequences. They completely change how management needs to think about and manage performance in these stores.

Today, many retailers still use transactions as a proxy for traffic. These transaction counts are used for, among other things, scheduling staff. As the above examples illustrates, if you scheduled staff based on transaction counts instead of prospect traffic, you would be seriously off the mark, and you would miss sales opportunities that you didn't even realize the stores had.

## Traffic and conversion to the rescue – again

By understanding the traffic and conversion profiles of each store, we can come to understand how the stores are really performing. We can determine which are truly the top performers and where the opportunities are. The chart below shows the traffic and conversion rate by store.

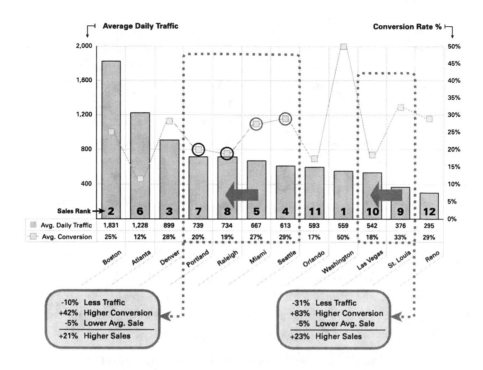

Washington ranked #1 in sales but had significantly less traffic than the other top-ranked stores. The strikingly impressive sales results in this store are being driven by a huge conversion rate; this store, more than any other, makes the most out of its relatively small traffic opportunity.

The Atlanta store is also notable, but not in a good way. This store had the second-highest traffic volume (or opportunity), but the best it could manage is a sixth-place sales rank. Think of the potential this store has! If it improved its conversion rate from 12% to 13% — just a single point — holding traffic and average ticket values constant, its sales rank would jump from sixth to fourth.

It's impossible not to compare stores when you see the results presented this way. St. Louis generated 23% higher sales than Las Vegas despite having 31% less traffic and a 5% lower average ticket – conversion rate was the difference. Miami and Raleigh are another interesting pair. Miami had 10% less traffic and a 5% lower average ticket but still managed to deliver 21% higher sales.

Even the most skeptical executive has to be intrigued by the possibilities traffic and conversion insights offer. Imagine how powerful this information could be in the hands of District Managers as they work to drive sales results across their stores. With only sales results and transaction data to reply upon, they're lost. They grope around in the dark, making random decisions that seem reasonable and logical based on the transaction data, but, in the light of traffic and conversion data, are blatantly wrong.

# Moving the right lever

As these examples show, each store has a unique traffic, customer conversion, and average ticket profile. The sales results the stores deliver are a function of these variables. The ultimate value in understanding these profiles is to identify what lever or levers will deliver the greatest impact on sales results for each store. Without the context that traffic and conversion data provide, this would not be possible.

For example, Atlanta had high traffic and low conversion. If management decided that in order to drive sales, it would launch an aggressive advertising campaign, what would the likely outcome be? This store already has more traffic than it can practically manage, so increasing traffic could hardly be the right decision. Or what if management decided that additional sales training was required to improve sales results in the St. Louis store? The store already has a high conversion rate and a reasonable average ticket – more sales training would likely have very little if any impact on this store's overall sales results. This store needs traffic!

The table below is an example of how traffic and conversion data can help reveal the most important sales lever for each store. Some stores have high customer conversion and average ticket but low traffic. These stores need advertising to increase traffic.

| STORE | AVERAGE DAILY TRAFFIC | CONVERSION RATE | AVERAGE SALE $ | SALES |
|---|---|---|---|---|
| North Chicago | 620 | 33% Conversion | $20 Average Sale | $4,092 |
| Northbrook | 385 Traffic | 48% | $35 | $6,468 |
| Highland Park | 500 | 29% Conversion | $40 | $5,800 |
| Lombard | 395 Traffic | 52% | $31 | $6,367 |
| Oak Park | 680 | 35% Conversion | $26 Average Sale | $6,188 |
| Downers Grove | 555 | 41% | $25 Average Sale | $5,689 |
| Elmhurst | 692 | 27% Conversion | $38 | $7,100 |
| Des Plaines | 420 | 38% | $33 | $5,267 |
| Arlington Heights | 388 Traffic | 42% | $33 | $5,378 |
| Cicero | 720 | 25% Conversion | $36 | $6,480 |
| Wilmette | 636 | 33% | $28 Average Sale | $5,877 |
| Joliet | 390 Traffic | 29% Conversion | $44 | $4,976 |
| Skokie | 550 | 45% | $19 Average Sale | $4,703 |
| West Chicago | 850 | 26% Conversion | $29 | $6,409 |
| Wheaton | 400 Traffic | 51% | $32 | $6,528 |
| East Chicago | 700 | 40% | $36 | $9,996 |
| District Average | 555 | 37% | $32 | $6,500 |

Some stores have ample traffic but need to improve conversion rates. This could mean more staff hours, better training, or perhaps an inventory re-set. Some stores have ample traffic and a reasonable conversion rate, but low average ticket value. Perhaps sales training to sharpen the staff's up-sell and cross-sell skills are in order. And, lastly, some stores have multiple issues, and a combination of tactics may be required to get sales performance on track.

With an understanding of what the most important levers are by store, management is able to target the right programs to the right stores. Not only does this knowledge help stores deliver better results; it also helps the Head Office make better, more cost effective program investment decisions.

# Finding opportunities and doing something about them

Sales outcomes are just outcomes. It's great if sales are going up, but knowing what's driving the sales is critical. Stores generally don't control traffic, but they do control what they do with traffic that comes in. Stores with low traffic but higher conversion and average sale need more traffic.

Traffic for these locations is the key performance driver. Stores with high traffic but low conversion and average sale need to focus on driving these two metrics. Perhaps it's staffing levels, perhaps it's training or inventory, but whatever the driver is, we know what it's not. It's not traffic.

Using traffic and conversion analytics to put store results in context cannot in and of itself change outcomes, but it does provide management with critical insights into how results are being driven, and more importantly, how to improve them.

*A constant flow of prospect traffic into the stores is absolutely key to a chain's growth and success.* So now let's turn our attention to how traffic and customer conversion can help retail marketers achieve that constant flow by making the most of every precious nickel they spend on advertising and promotions.

# Chapter 2.3

## Why Good Advertising Can Look Bad

Of the multitude of uses for traffic and conversion analytics, measuring the impact of advertising and promotional investments is among the most important. Beyond inventory and payroll, advertising is one of the largest and most critical investments retailers make, so it's reasonable to conclude that the head of Marketing would be among the most interested, maybe even <u>the</u> most interested, in measures that can provide answers to the fundamental question: Did our advertising work? Ironically, in my experience, marketers tend to be among the most skeptical and reluctant adopters of traffic and conversion analytics.

Despite the vast quantities of data, analytics, and sophisticated tools at their disposal today, marketers still lament the lack of measurability of their efforts. Yet measuring store traffic and customer conversion don't seem to be on the collective radar screens of retail marketers.

The simple fact is that store traffic and customer conversion are among the simplest and most effective ways to measure the impact of marketing investments. If your promotional investments are not driving more prospects into your stores, and/or lifting customer conversion rates, then what are they doing?

In this chapter we'll focus on why retail marketers need to open their minds to and enthusiastically embrace all the ways traffic and customer conversion analytics can measure the impact of marketing and promotional investments. When they do, they'll be able to measure the impact of their advertising investments, optimize programs to spend less and get more, and, once and for all, be able to confidently look the CEO in the eye and justify the investments and quantitatively support marketing decisions.

# Measurability – the Holy Grail

As a former marketing executive, I remember my constant struggle with measurability. How do we know if the marketing investments paid off? How do we know if they worked? These are fundamental questions that every retail marketing executive needs to know the answers to, but many do not.

While my own background may make me mildly sympathetic to the marketers' dilemma, it's undeniable that they work in a complex and pressure packed environment. There's nothing simple about retail marketing. From branding and media buying, to ad testing, research, creative execution, and much more, the Chief Marketing Officer and his/her team are called upon to make it happen. The CMO has stewardship over a significant budget, and there is considerable pressure to deliver sales results.

We've all heard it a thousand times: marketing is both art and science. While many of the decisions and elements of marketing are subjective (creative, for example), there is a considerable body of data and quasi-science that goes into decisions about buying media, ad effectiveness, and market share. There are established measures for certain elements of marketing programs, but according to surveys of marketers, there's plenty of uncertainty about what the programs are delivering.

Well, if there's so much uncertainty and lack of reliable marketing measures, then why are expectations so high for retail marketers to measure it? The simple answer: big budgets.

Large marketing budgets, tight margins, and razor thin profits – all drive the expectations. It is anathema to any business executive to make huge investments without having an understanding of the return on these investments.[1] It's downright reckless.

So, given the significant pressure to measure results, retail marketers are compelled to look for answers. They look for any clues they can find, sift through results, dive even deeper into the transaction data, maybe even conduct a focus group or two and try to draw conclusions about the impact of the investments and efficacy of their programs. The analysis is often based on anecdotal and qualitative data, wrapped in a formal

ROI presentation that gives it an air of quantitative reliability. Often the results of the analysis don't relate to sales performance, and the CMO and the rest of the executive team are left wondering what to do next.

Part of the problem is that retail marketers are simply ill prepared to provide the answers. Retail marketing education, while it regards campaign assessment as significant, provides students with too little instruction in measuring the effectiveness of marketing programs and no clear answers as to how to do the assessments.

While there is a plethora of marketing measures for the lucky direct marketer,[2] the retail marketer continues to struggle with brand studies, focus groups, and the ubiquitous and likely dubious ROI to try to make decisions and support investments. When the results are inconclusive or negative, the reaction is often to "stay the course" and continue to do what we've always done until more conclusive answers emerge.

Traffic and customer conversion data can bring far more light to these marketing decisions than transactional data, advertising awareness studies, or focus groups. Traffic and conversion rate are the fundamental metrics every retail marketer needs.

# Why good advertising can look bad

I did some work with a major hard goods retailer, and this is exactly what happened – their good advertising looked bad.

The Marketing team rolled up their sleeves, carefully assessed the media options, scrutinized and tested the creative, and then brilliantly executed a chain-wide, one-day promotional campaign that ran on the third Saturday of the month. This program represented a major financial investment, and the goal was clear: deliver a meaningful lift in top-line sales.

The campaign launched, and the marketing team held its collective breath. The sales results looked like the chart below. Not good.

Compared to other Saturdays during the month (and last year's comparative sales), results were embarrassingly underwhelming. Sales results for the day of the event were <u>down</u> 12% from the prior week and about flat compared to Saturday #1, when sales volume was downright lethargic. According to these results, the big promotion on Saturday #3 was an unequivocal failure.

| | Saturday #1 | Saturday #2 | Saturday #3 | Saturday #4 |
|---|---|---|---|---|
| Average Sales per Store | $75,250 | $85,000 | $74,400 | $81,600 |

If the goal is to deliver a lift in top-line sales, then the results are clear – the promotion didn't pay off. It didn't work. The numbers don't lie, and no matter how deep you dig into the POS transaction data, the conclusion won't change. Even worse, no one can explain why.

This is problematic because the CEO and CFO, among others, have distilled the whole advertising effectiveness question down to a very simple, but unfortunately incorrect proposition: an advertising investment should lead to improved sales results. If it doesn't, it's not working – or is it?

## Advertising and promotions create in-store sales opportunities.

*The fundamental problem with retail marketing is that its effectiveness is almost always measured by sales results.*

The expectation is clear: we invest a lot of money in advertising and promotions, and we expect a measurable increase in sales. This proposition assumes a direct, causal relationship between advertising and sales results. Notwithstanding bad creative decisions, media mix or general execution issues, if there were a direct causal relationship, then indeed sales would be the right measure for advertising and promotional effectiveness, and the more you invested in advertising, the more sales you would generate.

The root problem (and to a great extent it's a fallacy that marketers have perpetuated themselves) is that *there is not a direct, causal relationship between advertising and sales outcomes.* And, as my last example shows, advertising and promotional investments far too often have very modest or no material impact on sales results.

Now, many retail marketing executives know very well that advertising (even really effective advertising) doesn't necessarily translate directly into sales results. But no one seems to want to break the news to the CEO or CFO.

The CMO and his/her team get called on the carpet for the campaign post-mortem, which invariably includes a multitude of data indicating that the campaign reached the appropriate audience, that the media buy and mix were right, and of course, the good old pre- and post-awareness scores were off-the-charts positive.

So what went wrong? Why were sales underwhelming?

In the end, the marketers fall on their swords and vow to do better next time, and the discontinuity between the claim of advertising effectiveness and lack of sales results is written off as inherent in the vagaries of advertising – it's why advertising is considered both art and science.

It seems that the "art" is the part marketers can't seem to reliably measure.

As long as retail marketers use sales as the measure of success, they will remain condemned to marketing purgatory, where promotional impact assessment remains unachievable, and an eternity of "promote and hope" awaits. OK, a little dramatic, but true nonetheless.

## Stop looking in the till for answers.

Retail marketing investments can be measured, but the measure is not in sales outcomes. As the framework below indicates, first and foremost, retail advertising is the catalyst for driving <u>prospective</u> buyers into the store[3] (and to your website). Getting potential buyers into the store is critical – no traffic, no sale. Once the prospect visits the store, many things need to happen in order to convert the visit into a sale. If conversion takes place, then, and only then, does a sale occur.

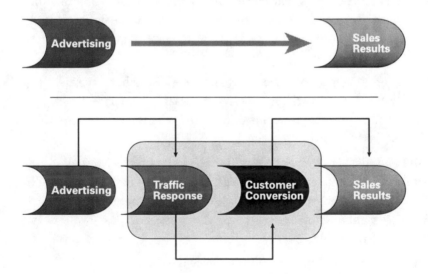

So now back to the big, one-day promotion example. Because this retailer tracked store traffic, we were able to determine how many prospects visited the store and what the customer conversion rate was. This additional context changed everything.

We know that sales were down by 12% on the promotion Saturday, compared to the prior Saturday, but we also now know that store traffic was actually <u>up 24%</u> from the prior week – delivering on average 3,100 prospects per store— more than any Saturday during the month. Unfortunately, we also know that customer conversion rates dropped dramatically on the promotion day.

Instead of the 68%-70% of the previous weeks, customer conversion rate sagged to an abysmal 48% — that's down a whopping 30% from the prior week.

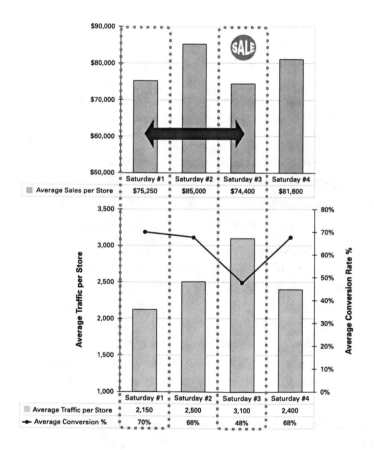

| | Saturday #1 | Saturday #2 | Saturday #3 | Saturday #4 |
|---|---|---|---|---|
| Average Sales per Store | $75,250 | $85,000 | $74,400 | $81,600 |

| | Saturday #1 | Saturday #2 | Saturday #3 | Saturday #4 |
|---|---|---|---|---|
| Average Traffic per Store | 2,150 | 2,500 | 3,100 | 2,400 |
| Average Conversion % | 70% | 68% | 48% | 68% |

After considering the additional context that traffic and customer conversion data provide, you reach an entirely different conclusion than from sales results alone. The promotion did indeed drive more prospects into the store, but unfortunately, the store was unable to successfully convert this traffic into sales. There's a whole host of reasons why these prospects didn't buy, and management certainly needs to investigate further to understand why. But at least you can now say categorically that the promotion did indeed work.

## Putting results in context changes everything.

Once a prospect visits the store, the advertising has mostly done its job. It has created a sales opportunity for the store. If marketing executives view advertising and promotional investments as investments in creating sales opportunities as measured by prospect traffic, the solve-for will be significantly clarified. The advertising objective should be to drive qualified prospect traffic into the stores — period.

The problem is that many retail marketing executives struggle with this idea; I struggle with why they struggle!

As I recall some of the heated debates I've had with CMOs over the years, I think there are several issues that have created this uncertainty.

- First, advertising and promotional investments are significant, and the outcomes unpredictable, so there's a lot of anxiety for the CEO, CFO, and others who have to explain the results (or lack thereof) to stakeholders. The notion of judging advertising investments by sales outcomes (as opposed to driving traffic) is so ingrained in senior management that it is heresy to suggest otherwise. I think Marketing leaders are in a very difficult spot. Who wants to tell the CEO and CFO that the $20M he invests annually in advertising and promotions doesn't directly drive sales outcomes?

- Second, the vast majority of retailers don't actually track prospect traffic in all their stores, so they simply don't have the data and consequently can't measure results. Sales transaction data are used as a proxy for prospect traffic (i.e., customer count is the number of sales transaction generated), but, as previously explained, sales transactions are not the same as prospect traffic counts and therefore do not provide an accurate picture of the results.

- Third, many retail marketing leaders sincerely don't believe that traffic is the best measure of their advertising and promotional investments. I can't blame the CMO. The notion of traffic as a measure of advertising effectiveness has not (yet) been embraced by the retail advertising industry or retail educators, so how should the CMO come to the conclusion that it should be? Meanwhile, the CEO and CFO are expecting to see an ROI on the marketing investments, and to even suggest that advertising doesn't lead to sales will either get you replaced (you're clearly incompetent) or your budgets reduced – if it can't drive sales, let's invest in other programs that will, like sales training.

In a meeting with a Senior Vice President of Marketing for a large general merchandiser, I engaged in exactly this discussion. His position was clear: he expects his advertising investments to generate sales. I used the chart below to help explain the process. I argued that if his advertising was effective and generated a significant lift in store traffic, then it was indeed effective, but it was very possible that the traffic didn't deliver the sales because the traffic didn't buy.

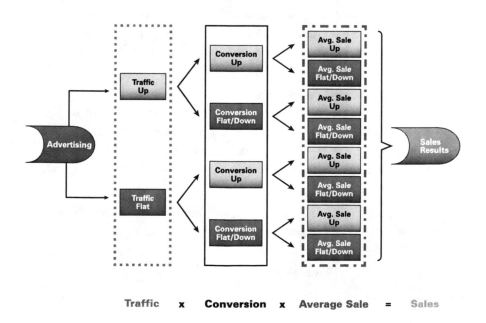

As a traffic and conversion analyst, when advertising or a promotional campaign is launched, I want to understand the changes in all three underlying variables that contribute to sales: traffic, customer conversion rates and average ticket.[4] By breaking down the results into the underlying drivers, you can start to understand what impact your marketing investment had. Let's look at each.

**Traffic Impact:**

The first, and in many ways most important question is: Did store traffic increase or not? Fundamentally, promotional activity should drive more prospects into the store. If your promotional activity does not deliver more store traffic, then it would be reasonable to conclude that it was ineffective.

There are three potential traffic responses: (1) traffic increases, (2) traffic remains flat, or (3) traffic decreases. It's unlikely that traffic will decrease when advertising is launched, but it is possible. Perhaps a competitor launches an aggressive program at the same time as you, or there is a massive weather event that prevents prospects from visiting your stores. In these situations, store traffic may very well be down despite your promotional efforts. However, beyond these extenuating circumstances, traffic volume should go up, and the results will be obvious and easily quantifiable – if you track traffic in your stores.

So if the goal of the promotional activity is to create more sales opportunities in the store, then traffic volume is the most meaningful measure of effectiveness. The assumption here is that the promotional activity will be targeted to qualified prospects, so that the more traffic a store receives, the more bona fide sales opportunities it has.

Given the above, the objective of your promotional activity should therefore be to *increase store traffic volume relative to current traffic or year-over-year comparable traffic volume*, while at the same time minimizing the cost of acquiring the traffic.

## Customer Conversion Impact:

Once we understand the traffic response, we then need to look at changes in customer conversion rate. As with traffic, there are three potential customer conversion outcomes: (1) conversion rates increase, (2) conversion rates remain unchanged, or (3) conversion rates decrease. It's important to understand customer conversion rate changes: these data give us important clues about how well the stores are performing and how well the promotional activity was targeted.

Let's start with decreasing conversion rates. It's common to see conversion rates sag during promotions that increase store traffic. Traffic volume and customer conversion tend to be inversely related, so when the store gets too busy, every prospect might not get served, and some may leave without buying. Just as in the previous promotion example, store traffic was up materially, but conversion rates dropped, and sales gains weren't realized. The trick is to either maintain current conversion rate levels or even increase them in the face of increased store traffic. If you can do that, sales will increase.

There are many reasons why customer conversion rates decrease significantly during a promotion. Perhaps the store is understaffed, or staff scheduling was misaligned with the traffic volume. Perhaps the store has the wrong inventory or not enough inventory. Perhaps the store is poorly merchandised, so prospects can't find what they were looking for. Perhaps there were long lines at check-out, and buyers abandoned their shopping carts. Regardless of why conversion rates fell, the point is, they did. *There is no point investing money in promotional activities that drive more prospect traffic into the store if the store is unable to service the traffic adequately*, and customer conversion helps you understand this fact.

There's a huge downside as well. The money you invested in the promotion was wasted, and, worse, if prospects visit the store, can't get served and leave without buying, there's a good chance they will be disinclined to visit again, and they might even tell others about their poor in-store experience, hurting future sales.

Another reason why customer conversion rates can sag is that the promotional activity is not well targeted. For example, a promotion that offers free giveaways to the first 100 people in the store may indeed drive traffic up, but if these people come into the store, collect their freebie and then leave, then obviously, conversion rates will decrease. The good news: you increased traffic; the bad news: they weren't legitimate prospects.

**Average Sale Impact:**

Given that sales are a function of traffic, of customer conversion rate and of average sale value, I'll briefly mention this final variable, despite the fact that most retailers already monitor average sale values closely. Generally, average sale values are influenced by factors within the store (e.g., the effectiveness of sales staff); however, promotions can influence average sale values in a very important way: loss leaders.

If the promotion features select products that are offered at deep discounts, it's possible that traffic and customer conversion can both rise – more prospects and more qualified buyers buying – but customers are mostly buying deeply discounted product and consequently average sales values are significantly lower. In this case, despite the increased traffic and a good conversion rate, sales results may appear underwhelming.

Context is critical, and without breaking sales results into the underlying drivers of traffic, customer conversion, and average sale, retail marketers will never have a complete understanding of what their promotional investments are delivering. If the marketing is not driving prospects to the store, this is a marketing problem. Review the marketing plans in detail, make changes, and experiment. If traffic is up, but customer conversion rates are down, that is, the stores are not converting the sales opportunities into sales, the store operations team needs to dig deep into the customer conversion data to understand why prospects aren't buying.

Getting poor sales outcomes from your promotional investments is forgivable – measure the results, adjust plans, experiment and try again. Failing to measure the impact of your promotional investments and continuing to do the same things over and over with the same inconclusive outcomes is unforgivable and reckless.

# Advertising effectiveness: seeing is believing

OK, enough of the theory, let's look at some more real-world examples. The chart below shows the traffic and customer conversion rate by day over the course of a month for a general merchandise retailer.

During the four-day sale that ran from May 12-15, it's clear just by looking at the chart that traffic levels were up – significantly. If you measured the average daily traffic counts during the sale period and compared them to the average for the other days of the month when the promotion was not in effect, you would find that average daily traffic was up over 120%. Moreover, conversion rates during the promotion averaged 18%, which was only slightly below the monthly average of 19%. And, despite average ticket being down 25%, average daily sales during the promotion were up 60%.

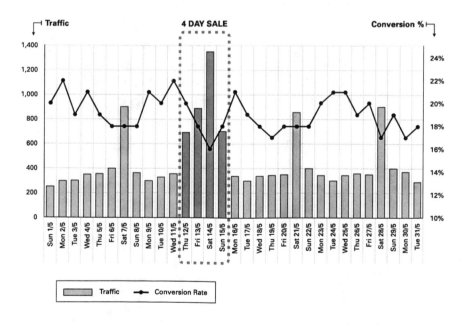

The promotion was clearly successful, and in this case, the sales results reflected it. But as significant as a 60% increase in average daily sales is, it actually understates the impact: traffic was up over 120%.

Beyond measuring the overall impact, our traffic and conversion data enable us to drill down further to better understand the impact during each day of the promotion.

The promotion kicked off on Thursday and ran through Sunday, and in addition to understanding the overall promotional impact, this retailer was also interested in understanding how the promotion performed by day of week. Using this same data set, we were able to easily provide the answer, and it was interesting.

Thursday had the biggest relative increase in traffic compared to the average Thursday for the month — up a whopping 100%. At the same time, customer conversion was up 17%. On Friday, traffic was up only 10% compared to the average Friday, while the conversion rate sagged by 5% compared to other Fridays.

On the Saturday of the promotion, traffic was up 53% compared to the other Saturdays in the month, and customer conversion rates were up by 8%. Sunday followed suit. Traffic was up smartly by 50% compared to other Sundays, but customer conversion rate dropped by 20%, again offsetting almost half of the gain created by the traffic increase.

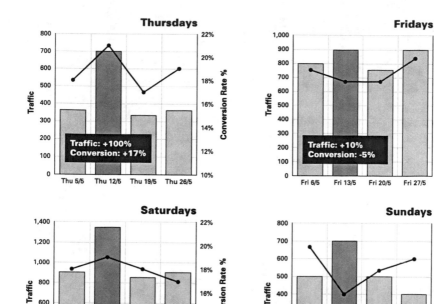

By breaking the results out by day of week, this retailer was able to understand how customers responded to the promotion each day, identify conversion rate sags on the Friday and Sunday, and then use these insights to adjust in-store stocking levels and staff schedules during promotions to improve customer conversion rates and ultimately drive higher sales. Good insights and easy to do, if you have the data.

# Comparing promotions

In the next example, a specialty soft-goods retailer was interested in understanding the impact of three different promotions over the course of the month. Specifically, the retailer wanted to know how the week #2 test promotion (which included an entirely new flyer) affected traffic and conversion compared to the standard creative of the flyers in weeks #1 and #3 promotions. The traffic and conversion chart is shown below.

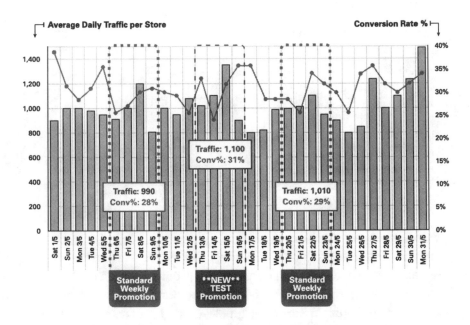

Compared to the week #1 promotion, week #2 had 10% higher average daily traffic, and customer conversion rate was up an impressive three points. More traffic and higher conversion rate – a double hit that, despite a lower average ticket, resulted in overall net sales rising almost 15% compared to week#1.

When we compared week#3 to week #2, we found the results were also positive. Average daily traffic was up 8%, and customer conversion was up two full points, or about 5%. Overall sales were up 8% in week #2, the test promotion week, compared to week #3.

As it turned out, there was, during the week #2 test promotion, no unusual weather or competitive behavior that would have influenced sales, so it's reasonable to conclude that the test promotion was successful.

Experimentation is the only way to discover new, potentially more effective approaches. Sometimes they work, and sometimes they don't. While it's never a great outcome to see sales slump, at least this retailer was able to measure results, understand what drove the sales outcomes, and then course-correct.

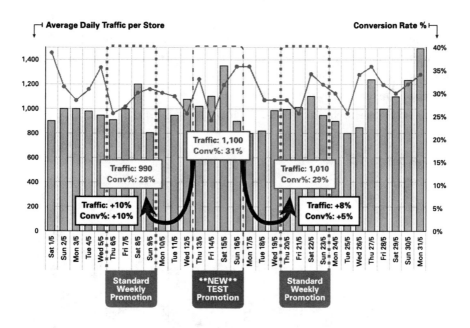

You might be asking what traffic and conversion tells you that the sales results alone don't. After all, sales were up almost 15% from week #1 and 8% from week #3, so wouldn't any marketers in their right mind deem the week #2 test promotion a success anyway? Very likely, but traffic and conversion provides a level of precision that sales data alone cannot.

In this case, the increase in sales was a result of not only more prospects in the store, but more visitors buying. Without traffic and conversion context, it would have been impossible to know what drove the sales results. Relying upon sales and transaction data would lead this marketer to believe that the sales lift was a result of the increased traffic, thus overstating the traffic impact, when in fact the sales lift was the result of a combination of traffic and increased conversion rates.

# Comparing promotions across markets

In the next example, a specialty hard-goods retailer was interested in understanding the impact of different media mixes in three major markets — Chicago, Denver, and Seattle. Overall chain traffic and customer conversion by day for the month of May (excluding the three test markets) is shown in the chart below.

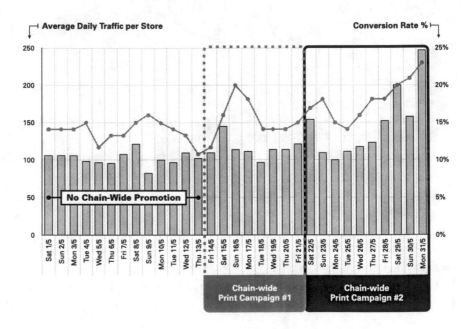

During the first two weeks of May, there was no advertising. In week #3, a national print campaign was rolled out to all markets and followed by a second, even heavier national print campaign in week #4.

Comparing the first print campaign in week #3 to the average of the first two weeks, we found that both traffic and customer conversion were up − 15%. Week #4 was up significantly more as the campaign ramped up. Compared to the first two weeks, traffic and customer conversion were up significantly — 40% and 30%, respectively.

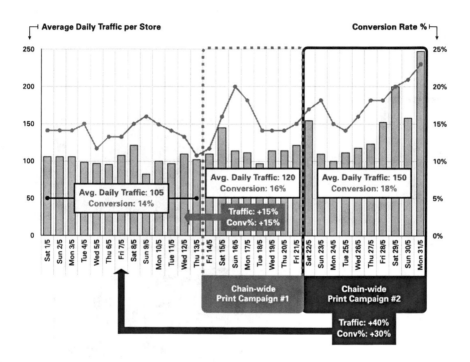

The point of the exercise was to use traffic and customer conversion data to better understand what impact, if any, different media mixes had in different key markets. The overall chain average gave us our baseline. Now on to the individual markets.

## Market #1: Chicago

In Chicago, there was no advertising during the first two weeks of the month, and the two print campaigns generated results that were directionally similar to the overall chain average. The results are shown in the chart below.

Traffic and customer conversion were up in weeks #3 and #4. However, the gains in traffic and conversion in week #3, compared to the first two weeks, were much more modest than the chain-wide results. Week #4 results were even stronger than the chain results, with traffic up 60% and customer conversion up 30%.

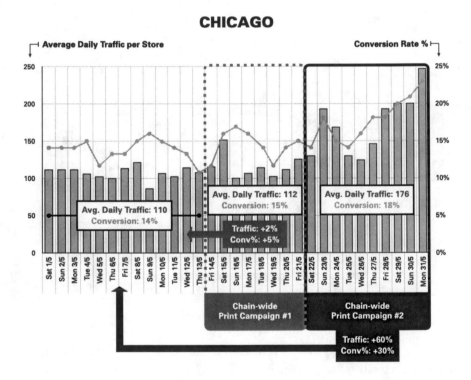

## Market #2: Denver

A key question the CMO wanted to answer was: what impact, if any, did incremental investments in advertising have on traffic and conversion rate results? He selected Denver as one of his test markets, and here's where things started to get interesting.

In Denver the national print campaigns were augmented by an aggressive radio campaign that was scheduled during week #3, as shown in the chart below.

Compared to the chain average, the first two weeks in Denver were very similar, in both traffic and customer conversion. However, the results were dramatically different in week #3 – traffic was up 40%, and customer conversion rate, up 36%. compared to the first two weeks.

The combination of radio and print dramatically increased traffic to the stores. And not only was there more traffic in the store, but there were also more buyers, as evidenced by the increase in conversion rate. In week #4, the print only campaign rolled along but failed to deliver the traffic lift that week #3 did. The addition of radio to the campaign in week #3 clearly had a positive impact.

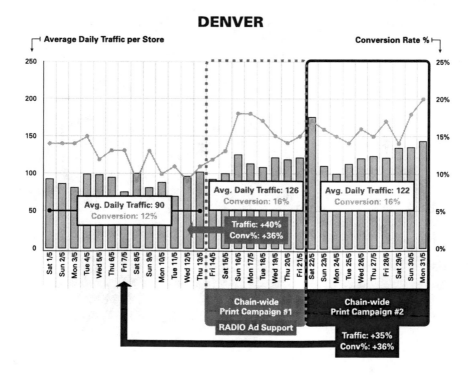

**DENVER**

## Market #3: Seattle

The third and final test market was Seattle, and this one was of particular interest to management because it was here that the company had been struggling for some time. In an effort to kick-start sales, the CMO invested in a double shot, with radio advertising to augment the print campaigns in weeks #3 and #4. The results are shown in the chart below.

As in Denver, the Seattle print campaign was augmented by radio, but the results were nothing like Denver's. Traffic, conversion, and sales were basically flat in weeks #1-#3, and despite the fact that weeks #3 and #4 included radio advertising, the impact on both traffic and customer conversion, compared to the first two weeks, was negligible. Seattle remained a mystery, and the CMO needed to go back to the drawing board.

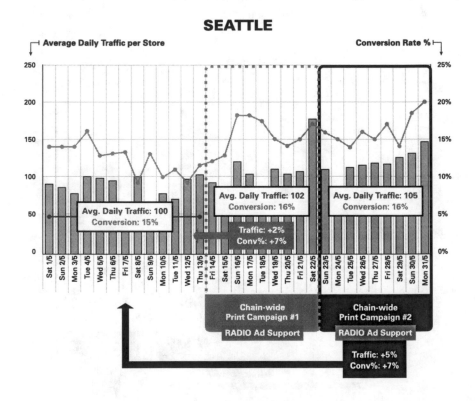

So what, in the final analysis, did this retailer learn that he couldn't have learned without traffic and customer conversion data?

First, that Chicago, which had the same advertising effort as all other markets, had a bigger lift the last week compared to the third week. Ensuring staff are ready the next time this happens could help deliver even better sales results.

Second, the retailer learns that the additional spend on radio in Denver had a powerful impact on traffic volume and customer conversion. Adding radio to the print in week #3 delivered better results than a ramped-up print-only campaign in week #4. Without traffic and conversion, the retailer would have never known just how effectively the extra advertising drove traffic.

And, finally, management learned that the advertising program in Seattle had little impact. Not only did it not generate materially more prospect traffic to the store, but conversion remained lethargic as well. Management needs to totally re-think Seattle.

When promotional activities don't deliver the expected sales lift, marketers often wonder if the stores simply failed to execute. They say things like "The stores were busy, but I'm not sure the store sales teams made the most of it." With traffic and conversion data, you don't have to speculate – the results are clear.

# Promotional Impact – variations by store

Measuring promotional impact chain-wide is important, but ultimately, you need to understand traffic and conversion response right down to the store level. As the next real-world example will show, every store is unique, and the impact of a promotion can be very different.

We monitored the traffic and customer conversion rates for a sample of six big-box specialty stores, all located in Atlanta. Our goal was to help this chain understand what impact their flyers were having on traffic and customer conversion rates, overall and by store.

We analyzed the traffic volume and customer conversion rates for the stores over a six-month period, comparing results when flyers were in effect (we labeled these "flyer days") to days when flyers were not in effect ("non-flyer days"). For both flyer and non-flyer days, we excluded holidays, special events, and days when bad weather may have influenced results. The results are shown in the table below.

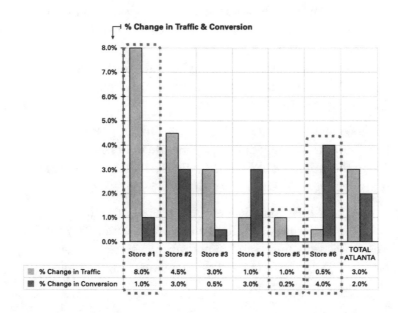

| | Store #1 | Store #2 | Store #3 | Store #4 | Store #5 | Store #6 | TOTAL ATLANTA |
|---|---|---|---|---|---|---|---|
| % Change in Traffic | 8.0% | 4.5% | 3.0% | 1.0% | 1.0% | 0.5% | 3.0% |
| % Change in Conversion | 1.0% | 3.0% | 0.5% | 3.0% | 0.2% | 4.0% | 2.0% |

Naturally we hypothesized that flyer days would have higher traffic and/or higher customer conversion rates than non-flyer days, and when we ran the numbers, that is exactly what we found. However, what was surprising was how the traffic and conversion responses varied so much by store.

All six stores' combined flyer days had 3% higher traffic and 2% higher customer conversion rates than non-flyer days. Traffic up and conversion up – this is a good thing. At store #1, traffic spiked by 8% on average compared to non-flyer days, and customer conversion rate was up 1%. Clearly, customers who shop at this location are very responsive to flyers.

Store #5 was very interesting, but for exactly the opposite reason: lack of response. There was very little difference in store traffic or customer conversion rates during flyer days compared to non-flyer days. In this case, the flyers had virtually no impact.

Store #6 was curious because the flyers didn't seem to attract more traffic into the store, but customer conversion rates were up by 4% compared to non-flyer days. The increase in conversion may have been driven by the featured items in the flyer, or perhaps by better in-store execution. In any event, the traffic needle didn't seem to move.

*Knowing the promotional response by store is important* for several reasons. First, with an understanding of the response profile, store management can better prepare the store and deliver stronger results.

The manager at store #1, knowing that his store experienced a consistently large lift in traffic, started scheduling additional sales staff on flyer days, and customer conversion rates and overall sales increased further. This manager already knew his store was busy on flyer days, but he didn't know by how much. The additional context traffic and conversion data provided enabled him to build a case for the additional sales resources he needed.

At store #5, the manager prepared for promotions by coaching his staff to spend more quality time with the prospects that did enter the store. The Store Manager, now armed with traffic and conversion data, understood that flyers didn't necessarily deliver more overall traffic to his store, so he had his staff focus on improving conversion rate and average ticket for the traffic he did get. And the manager at store #6, realizing that buying behavior increased, made sure his check-outs were running smoothly and that inventory levels were up on the featured SKUs.

# Other measurement challenges

The examples above all seem to fit nicely into discrete, tidy packages. But as we all well know, it's not always so clean and simple. The chart below shows the promotional activities of a general merchandiser over the course of a month.

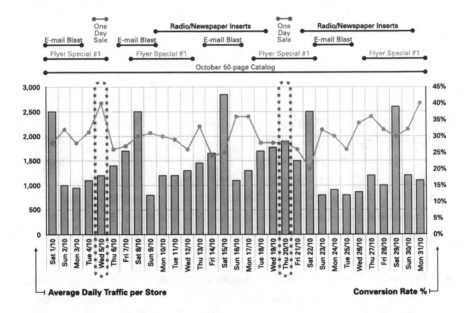

Obviously, there's a lot going on here. There's not just one flyer or one promotion; there's a whole bunch of them, and they overlap. Throw weather into the mix, and you start to wonder exactly what, if anything, you can discern from the results. It's a fair question. With so much going on, even with the benefit of traffic and conversion analysis, it's difficult to get a handle on what's driving what. And some retailers use this complexity as an excuse for not measuring – "it's immeasurable, so why bother?"

Unquestionably a promotional plan like the one shown above presents measurement challenges, but that doesn't mean you shouldn't try. While traffic and customer conversion analysis will not magically make it any easier to precisely measure every aspect of a complex promotional schedule, they will provide additional context and insights that you could not have had otherwise.

When retailers aggressively promote, layering campaign on campaign, a solid 52 weeks of the year, another way to come at the marketing effectiveness question is to ask, "What would happen if you took something away? If you ran one less flyer, reduced the size of some of your print ads or discontinued one flight of radio?"

When your only measure is sales, the risks seem high – what if sales go down? Without context, it's a guess; it seems more risky. However, when you have traffic and conversion data, you have the context you need to confidently experiment. Experimentation is the only way to discover new, potentially more effective approaches; however, experimentation without adequate measures is little more than gambling.

# Traffic is a leading indicator.

Most typically advertising investments are made with the intent to drive incremental traffic into the stores, however it may well be that advertising is needed just to maintain the traffic you already have. Aggressive competitors, changing customer wants, or other macro factors can cause traffic to wane in your stores. The chart below clearly shows the systemic year-over-year declines in average daily store traffic across this apparel chain.

In this case, the significant reduction in store traffic contributed to a slight increase in customer conversion rates (remember: traffic and conversion tend to be inversely related), so the overall traffic declines looked less dramatic based on the sales results alone. The traffic counts told the real story – across the chain, traffic was down by 20%, and the trend was continuing. This retailer needed to take decisive action to get prospects back into the store, and that's exactly what he did.

*Traffic is a leading indicator of a chain's health,*[5] and when it starts to wane, the number of sales opportunities is shrinking. Sales results will ultimately follow, because customer conversion gains that can naturally occur because of reduced traffic aren't enough to offset the traffic decreases. Still, advertising alone won't save you. Even if it brings prospects into the store, you must still convert if you're going to improve sales.

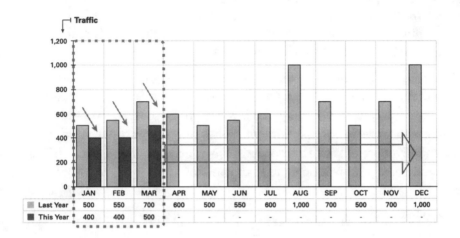

## Measuring promotional impact: test or guess

Regardless of what your advertising or promotional strategy is, if the objective is to drive a sales response, then the only way to really understand what happened is to put the results in context. It's not good enough that sales increased when you launched your promotion or advertising campaign. You need to understand which levers moved so that you can assess the impact, replicate the successful programs, and discard the unsuccessful ones.

Measuring the impact of advertising and promotional activities with sales results alone is tantamount to guessing. Sales are up, it worked; sales are flat, it failed. Without a doubt, this binary thinking has led to many sub-optimal marketing decisions.

I wonder how many potentially effective campaigns or promotions were discarded because the sales needle didn't move, when in fact, traffic was up materially, but the stores failed to <u>convert</u> the traffic, and the resulting sales were underwhelming. I also wonder about how many campaigns were repeated over and over, because there appeared to be some sales lift when the campaign first ran, but in reality store traffic didn't increase at all, and it was the effective store execution or maybe the new sales training program that delivered higher conversion rates. Sales were up despite the ineffective advertising, thanks to Store Operations, but Marketing got the credit.

Think about the marketing investments you make today. What if you could spend 5% less and still generate the same amount of traffic in the stores? What would that be worth? What if, for the same marketing budget, you were able to drive 10% more traffic into your stores? What would it be worth? With traffic and customer conversion, data you can begin to answer these questions and actually quantify the results.

Traffic and customer conversion data are completely objective measures uninfluenced by subjective opinion and sample error, unlike so many other retail marketing measures. The data are relatively inexpensive to collect and don't require a genius to extract useful insights. When implemented chain-wide (which you should do if you are serious about this), you have a comprehensive view, with data that can be analyzed hourly, by region, district, media market, store format and ultimately, by individual store. Traffic and customer conversion analysis was made for retail marketing!

The point of advertising and promotions is to create sales opportunities in the stores. Great advertising or an irresistibly compelling promotion can't guarantee sales, but they should deliver prospects to the store. And if they do that, they worked, and traffic and customer conversion analysis can quantitatively prove it. Retail marketers who have traffic and conversion data at their disposal have a significant advantage over to those who don't.

Part one is getting prospects to visit the store, and that's what advertising can do; part two is converting these prospects into buyers. Of all the factors that influence customer conversion, none is more important than those related to staffing, and that's where we turn our attention next.

# Chapter 2.4

## Staffing for Conversion

When I talk to retailers about optimizing staff scheduling with traffic and customer conversion insights, I'm almost always met with apprehension and even a mild disdain – "optimize" staffing? Yeah, right.

Admittedly, staffing is hard. There are no silver bullets, but it is significantly harder without the benefit of traffic and customer conversion analytics to help you make better decisions and improve your results.

For most retailers, labor expense represents one of the single largest, discretionary expense items in the business. The bottom-line benefits of getting staff scheduling right are significant, and that's why retailers spend so much time, attention and money on this issue. Unfortunately, despite the heroic effort, it still eludes most retailers. It's a little disturbing to see many retailers trying to manage staff scheduling using old heuristics, basic spreadsheets, or gut instincts.

The first step is to realize that "optimizing" staff is not a discrete task that, once accomplished, will remain neatly in place or solved – OK, staff are optimized, done. What's next? Optimizing labor is like a giant Rubik's Cube problem: a complex, multidimensional mind-bender with a vast array of permutations and variables, many of which you can't even control – all with the overarching, virtually unsolvable goal of minimizing labor expense while maximizing customer service and sales results.

As if this isn't hard enough, throw in labor standards and government regulations that can vary by state and province – it's not hard to understand why you get a collective groan from retailers when anyone talks about "optimizing" staff.

While traffic and customer conversion analytics are not the panacea to staffing challenges, they do provide critical context and enable retailers to make better staffing decisions and yes, optimize staffing. There are some basic actions every retailer can take to improve scheduling, and this chapter will show you what they are.

## Staffing to traffic – <u>not</u> transactions

As obvious as it seems, the very first step is to ensure that your staff resources are scheduled relative to the prospect traffic coming in the door. Staffing to traffic is a fundamental principle — have staff available when prospects are visiting the store.

The key problem with trying to accomplish this is that most retailers don't have traffic data and therefore are forced to use transactions as a proxy for traffic.[1] As I've repeated ad nauseam throughout this book, transactions represent only the number of lucky visitors who actually made a purchase, and so this transaction number will certainly be lower than the actual total number of prospects who enter the store and are represented by the gross traffic count.

As the chart below shows, this retailer's traffic pattern is very different from its transaction pattern.

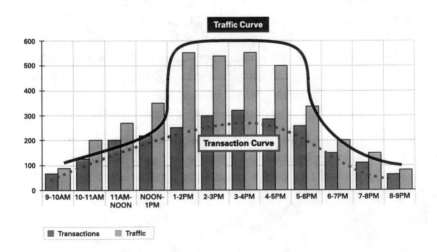

Some retailers may be reluctant to consider this disparity, because they're afraid their already high salary expenses will be even higher — how can they not be, if traffic count is higher than transaction counts? And if I'm using transactions to schedule staff today, then I must be understaffing. If this is the question that comes immediately to mind, then you already know the answer, but rather than deal with it, it's simpler to plead ignorance.

That said, we shouldn't jump to the conclusion that more staff is needed. First, let's schedule the existing resources to traffic patterns, so that at least we have the timing right. In fact, a simple realignment of existing staff resources can potentially deliver higher customer conversions, sales, and better customer service, without spending an extra nickel.

# Mapping traffic patterns: by month, week, day and hour

The idea of staffing to traffic is simple enough, but when you start to map traffic patterns and how they change, you soon realize that in practice, it's not as simple as it looks. Traffic is influenced by many factors and is constantly changing: by day-of-week, by season, by promotional activities, by competitors' activities, holidays, and, of course, by the weather. And the constantly changing conditions have a unique effect on each store.

Let's start by mapping seasonality. The chart below, showing average daily traffic by month, provides a high-level starting point for deciding how staff resources should be distributed by month over the course of the year in this store. For the apparel retailer shown in the chart below, average daily traffic volume is low in January and February, starts to build from March, and remains moderate and consistent through June. Since this retailer caters in part to the back-to-school market, traffic picks up again in July and hits its annual peak in August, before dropping back down to moderate levels from September until December, when traffic again spikes, for the holiday selling season.

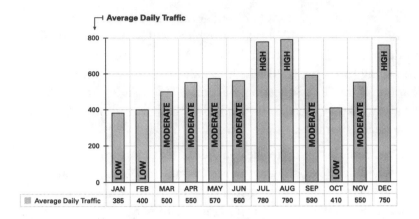

| | JAN | FEB | MAR | APR | MAY | JUN | JUL | AUG | SEP | OCT | NOV | DEC |
|---|---|---|---|---|---|---|---|---|---|---|---|---|
| Average Daily Traffic | 385 | 400 | 500 | 550 | 570 | 560 | 780 | 790 | 590 | 410 | 550 | 750 |

At the most rudimentary level, staff resources over the course of the year should be aligned with the seasonal patterns of this store. While it's true that patterns can vary, the overall seasonality of a chain tends to be less variable than hourly or even daily patterns. Traffic defines the sales opportunity, so the retailer who wants to make the most of the opportunity should, as a starting point, make sure that resources are scheduled on the basis of these general trends.

We can further refine the monthly patterns to weekly, as shown in the chart below. With the benefit of year-over-year data, not only can we refine our distribution to a weekly level of granularity, but we can also apply comparative year-over-year traffic trending. As you can see, year-over-year traffic was down considerably in the first six weeks of the year but has picked up, and the last six weeks show strong gains in year-over-year traffic.

Now that we've mapped monthly and weekly traffic, let's drill down to the variances by day of week for a particular month. As the chart below shows, and as every retailer intuitively knows, traffic volumes vary by day of week. The first step in aligning staffing is to make sure we have our day-of-week labor distribution right.

**Average Daily Traffic**

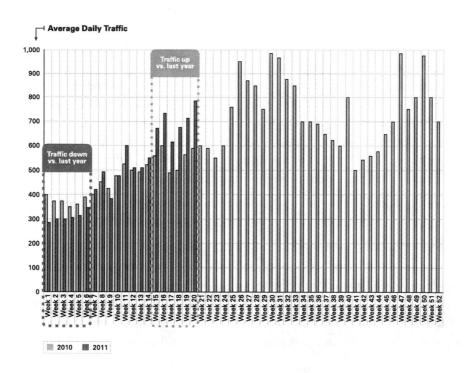

Traffic down
vs. last year

Traffic up
vs. last year

**Average Daily Traffic**

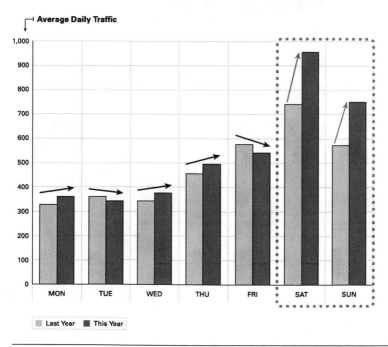

MON    TUE    WED    THU    FRI    SAT    SUN

Last Year    This Year

It's clear that if we look at the average daily traffic by day of week, traffic volume Monday through Wednesday is very consistent, at about 350 counts per day. On Thursday and Friday, traffic picks up to about 500 to 600 counts; it hits its peak on Saturdays, with over 900 average counts logged, and then slips back to 700 on Sundays. At the most basic level, staff in this store should be distributed to match these daily traffic totals. Remember, every store is unique, so you shouldn't assume that every store in your chain will have the same pattern – in fact, I can almost guarantee you that it won't. Review patterns by store – every store.

Once you have your overall day-of-week distributions mapped, then you need to map daily traffic by hour to further refine your staff distribution.

The chart below shows average daily traffic by hour on Wednesdays for a specialty retailer. As is clear, traffic is very low from opening until noon, at which time traffic volume builds, with maximum hourly traffic between 1 PM and 2 PM. Traffic then declines throughout the day. From these data, it's clear how staff should be scheduled: minimal staff from opening until noon, then less staff from 5 PM until close. So far, so good.

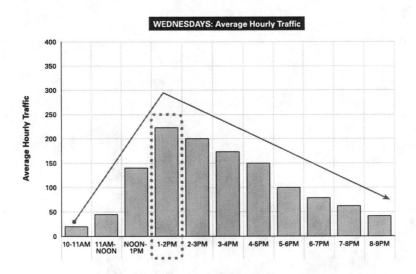

Now if every other day of the week looked like the chart above, things would be easy, but unfortunately, they don't. Traffic patterns for the same store are very different on Fridays and Saturdays, as shown in charts below.

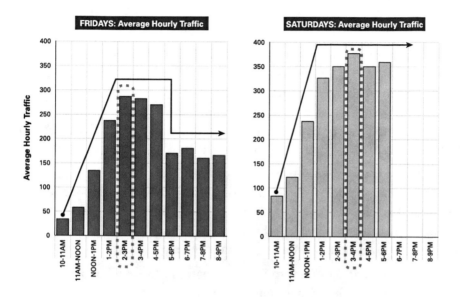

On Fridays, traffic spikes at 2 PM remains strong until 5 PM, and is lower but steady until close. On Saturdays, traffic starts slow but jumps at noon and remains very high through the remainder of the day. The transaction "traffic" for this retailer looked very different, and it didn't resemble the traffic patterns at all.

The process is not complicated, but if you don't have traffic data, it's simply impossible. Because every store is unique, the process needs to be completed for each location – resist the temptation to generalize or distribute resources based on "standard" patterns created by averaging trends over some number of stores. There is no such thing as a "sister" store, so don't bother. Of course it's more work to do this store-by-store, but it's also the only way to truly optimize staff schedules based on the requirements for each store. The benefits of doing this right will far outweigh the extra work it takes to map traffic trends by store.

# Staffing for holidays and events

Beyond aligning staff resources to general monthly, daily and hourly traffic trends by store, retailers also need to pay close attention to traffic patterns during holidays or events, when traffic patterns can change radically and where many retailers miss sales opportunities. This is where we often see conversion rates sag terribly.

 Black Friday is a retailing tradition that falls on the Friday after Thanksgiving in late November and represents the busiest shopping day of the year for most retailers in the United States. The chart below shows average traffic by day for a general merchandise chain. The huge spike in traffic –some 2,250 counts or almost 1.5 times as much traffic as the busiest Friday in November – is plain to see in the chart below.

The fact that a major holiday or event will have significantly higher traffic volume may not seem like a startling revelation for most retailers; however, knowing the actual traffic counts instead of just transaction counts will enable retailers to fully understand just how big the sales opportunity was and how well stores made the most out of it.

As interesting as it is to know the overall chain traffic for a holiday or event, the real value comes in understanding how traffic varies by individual store. For this retailer, overall chain traffic on Black Friday was up 1.5 over an average Friday in the month of November, but traffic volume varied dramatically by store.

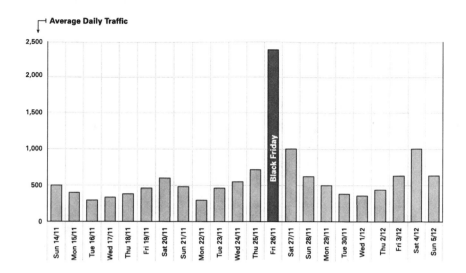

**Average Daily Traffic**

Traffic by hour for Store A is represented in the chart below. Overall, traffic on Black Friday was up 75%, compared to an average Friday. On an hourly basis, traffic volume was extremely high in the first two hours of the day, undoubtedly as door crashers inundated the store as soon as it opened. As the day progressed, traffic remained strong relative to typical Friday hourly volumes, but starting at about 1 PM, the variance became less significant, and by 3 PM on Black Friday, traffic was virtually the same as a typical Friday.

If every store in the chain looked like this one, the staffing problem would be easy to solve – have all hands on deck from opening until about 4 PM, then ramp down to normal Friday staff levels. Makes perfect sense, as long as the other stores have the same pattern, but the complication, of course, is that they do not.

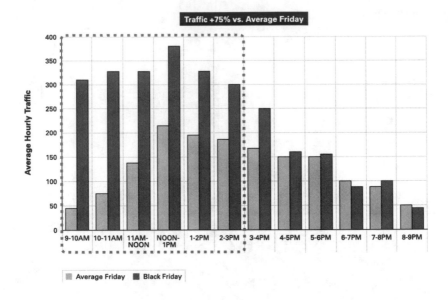

Traffic +75% vs. Average Friday

Average Friday ▓    Black Friday ■

Traffic by hour for Store B, in the same chain, is depicted in the chart below. In this case, overall traffic on Black Friday was up 175% over an average Friday.

As the hourly traffic chart below clearly shows, not only was traffic extremely high from opening, just as in Store A — it remained extremely high throughout the entire day, except the last couple of hours. With this analysis, you would schedule your staff resources differently from Store A, but of course, you could do this only if you understood the traffic patterns. If you don't have traffic data, I guess, you guess. Not good.

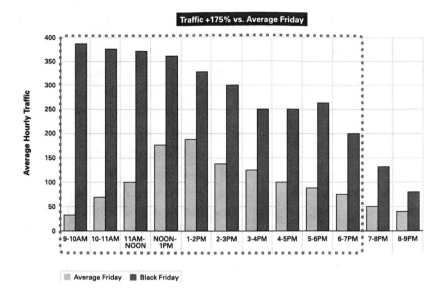

Average Friday    Black Friday

Getting staff properly aligned to traffic is one of the most important actions management can take in making the most of a holiday or major event. Increasing staffing levels by over 175% may not be realistic for most retailers, but understanding what the traffic is likely to look like and being prepared for it will go a long way towards helping you make the most of it. Even if customer conversion rates do sag somewhat in the face of a massive influx of store traffic, you will be in a position to capture more than you would have otherwise.

I cannot emphasize it enough – *every store is unique, and retailers need to think about scheduling on a store-by-store basis.* As the example above illustrates, what works in one store may not in another. And the results weren't just a market variance. As it turned out, both store A and B were actually located in the same major metropolitan market. Retailers who fail to understand these differences are destined to underperform.

# Customer conversion and staffing

Aligning staff resources to traffic is an important first step in optimizing your staffing, but it's just that — a first step. When you combine traffic with customer conversion, you begin to clearly see where the sales opportunities are being lost – where the conversion "leaks" are occurring and where you need to focus your staffing in order to plug them.

The chart below shows the traffic and customer conversion rates by hour for a specialty retailer. When you look at data in this way, it's not hard to see where the customer conversion leaks are occurring. As traffic builds from noon to 4 PM, customer conversion rates sag significantly. These drop-offs represent lost sales opportunities. Scheduling staff to traffic should go a long way towards minimizing the customer conversion rate dips, but staffing to traffic alone may not necessarily eradicate all drops in the conversion rate.

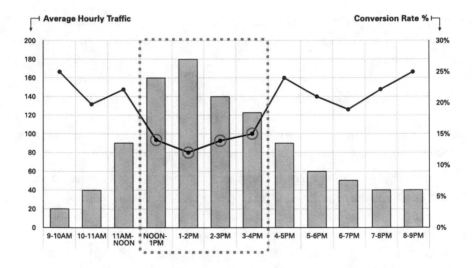

Charts like the one above are tell-tale signs that staff is not properly aligned with traffic. The sags in customer conversion rate imply that customers are visiting but not buying, which further suggests that they aren't being served — and that's why conversion rates are sagging. Customer conversion helps to further refine staff alignment.

When staff is aligned, traffic and customer conversion trends should look something like the chart below. As you can see, customer conversion rates are relatively smooth and consistent across all day parts. There are no wild conversion swings, especially during the busiest hours – customers are being served and being converted. Staff resources are properly aligned – <u>and</u> staff are performing well.

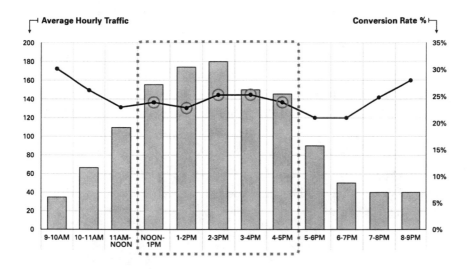

If retailers can have the right amount of human resources correctly distributed so as to follow the ups and downs in traffic, they'll be in the best position to maximize sales results.[2] And by also analyzing where customer conversion rates are sagging, retailers will be able to further refine their decisions about where staff resources need to be deployed relative to the traffic opportunity.

But there's one small complication that also needs to be considered – the staff itself.

Up to this point, the underlying assumption has been that all staff is created equal – but of course, as every manager can tell you, that there are stars, grinders, and floaters; one hour of "floater" Associate time will not deliver the same results as one hour of "star" Associate time.

# More staff, less staff – the right staff

Aligning staff resources to traffic does not necessarily mean adding staff. The idea of staff optimization is to match the resources you have with the opportunity, as defined by traffic through the door. All retailers say that they have limited resources and that staff hours, in particular, are very precious and very hard to get more of. That's why it is so critically important to make sure these limited resources are being used when they will have the greatest impact – when traffic is in the store.

The following example will help illustrate. The chart below shows traffic and customer conversion by day for a flagship location of a national apparel retailer. Traffic on four Wednesdays during the month was relatively consistent; however, the customer conversion rate of only 14% on May 18 was significantly lower than the other Wednesdays, when conversion rates were over 20%.

In an effort to better understand what happened to customer conversion on May 18, we compared the traffic and conversion from the prior Wednesday, May 11, to look for answers.

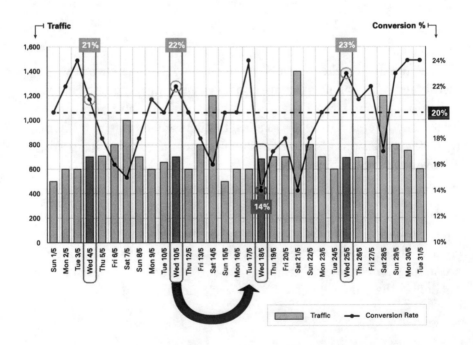

While these two Wednesdays had very similar levels of store traffic, the sales results were very different. May 11 had 43% higher sales than May 18, despite having the exact same amount of traffic – 700 counts – and a lower average ticket. The average ticket on May 11 was only $65, versus $72 on May 18. How is this possible? If we compare store traffic, customer conversion, average sale and labor hours, the answer becomes clear – conversion.

On May 11, the store had 95 labor hours, versus only 88 hours on May 18 – that's about 8% more. The store had more staff to service the same amount of traffic, and the result was significantly higher sales. The store spent 8% more on labor, but in return, generated 43% higher sales – not a bad trade. The results are summarized in the illustration below.

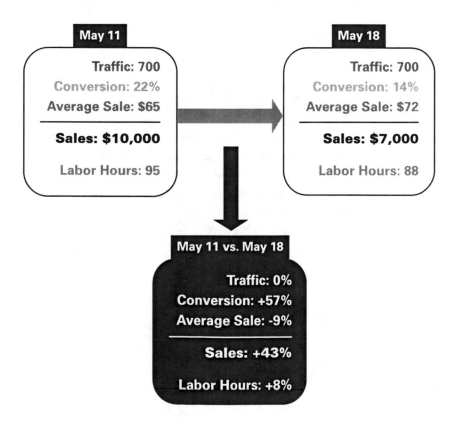

In order to understand the impact further, we analyzed the hourly results for both days. These are shown on the charts below.

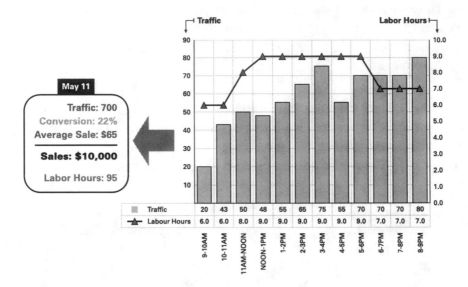

When we compare store traffic by hour to labor hours, we can see that on average, 8.5 hours of labor were available on May 11, and, generally the labor distribution matched traffic volume well. In fact, the store could have done even better: as you can see, in the last three hours of the day, traffic levels were at their highest, but staff hours were reduced. So, as good as the day was, it could have probably been even better if some of the early morning staff hours were reallocated to the end of the day, when traffic was much higher.

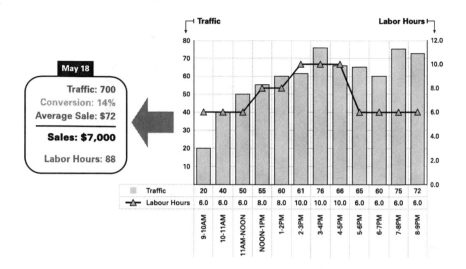

| | | 9-10AM | 10-11AM | 11AM-NOON | NOON-1PM | 1-2PM | 2-3PM | 3-4PM | 4-5PM | 5-6PM | 6-7PM | 7-8PM | 8-9PM |
|---|---|---|---|---|---|---|---|---|---|---|---|---|---|
| | Traffic | 20 | 40 | 50 | 55 | 60 | 61 | 76 | 66 | 65 | 60 | 75 | 72 |
| | Labour Hours | 6.0 | 6.0 | 6.0 | 8.0 | 8.0 | 10.0 | 10.0 | 10.0 | 6.0 | 6.0 | 6.0 | 6.0 |

**May 18**

Traffic: 700
Conversion: 14%
Average Sale: $72

Sales: $7,000

Labor Hours: 88

On May 18, however, not only did the store have fewer total labor hours available compared to May 11, but the distribution of these hours relative to store traffic was also misaligned – especially during the last four hours of the day, when conversion rates slumped significantly.

Analyzing traffic and conversion along with labor hours and scheduling can reveal profound insights.

# Traffic and conversion as a performance management tool

As noted, the underlying assumption so far has been that all Associates perform equally well, which is not really the case. With store traffic and customer conversion data, retailers can better understand Associate performance and learn who's who.

The chart below shows the average daily traffic by day of week, with the corresponding customer conversion rates.

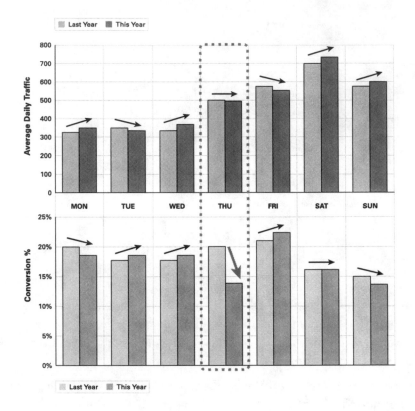

As the chart clearly shows, overall traffic levels Monday through Thursday have remained relatively consistent – not much change at all from the prior year. Customer conversion is fairly consistent Monday through Wednesday, but Thursday is significantly off. Traffic remained consistent, but Thursday's customer conversion rates decreased by 10 points – what's that about?

Upon further investigation, it was discovered that total labor hours hadn't changed on Thursdays from a year ago, but the schedule did change. One of the top performing Associates switched from Thursdays to Tuesdays – the negative impact on customer conversion is very apparent.

So it's just not the amount of labor hours, but it's what you do with the hours that really count. By measuring traffic and customer conversion, we can understand sales performance versus the sales opportunity, which you simply cannot do without traffic and customer conversion.

To sum up: Managers should compare traffic levels to customer conversion rates to look for conversion rate sags. You may need more staff hours; you may need to simply redistribute your labor hours to better match traffic; or it may be that your labor hours and distribution relative to traffic are fine, but the Associate(s) you have working at a given hour may be underperforming. With traffic and customer conversion insights, you narrow down the potential causes and have the context you need to solve them.

# Assisted versus self-help: staffing and retail environments

The type of retail environment you operate in also has a lot to do with how you should think about staff scheduling.

Of course, understanding an individual Associate's performance is easier to do when your stores are relatively small and you only have three or five Associates working at any given time. It is significantly harder to do when you operate large-footprint stores, thousands of square feet in size and you have 20, 50 or even 100 or more Associates working at any given time. That said, the principle is essentially the same: match staff resources to prospect traffic.

Beyond store size, the types of products sold and the level of service required are also important considerations. Let's look at two general cases:

- **high involvement, assisted sales environments:** Any sales environment where Associate assistance is needed to help prospects shop and ultimately complete the sale can be characterized as an "assisted" sales environment. Jewelry, high-end furniture, mattresses, and even exclusive boutique clothing come to mind here. In these environments, understanding traffic is particularly critical, as every prospect will certainly require assistance. Ensuring that staff schedules are aligned with store traffic is vital.

The other fact about these high assistance retail environments is that at some point, traffic will be higher (sometimes significantly higher) than the number of Associates available to service them. If you have a jewelry store with five really great Associates working, the sixth prospect that walks into the store has to wait. While it may not be practical or cost effective to increase staffing levels based on these periodic spikes, arming staff with an understanding of when these traffic spikes are likely to occur, based on the historical patterns, can go a long way in helping them prepare for and effectively "triage" the prospects, thus maximizing customer service and ultimately conversion rates. It's hard, but it's even harder when you don't have traffic and customer conversion data.

- **self-help, unassisted sales environments:** Any retail environment where prospects can shop and purchase with little or no assistance from an Associate can be defined as a "self-help" or "unassisted" sales environment. Think big-box home improvement retailers, general merchandisers, and department stores as obvious examples. In these environments, prospects can wander the aisles, browsing and interacting with merchandise. Depending on the item they are interested in, they may or may not require assistance. These stores generally receive very high volumes of store traffic, and the staff imperative often comes down to making sure there's enough staff, aligned with store traffic, with the right type of staff working.

In self-help retail environments, the key to driving sales results is to manage check-out traffic and transaction processing as efficiently as possible. Customers found what they were looking for, their shopping carts are full, now take their money, quickly, so that they can be on their way.

Managers operating in this type of environment should use traffic and conversion to align staff resources to traffic and then pay particular attention to customer conversion rate sags. These can often occur because of long line-ups at the check-out, so managers need to pay particular attention to cashier staffing to ensure that customers are being processed quickly during the peak traffic hours.

These two cases are the opposite ends of the retail service continuum. Many retailers might fall somewhere in between, requiring some level of assistance that can also vary according to the type of product a prospect is interested in. For example, a general merchandise retailer may have an electronics department within the store selling high-end TVs. Even though the store carries plenty of self-help items, any prospect interested in a TV will need Associate assistance.

Whatever the retail environment is, having store traffic and customer conversion data will help you better align your staff resources, identify and plug customer conversion leaks, and ultimately enable you to deliver better customer service and generate higher sales.

# Training program development and performance measurement

Measuring the impact of training programs is another important area where store traffic and customer conversion can be invaluable.

Every year retailers invest millions of dollars on retail training programs, the majority of which are related to customer service and sales skills. Ostensibly, executives are looking for the payback in improved sales outcomes or at least in improved customer experience scores. Unfortunately, and much to the chagrin of the VP of HR, the sales results don't always reflect the time, effort and money that went into the training programs. And, as much as the executives agree that training is a good thing to do, without the sales results to back it up, it's difficult to invest more.

Here's an example. In an effort to improve sales performance, an electronics retailer decided to test a sales training program in a select number of stores. A district of nine stores was selected, and in order to measure the impact, four stores received the sales training, while the other five did not.

The hypothesis was simply that the stores that received the sales training should show better year-over-year comparative sales results than the stores that didn't. A month after the training was completed, the year-over-year comparative sales for the nine stores in the district were compared, as you see in the chart below.

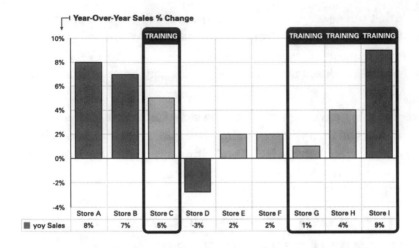

Year-Over-Year Sales % Change

| | Store A | Store B | Store C | Store D | Store E | Store F | Store G | Store H | Store I |
|---|---|---|---|---|---|---|---|---|---|
| yoy Sales | 8% | 7% | 5% | -3% | 2% | 2% | 1% | 4% | 9% |

On the basis of the sales performance, the impact of the sales training is mixed. Both Store C and Store I, which received the training, showed great performance, delivering comp sales increases of 5% and 9%, respectively. However, as good as these results are, there are two problems: first, Store A and Store B both delivered sales improvements as good as or better than these, and they didn't receive any additional training; second, Store G and Store H both received the training, but their sales results were comparatively poor. The training was inconclusive at best.

This scenario has played out countless times in boardrooms across North America – more inconclusive, mixed results that don't provide management with any comfort about whether this program made any difference. Oh well, on to our next program – maybe the next one will be more conclusive. What else is management to do with sales results like these?

What if instead of just analyzing the sales results, HR also had the benefit of store traffic and customer conversion data to help understand how the stores performed, beyond the sales results?

The sales results are the sales results, and no matter what additional data you analyze, you won't change the outcomes. However, putting the results in context can significantly change how management assesses the training program. The chart below shows the nine stores in the district, but instead of sales, the chart shows the year-over-year change in store traffic volume and customer conversion rates by store.

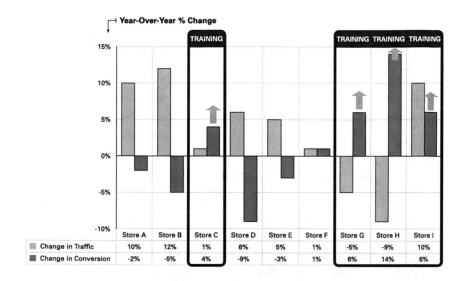

| Year-Over-Year % Change | Store A | Store B | Store C | Store D | Store E | Store F | Store G | Store H | Store I |
|---|---|---|---|---|---|---|---|---|---|
| Change in Traffic | 10% | 12% | 1% | 6% | 5% | 1% | -5% | -9% | 10% |
| Change in Conversion | -2% | -5% | 4% | -9% | -3% | 1% | 6% | 14% | 6% |

Breaking out store traffic and customer conversion to see year-over-year change produces a very different perspective on what impact the training actually had. The first thing you notice in these results is that year-over-year customer conversion rates were significantly higher in the stores that received training. Given the nature of the training, we would expect to see customer conversion rates increase (i.e., the stores did a better job of selling to the prospects who visited), and that's exactly what happened – the training was very effective.

The reason why the positive impact of the training is not reflected in the sales results is also now clear: traffic. Stores G and H both received sales training, and customer conversion rates are significantly up, but unfortunately traffic is down – way down. The decrease in store traffic is what caused overall sales to look poor, not the sales performance of the Associates in the store. And, just as traffic was the culprit in keeping sales results down at Store G and Store H, it was exactly what made the performance at Store A and Store B look so good.

These stores didn't receive any sales training, and despite having poor year-over-year customer conversion results, were able to generate high year-over-year sales because they had so many more prospects to sell to. Now how would you assess the sales training program?

# Incentives and compensation based on conversion

Customer conversion is an important measure of store-level performance, so it's reasonable to want to create incentives to encourage it. However, as with any compensation program, care must be exercised in designing a program that can't easily be "gamed." Here are a couple of suggestions for designing compensation programs that include customer conversion.

1) Make conversion one element of an overall program: depending upon the traffic counter technology used, it may be possible for staff to reduce total traffic counts by blocking sensors. The net effect of this behavior is that traffic counts go down and customer conversion rates go up – if you have a bonus plan based solely on customer conversion rates, you might find yourself paying out without seeing any gain. To avoid this situation, ensure that your bonus plan is driven by overall comp sales, average ticket and customer conversion rates. Any plan that doesn't pay out on customer conversion alone will go a long way to keep Associates focused on the real prize – driving overall comp sales.

2) Base customer conversion bonus targets on total store versus individuals: because you can't easily attribute traffic to individual Associates, you can't precisely measure customer conversion rates down to the individual Associate. It's really challenging to set individual conversion goals. Furthermore, setting overall store targets, such that all Associates need to pull their weight in order to achieve the overall goal, can create a useful team dynamic. After all, it takes everyone's effort to serve customers and create conversion, so it makes sense that the targets and rewards be team oriented.

There's no shortage of interesting and creative ways to create incentives and compensate staff. Traffic and customer conversion not only provide important context for HR to design and implement these programs, but customer conversion itself is a very useful compensation or bonus plan metric – another reason why it's such a great and versatile metric.

# Labor Force Management tools are powerful but not perfect.

Labor force management (LFM) tools play a critical role in retailing today. LFM systems run the gamut, from basic time-and-attendance systems to sophisticated, end-to-end systems that cover everything from time tracking and scheduling to performance management and compensation. While I do realize that LFM systems often do much more than just scheduling, scheduling is still a very critical element of labor force management and an area that continues to vex many retailers.

No matter how sophisticated the LFM system is, if the retailer doesn't have traffic count data as an input into the scheduling system, it just won't be right. There is no algorithm or software coding that can adequately "guess" at traffic levels. When store traffic data is not available, these systems ostensibly rely on transactions as a proxy for traffic.

The transaction may be factored up by some number to calculate or estimate store traffic counts, but it just won't be right.[3] And that's why even the best scheduling systems come up short – they just don't have the right input. Store traffic counts. LFM systems are powerful tools for retailers, and traffic and conversion data make them work even better.

You now know what missed opportunities look like – not pretty. You also now know how you can use traffic and conversion insights to get more out of our marketing investments and optimize labor. This is all great stuff, but knowing and doing are two very different things, and it's only through doing that your results get better.

So, how do you action these insights to drive sales results? That's where we go next.

# Part 3

## Leveraging Insights
## to Drive Performance

# Chapter 3.1

## Driving Sales Performance with Conversion

There are really only two good reasons for retailers to invest in programs like traffic and conversion analytics: they help save money or make money. Traffic and conversion analytics can do both.

Across every segment, from specialty luxury to discount merchandisers, retailers are obsessively focused on ways to squeeze more cost out of the system. Given the tight margins in retailing, it's not hard to understand why. There are plenty of expense lines to prune, and retailers have become very adept at pruning them. Being cost conscious and managing expenses tightly is an important part of what every good retail operator must do.

But what about the top line?

Every retailer lusts after positive comp sales. They separate retail winners from the losers. And while retailers have become very adept at managing expenses, it seems that when the discussion turns to what they need to do to drive comp sales, there's a whole lot less to talk about.

Invariably, the discussion boils down to (1) getting more buyers into the stores; and (2) increasing average ticket. The first objective is achieved through advertising and/or promotion to stimulate visitation, and the second is achieved by having store personnel focus on up-selling and cross-selling. This "two-trick pony" mentality to driving comp sales is so well entrenched it's almost axiomatic. As one stock market analyst summed it up on an earnings call with a major retailer, "Congratulations on the good quarter. Was it ticket or traffic that drove your positive comps?"

There's a third trick the retail sales pony must learn, and it's one that most retailers today completely ignore: **customer conversion**.

As we will see as we explore the subject in depth in this chapter, not only is customer conversion another important way to drive comp sales; for some retailers, it may be even more important than average ticket.

## The three key sales drivers

Sales are a function of three variables: (1) prospect traffic, (2) conversion rate, and (3) average sale. So sales performance can be driven by increasing any one individual variable while holding the others constant — or by moving multiple variables in a positive direction.

As the example below shows, a 10% lift in sales can be achieved by increasing prospect traffic from 800 to 890 counts, while holding conversion rate and average ticket constant. Alternatively, with 800 prospect counts and a 30% conversion rate, the store can achieve the 10% lift by increasing average ticket from $30 to $33. Finally, the 10% sales lift could be achieved by selling to more of the 800 prospects visiting the store. If, instead of converting only 30% of the traffic, the store converted 33% of the traffic into buyers, then, even at the same $30 average sale, overall sales would increase by 10%.

So while it may appear at first glance that each of the three drivers can equally deliver improvements in overall sales, it becomes clearer, as we explore each in detail, that they are not equal at all.

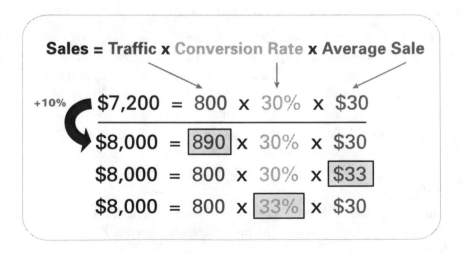

# Traffic:

Driving more prospects into your stores is a good idea. Traffic, after all, is the lifeblood of retailing. But prospects just don't decide to show up; driving additional prospect traffic to your stores requires some kind of stimulus. The most common traffic stimulus is advertising and/or promotion. While there's a vast array of advertising and promotional vehicles retailers can and do employ to drive traffic, they all generally have one common attribute – they cost money. As noted in Chapter 2.3, retailers collectively spend billions on advertising annually in an attempt to drive more buyers into their stores and ultimately increase sales.

It's important to remember that advertising drives not buyers but <u>prospects</u> to the store. Buyers are part of the prospect traffic group; some of these prospects will become buyers, and the others won't. This unconverted prospect traffic represents a significant lost sales opportunity. A campaign may be very effective at driving traffic levels up in the stores, but if at the end of the day, customer conversion rates and/or average ticket values decrease, overall sales may not necessarily increase – or increase enough to justify the investment.

*Investing precious budget dollars to drive more prospect traffic to your stores when you may not be adequately serving the prospects you already have doesn't make sense.* Unfortunately, this is exactly what many retailers do, week in and week out, throwing money at advertising and promotions without the faintest clue as to what impact they're actually having on sales or what the ROI actually is.

To drive conversion, remember that *traffic and customer conversion rate tend to be inversely related.*[1] As traffic levels go up, customer conversion often goes down. As I explained in Chapter 1.4, it's not hard to understand why this happens. As the store gets busier, it's harder to find an Associate to help, the check-out lines get longer, and service levels generally decline. Or perhaps the store misplaced (or simply didn't receive) its shipment of items that were featured in the promotion. Prospects might have come looking for the item — but left when they learned the store didn't have the item or ran out. Whatever the cause, the net effect is that more people came to the store but left without buying.

As the example below shows, if the advertising successfully drove 10% more prospect traffic to the store (even if the store maintains its $30 average ticket), and if the customer conversion rate decreases from 30% to 28% (not atypical), the overall sales lift would be only 4% instead of the 10% it should be, given the traffic increase.

The moral of the story is this: traffic is good, but your stores need to be prepared for increased prospect volume if you're going to get the return you're looking for. If conversion sags, you won't get everything you should from your advertising investment.

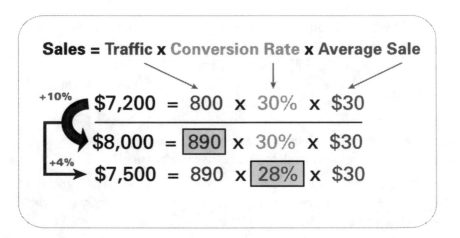

## Average Ticket

If there is one variable that retailers universally accept as the sure way to deliver improved comp sales, average ticket is it. Selling more to each buyer. The pursuit of higher average ticket values is worthwhile, and it's an objective in which retailers invest heavily.

Retailers employ various strategies to drive up average ticket values. They conduct sales training to increase Associates' effectiveness at up-selling and cross-selling. This is especially important in sales environments where Associate assistance is required – think shoes, jewelry, electronics and apparel. In retail environments where customers self-help or where less Associate assistance is required, average ticket can be increased through effective plan-o-grams and compelling merchandising programs that make products irresistible to the impulse shopper.

In an attempt to drive up average sale values, many retailers urge their Associates to focus on increasing the number of SKUs or units per transaction (UPTs). The thinking here is that framing the objective in terms of the number of line items on the sales receipt is conceptually easier to internalize than the notion of average ticket or average basket. But regardless of how you communicate it, it amounts to the same thing – sell more to buyers.

Every retailer should try to maximize average ticket values, and practically every retailer striving to improve results is already working hard in this area. Even the most junior Associate is keenly aware of the virtue of driving average sale.

Anything that store-level personnel can influence is, by definition, important. But as important as driving average sale is, I question whether it deserves the time and attention it gets, both as a focus for store Associates and in proportion to its ability to deliver overall sales results.

The chart below shows a district of ten specialty stores ranked from highest average ticket to lowest. I've also embedded the sales rank for each store in the bar.

It's curious that of the four stores with the highest average ticket values, only one, St. Louis, actually has high sales performance – it ranked number one! The other stores — Denver, Raleigh and Tampa — have the lowest sales ranks of the entire set. At the other end of the chart, we find Reno. This store ranked second in overall sales but had the lowest average ticket of the entire set.

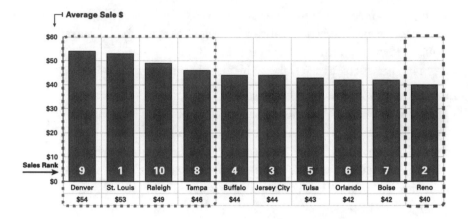

What does this say about the relationship between average ticket values and overall sales? Short answer: the two aren't as closely linked as we might have thought.

As heretical as it sounds, is it possible that retailers are too focused on driving average ticket? Frankly, I think so. An example will help illustrate.

# Average sale impact on overall sales rank

Given that so much has already been done in trying to drive up average ticket values, I'm skeptical that any retailer can dramatically improve overall sales results just by focusing on improving average ticket values. We analyzed the sales results for a nine-store district of an apparel chain. The sales rankings for the month, from highest average daily sales to lowest, are shown in the chart below.

The ninth-ranked store had a $31 average ticket, which was not bad compared to the other stores. So we asked, "What would happen to its sales rank if it increased its average ticket from $31 to $41 – that's a $10 (or 32%) lift in average ticket?" Not only is this a big increase for the store, but it would also be a higher average ticket than any other store in the district, by 20% (or $7).

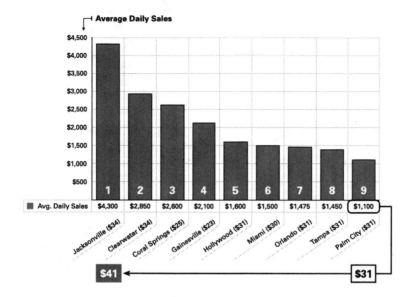

| | Average Daily Sales | | | | | | | | |
|---|---|---|---|---|---|---|---|---|---|
| | 1 | 2 | 3 | 4 | 5 | 6 | 7 | 8 | 9 |
| Avg. Daily Sales | $4,300 | $2,850 | $2,600 | $2,100 | $1,600 | $1,500 | $1,475 | $1,450 | $1,100 |

Jacksonville ($34) · Clearwater ($34) · Coral Springs ($25) · Gainesville ($23) · Hollywood ($31) · Miami ($30) · Orlando ($31) · Tampa ($31) · Palm City ($31)

$41 ← $31

Surely this will impact the comparative sales rank of the store significantly. The only question is: by how much?

We re-ran the sales rankings with the new $41 average ticket value for the ninth-ranked store. The results can be seen in the chart below. Much to our surprise, and that of the retailer, a 32% lift in average sale had no impact of the overall sales rank of this store compared to the others in the district. The ninth-ranked store was still ninth.

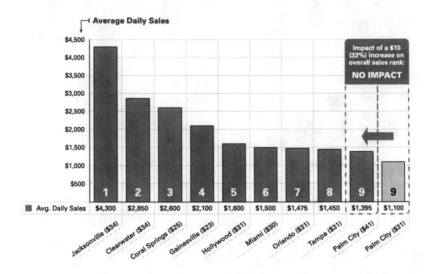

| | Average Daily Sales | | | | | | | | |
|---|---|---|---|---|---|---|---|---|---|
| | 1 | 2 | 3 | 4 | 5 | 6 | 7 | 8 | 9 | 9 |
| Avg. Daily Sales | $4,300 | $2,850 | $2,600 | $2,100 | $1,600 | $1,500 | $1,475 | $1,450 | $1,395 | $1,100 |

Jacksonville ($34) · Clearwater ($34) · Coral Springs ($25) · Gainesville ($23) · Hollywood ($31) · Miami ($30) · Orlando ($31) · Tampa ($31) · Palm City ($41) · Palm City ($31)

Impact of a $10 (32%) increase on overall sales rank: **NO IMPACT**

I'd like to tell you that this was merely some analytic sleight of hand, but it wasn't. The shocking fact is that *even significant improvements in average ticket values may have very modest overall impact on sales.* Yes, it's true, a 32% increase in average ticket does mean that the store is up 32% in sales using the numbers above, but my point is: So what? In the broader context of district results and rankings, it meant little – this significant improvement had very little impact on overall sales. Shockingly little.

We did a similar analysis across a spectrum of retail segments from high-end luxury goods to mass-market general merchandisers and everything in between, and we came to the same conclusion: average ticket had far less impact on overall sales results than almost anybody had expected. Focusing on driving up average sales values can only take you so far.

# Average ticket myopia?

I realize that the suggestion may seem strange, but in my experience retailers are universally focused on driving average ticket values as a strategy for improving store sales performance. The problem with putting too much emphasis on average ticket is that you potentially hurt customer conversion rates, and that can often have a much more profound impact on sales.

Here's a scenario: a prospect enters the store. The Sales Associate does an excellent job of engaging the prospect. They start to talk; the Associate shows the prospect a number of great outfits; the prospect tries on several. Bingo – the prospect is converted into a buyer. She's taking the new $100 outfit.

Wanting to deliver great service and trying to get the average ticket up, the Associate begins to show the prospect all the wonderful accessories that suit her outfit perfectly. After some time, the two are really hitting it off, and the prospect agrees to add the lovely $20 scarf the Associate suggested. Well done, Sales Associate, well done.

This is textbook retail selling, and it resulted in a 20% lift in the sale ticket. What's not to like? The Sales Associate performed her job brilliantly. She delivered excellent customer service, resulting in an outstanding in-store experience, the customer was delighted and made a purchase – she might have even filled out a most flattering satisfaction survey. Everyone's happy, right?

No, not everyone.

While the Associate was delivering the brilliant service, five other prospects entered the store. These ladies couldn't get the attention of the Associate who was so focused on delivering brilliant customer service and driving up her average ticket that she hardly noticed, let alone acknowledged them. These prospects wandered around and then finally left the store. Not only did they not buy, they weren't very happy about not being served. These folks didn't fill out a survey.

I realize that the training guide doesn't say ignore other prospects, but, as in the example above, this Sales Associate was just trying to do the right thing. She didn't intentionally or maliciously ignore the other prospects;

she was just focused on delivering great customer service and increasing her average sale – just as she was taught.

I'm not suggesting that retailers should no longer concern themselves with average ticket. It comes down to this: if Associates are so focused on delivering great customer service to any individual prospect that they let five other prospects come and go without being served, it's a bad trade-off for the business. And the sad fact is that retailers do it many times, every day.

Let's turn our attention to the third (and my favorite) sales driver, conversion.

# Conversion Rate

The third way to drive sales is to sell to more of the prospects that come into your store. I know this may seem like an obvious point, but unless you are measuring prospect traffic and calculating customer conversion rate, you don't have a clue as to whether or not your stores are doing a good job of converting the traffic that's already in your stores.

*Customer conversion is truly a powerful and unique metric. Unlike any other retail performance metric, it measures how a store performs versus its sales opportunity.* Think about it. Prospect traffic defines the opportunity size, and customer conversion measures sales performance versus the traffic opportunity – every hour of every day. No other metric can do this.

Yet many retail executives simply ignore customer conversion, in part because they can't measure it. They don't count prospect traffic and therefore have no way of calculating their conversion rate. These retailers simply and erroneously assume that all the prospects that visited the store and intended to buy....did buy. This is a false and costly assumption.

Many didn't buy, and for various reasons. And unlike average ticket values, which tend to be more consistent across stores, customer conversion rates can vary significantly across stores. The chart below shows the customer conversion rates by store for the same nine-store district.

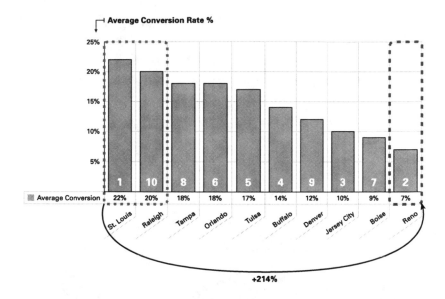

In this group of stores, the variation from highest average ticket to lowest was 30%. For these same stores, conversion rate variance from highest to lowest was over 200%.

# Conversion rate and average sale: variables that store-level personnel can influence

There are really only two variables store-level personnel can influence in order to drive sales: (1) the number of people they sell to; and (2) how much they sell to each buyer. The first is measured by customer conversion and the second by average sale. Stores don't control traffic.

In many ways, average sale is a measure of the "depth" of relationship that any one of your store Sales Associates has with an <u>individual</u> prospect. It is widely understood that the more a sales person knows and understands about an individual prospect's needs, wants and desires, the more likely the Associate will be able to help the prospect to fulfill them. This is generally believed to be a significant factor in increasing average sale value, which is well-understood as a key sales performance driver.

If average sale is a measure of the depth of relationship, then customer conversion rate is a measure of the "breadth" of relationships all your Associates collectively have with all the prospects that enter the store. And while average sale is critical and worth trying to maximize, customer conversion rate is even more significant, in several important ways.

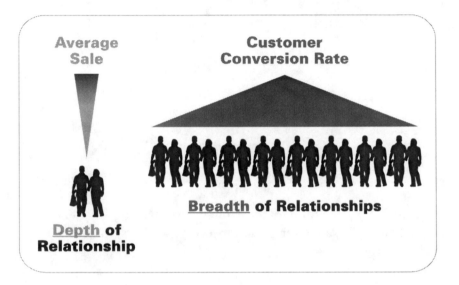

## Optics matter: Framing the objective in achievable terms

Let's consider the case where we're trying to drive a 10% lift in sales. Of course, a sales lift can be achieved by either increasing average ticket values and/or by increasing conversion rates. However, when it comes to training store-level personnel in improving sales, I think conversion rate is not only conceptually easier to understand but potentially even easier to achieve. An example will help illustrate.

In order to deliver a 10% increase in sales, the Store Manager needs to increase average sale from $50 to $55. This might not seem like much, but most managers would agree that up-selling and cross-selling your way to a $55 average ticket from $50 is no cakewalk.

Part of the problem is that many Associates have a hard time with their role in the process. Either they feel uncomfortable asking for the add-on sale, or they simply don't ask for it — or at least not in a compelling way. They think, "Hey, I got the sale; I don't want to push too hard." Also, shoppers are so accustomed to being up-sold that many are programmed to say no. The old "did you want an apple pie with your order, sir?" line simply doesn't work the way it used to.

Nevertheless, if, in this case, the Store Manager could increase average ticket by $5, based on the traffic through the door and the current conversion rate of 40%, he/she would deliver a 10% lift in sales.

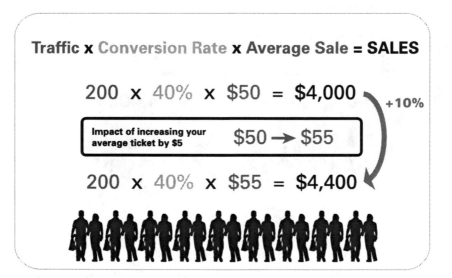

The other way to come at this is to focus on customer conversion. What if, instead of asking the Store Manager to increase the average sale by $5, we asked him/her to focus on selling to just <u>one</u> more customer per hour? Sure, go ahead and do all your good up-selling and cross-selling, just as we taught you, but don't get too hung up on it. Over the course of an eight-hour day, selling to one more customer per hour would produce – you guessed it – a 10% lift in sales. Here's the math to prove it.

In the base case, the store had 200 traffic counts and a 40% conversion rate, producing 80 sales transactions (i.e., 200 counts x 40% conversion rate = 80 sales transactions). Delivering eight more sales transactions – just one more per hour – based on the same 200 traffic counts, would result in 88 total transactions for the day. With 88 sales transactions, the customer conversion rate would have increased from 40% to 44% (88/200 = 44%), and, assuming the average ticket value stayed the same at $50, total sales would be $4,400, or 10% higher than before.

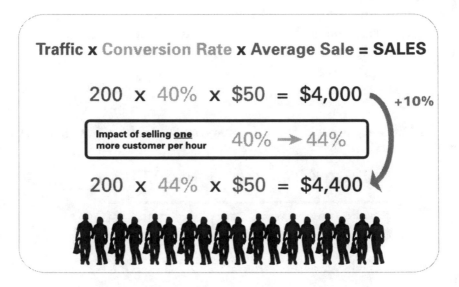

**Traffic x Conversion Rate x Average Sale = SALES**

200 x 40% x $50 = $4,000  +10%

Impact of selling **one** more customer per hour  40% → 44%

200 x 44% x $50 = $4,400

No one would dispute the importance of average sale as a key driver of overall sales performance, but to focus on it to the detriment of customer conversion – or even without any regard to customer conversion – is to leave money on the table. Lots of it.

The question to ask is: how much higher will sales be if I spend more time with this one prospect rather than talking to some number of other prospects and converting most or all of them into sales? Making prospects feel rushed or pressured would obviously not be a good idea; however, balancing the time spent with any given prospect, while trying to reach as many prospects as possible, will yield the best overall results.

# Trading off average sale
# for customer conversion

At first blush, one might hypothesize that average sales and customer conversion are somewhat conflicting objectives. The thinking goes something like this: in order to drive average ticket, Sales Associates need to engage the prospect, really get to understand his/her needs, and then make suggestions and offer opinions about other items that might be of interest. This takes time and attention. If the Associate is too distracted with every prospect that comes into the store and is simply running around, then the prospect may feel underserved. Not only might the sale be lost, but also, even if a sale is made, it's likely that average sale values will be lower, because Associates aren't spending enough quality time with individual prospects.

It's an interesting question. If you drive up customer conversion only to see average sale values plummet, resulting in only modest sales gains...I agree, what's the point?

We were so intrigued by the question that we set out to find the answer by analyzing average sale and customer conversion data for a wide range of retailers. Specifically, we plotted the average sale values by store, from highest average sale to lowest. Then we overlaid customer conversion rates for the corresponding stores.

If average sale values and customer conversion rates were indeed trade-offs, it should look something like the chart below. As you can see the in this hypothetical case, the higher the store's average sale, the lower the conversion rate. And the lower the average sale, the higher the conversion rate – average ticket and customer conversion are trade-offs. While we didn't expect real data to look this linear, if average sale and customer conversion were indeed trade-offs, the actual data should follow the general pattern.

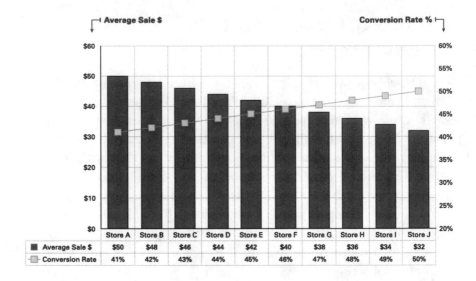

| | Store A | Store B | Store C | Store D | Store E | Store F | Store G | Store H | Store I | Store J |
|---|---|---|---|---|---|---|---|---|---|---|
| Average Sale $ | $50 | $48 | $46 | $44 | $42 | $40 | $38 | $36 | $34 | $32 |
| Conversion Rate | 41% | 42% | 43% | 44% | 45% | 46% | 47% | 48% | 49% | 50% |

Going into the analysis, we did expect to see some trade-off between average sale values and customer conversion rates. However, we expected that the trade-off would be modest and the net effect would be more positive for stores with high customer conversion rates. But what we actually found when we plotted real data was surprising.

We started with a group of stores from a general discount merchandise chain. As the chart below shows, this retailer's average sale and customer conversion rate are not mutually exclusive or conflicting. In fact, *stores that had the highest average sale values were often the stores that also had the highest customer conversion rates.*

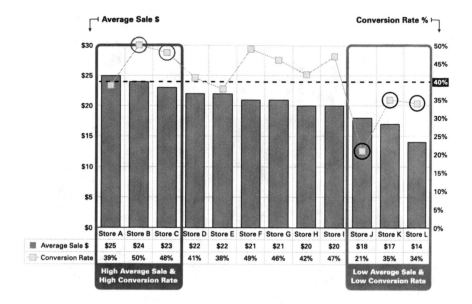

| | Store A | Store B | Store C | Store D | Store E | Store F | Store G | Store H | Store I | Store J | Store K | Store L |
|---|---|---|---|---|---|---|---|---|---|---|---|---|
| Average Sale $ | $25 | $24 | $23 | $22 | $22 | $21 | $21 | $20 | $20 | $18 | $17 | $14 |
| Conversion Rate | 39% | 50% | 48% | 41% | 38% | 49% | 46% | 42% | 47% | 21% | 35% | 34% |

**High Average Sale & High Conversion Rate**

**Low Average Sale & Low Conversion Rate**

Looking at the three stores with the highest average sale values (ranging from $23 to $25), we can see customer conversion rates ranged from 39% to a high of 50%. The chain's average conversion rate was 40%. All three stores had conversion rates close to or well above the average district customer conversion rate, and the stores with the second- and third-highest average sale values in the group also had the highest customer conversion rates.

At the other end of the scale, we can see that the three stores with the lowest average sale values (ranging from $14 to $18) also had some of the lowest customer conversion rates. In fact, the bottom three stores in average sale had the worst customer conversion rates of the entire data set.

At first we thought the findings were anomalous. How could this be? We thought perhaps the results in this case were somehow a function of this particular category or chain. So we kept digging and moved on to some other categories and chains.

The next analysis we conducted was on a set of stores in the cosmetics category. The results are shown in the chart below. Again, high customer conversion and average sale values were not mutually exclusive.

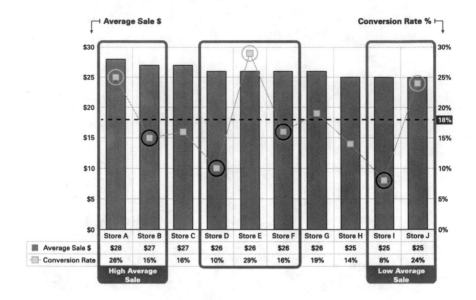

| | Store A | Store B | Store C | Store D | Store E | Store F | Store G | Store H | Store I | Store J |
|---|---|---|---|---|---|---|---|---|---|---|
| Average Sale $ | $28 | $27 | $27 | $26 | $26 | $26 | $26 | $25 | $25 | $25 |
| Conversion Rate | 26% | 15% | 16% | 10% | 29% | 16% | 19% | 14% | 8% | 24% |

In this data set, average ticket values were very consistent across all stores, with only a $3 spread between the highest and lowest. But conversion rate was an entirely different story.

Store A had the highest average ticket and the second highest conversion rate. Store E, only in the middle of the pack in average ticket, delivered the highest conversion rate, and Store J, with the lowest average ticket, had the next highest conversion rate. Seeing the data in this way raises a simple question: if these stores can achieve a high conversion rate <u>and</u> deliver these average ticket values, why can't the other stores perform comparably?

For example, Store D, E and F, all had a $26 average ticket, but Store E converted a whopping 29%, while Store D and Store E could only manage 10% and 16%, respectively. Why?

Our last example is in women's apparel, but the conclusions didn't change. The average customer conversion rate for the group was 36%, but again, *some of the highest conversion rates were achieved by stores that had the highest average sale values*. Stores A, B and D had the highest average ticket values and were among the leaders in conversion rates.

You'd think that the conversion rates might be a little lower in stores with high average sale values, compared to stores with low averages, but that's just not what the data showed. As in the other cases, at the low end of the average sale value scale, lo and behold, we find some of the lowest customer conversion rates of the group!

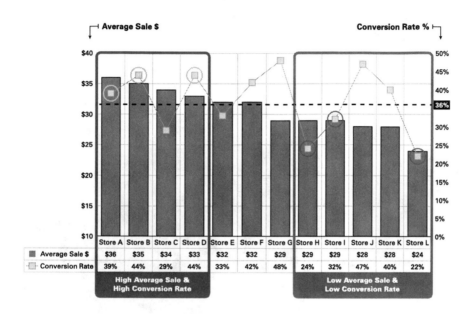

| | Store A | Store B | Store C | Store D | Store E | Store F | Store G | Store H | Store I | Store J | Store K | Store L |
|---|---|---|---|---|---|---|---|---|---|---|---|---|
| Average Sale $ | $36 | $35 | $34 | $33 | $32 | $32 | $29 | $29 | $29 | $28 | $28 | $24 |
| Conversion Rate | 39% | 44% | 29% | 44% | 33% | 42% | 48% | 24% | 32% | 47% | 40% | 22% |

These are just three of the dozens of examples we studied, and in every case, we saw similar results. *Higher customer conversion rates and higher average sales are not mutually exclusive.* The best performing stores did both well and the underperformers seemed to do both poorly.

# Average sale + customer conversion = sales results?

So if customer conversion rate and average sale are the two metrics that, when combined, provide the best measure of overall in-store performance, then it follows that stores with higher average sales and conversion rates should also be stores that deliver the best overall sales results, right?

It was simple enough to include sales results in our analysis of average sale value and customer conversion rate. In the chart below, a district of general merchandise stores is arrayed from high average sale to low, with its corresponding customer conversion rate overlaid, just as we did for the previous examples. However, with this grouping we also embedded the store's overall sales rank within the bar, so that in addition to its average sale value and conversion rate, we can see its comparative sales rank. Again, the findings were very interesting.

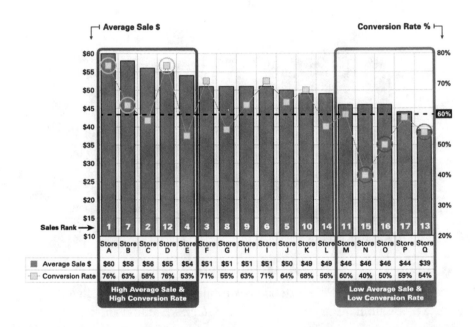

| | Store A | Store B | Store C | Store D | Store E | Store F | Store G | Store H | Store I | Store J | Store K | Store L | Store M | Store N | Store O | Store P | Store Q |
|---|---|---|---|---|---|---|---|---|---|---|---|---|---|---|---|---|---|
| Sales Rank | 1 | 7 | 2 | 12 | 4 | 3 | 8 | 9 | 6 | 5 | 10 | 14 | 11 | 15 | 16 | 17 | 13 |
| Average Sale $ | $60 | $58 | $56 | $55 | $54 | $51 | $51 | $51 | $51 | $50 | $49 | $49 | $46 | $46 | $46 | $44 | $39 |
| Conversion Rate | 76% | 63% | 58% | 76% | 53% | 71% | 55% | 63% | 71% | 64% | 68% | 56% | 60% | 40% | 50% | 59% | 54% |

As the chart shows, while the stores with the highest average sale values and customer conversion rate are among the best performing sales stores, they didn't always deliver the highest sales. For example, Store E, the fourth-ranked store in sales, had a lower average ticket and lower customer conversion rate than Store D, the twelfth-ranked sales store – how is this possible? Store Q (13th in sales) and Store P (17th) are also interesting. Store Q had a significantly lower average ticket ($39 versus $44) and a lower conversion rate (54% versus 59%) than Store P — yet managed to rank  higher in sales.

This all seems crazily counter-intuitive. How do we reconcile these findings with the idea that average ticket and customer conversion rate are the combined metrics that best determine in-store performance?

# Sales results can mask good in-store performance.

In my experience, most Store Managers not only want to deliver positive comp sales — they also want to look good compared to other stores in the chain. Unfortunately, comparative store performance is largely measured by a single, blunt metric – sales. The problem is that sales results can actually mask the true performance of a store. Here's an example.

The chart below shows the average daily sales by store for a district of apparel stores in Texas. Stores are ranked from highest average daily sales to lowest, one through ten. If I asked you to identify the three best performing stores, which would you choose? Obviously, you would choose the ones with the highest average daily sales.

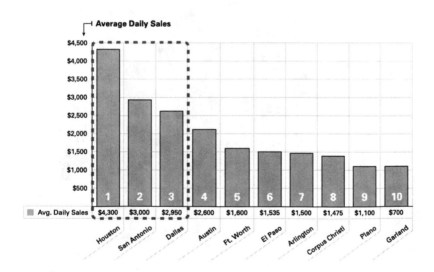

So far, so good. These results are irrefutable. There's nothing I'm going to say that will change them. However, instead of evaluating performance only on sales results, what if we looked at these stores with respect to the variables that actually measure a store's performance: average ticket and customer conversion rate?

The chart below shows the stores arrayed from highest to lowest average ticket, with corresponding customer conversion rates. I've also embedded the store's sales rank, so that we can compare average ticket and conversion rate to overall sales results.

This is where things start to get really interesting.

Let's start with the #1 sales ranked store. As you can see, this store had one of the <u>highest</u> average ticket values, but it also had one of the <u>lowest</u> customer conversion rates. The #3 sales-ranked store was similar – it had a high average ticket but a below-average customer conversion rate. Both stores generated the best sales results, and it appears that the high average ticket values had a lot to do with it. Furthermore, you might argue that, based on the data, the comparatively low customer conversion rate didn't seem to hurt sales results.

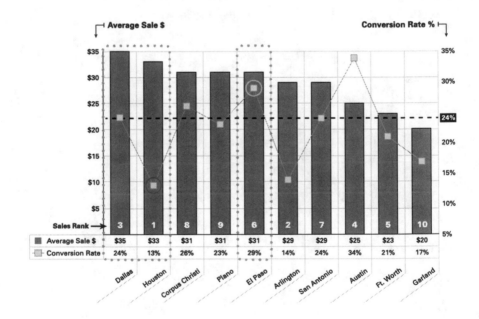

| | Average Sale $ | | | | | | | | Conversion Rate % | |
|---|---|---|---|---|---|---|---|---|---|---|
| Sales Rank ➔ | 3 | 1 | 8 | 9 | 6 | 2 | 7 | 4 | 5 | 10 |
| Average Sale $ | $35 | $33 | $31 | $31 | $31 | $29 | $29 | $25 | $23 | $20 |
| Conversion Rate | 24% | 13% | 26% | 23% | 29% | 14% | 24% | 34% | 21% | 17% |
| | Dallas | Houston | Corpus Christi | Plano | El Paso | Arlington | San Antonio | Austin | Ft. Worth | Garland |

While the high sales ranks of the #1 and #3 stores may be explained by the high average ticket values they generate, the store that had the highest combination of average ticket and customer conversion rate – the variables that, as I say, best define in-store performance – was El Paso. But El Paso only had an overall sales rank of sixth. How can this be? If average ticket and customer conversion rate define in-store performance, why doesn't it translate into high sales rank?

While it makes perfect sense for stores that have low average ticket values and low customer conversion rates to have poor overall sales results — and consequently low comparative sales rankings (just as they do on the right-hand side of the chart) — it's a little harder to understand the stores that have high average ticket values and high customer conversion — but still generate relatively low overall sales ranks. But it's perfectly logical. Here's why.

A store's sales rank and its actual in-store performance are not the same thing. A store could be a very good performer but have a low sales rank, as with the 6th-ranked store in the example above. Conversely, a store could have a high comparative sales rank and be an underperformer, just like the store ranked #1 in sales in the example above. The answer to this apparent enigma is one word: **traffic**.

Stores don't control traffic. Store-level personnel can only control what they do with the traffic they receive in their stores. If their store happens to be in a poor location in a bad mall, it could very well be that they do an excellent job of servicing customers, as measured by high customer conversion and average ticket values, but if the traffic is so low in their store, despite this outstanding in-store performance, its overall sales results will look comparatively poor. The store can't help that.

Comparatively poor sales results and ranking don't change the fact that from an in-store performance perspective, staff is doing a great job. Similarly, the store located in a high traffic, demographically blessed location may have abysmal customer conversion rates and poor average ticket values, but still generate high sales and consequently high sales rank.

The sales rank is inconsequential! This store is still underperforming compared to its opportunity. Moreover, the sales rank is irrelevant because we're comparing apples to bananas to oranges.

*Traffic is the critical context in which store performance needs to be considered.* Without the benefit of traffic data, you can never fully understand how a store is performing, and, as I've shown, sales results alone can't be the answer.

If we ignore sales rank and identify the three stores that had the best combination of average ticket and customer conversion rate, the three top-performing stores would be the ones shown in the chart. In this case, the #1, #2 and #3 best-performing stores had sales ranks of #6, #4 and #3, respectively.

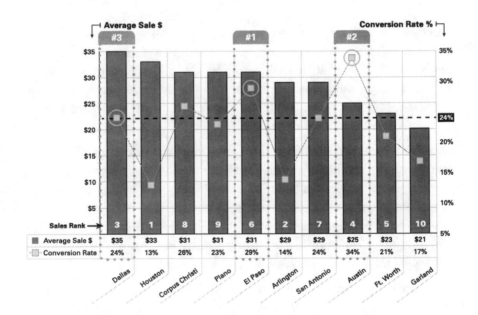

| | Dallas | Houston | Corpus Christi | Plano | El Paso | Arlington | San Antonio | Austin | Ft. Worth | Garland |
|---|---|---|---|---|---|---|---|---|---|---|
| Sales Rank | 3 | 1 | 8 | 9 | 6 | 2 | 7 | 4 | 5 | 10 |
| Average Sale $ | $35 | $33 | $31 | $31 | $31 | $29 | $29 | $25 | $23 | $21 |
| Conversion Rate | 24% | 13% | 26% | 23% | 29% | 14% | 24% | 34% | 21% | 17% |

So we if we revisit the original chart that ranked stores by average daily sales, but this time highlight our #1, #2 and #3 stores based on in-store performance instead of average daily sales, the chart would look like this:

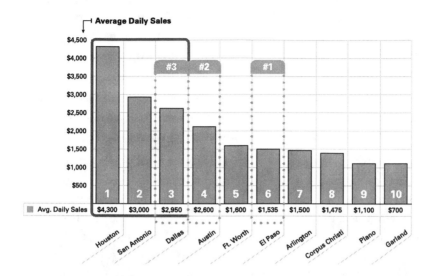

If this appears somewhat confusing, I understand. The data say that sales rank and in-store performance rank don't seem to correlate in any obvious way. So it's reasonable for you to ask, "What does it mean?" and "How can I put these insights to practical use to drive performance in my stores?" The next section will help you do just that.

# Comparing stores with different opportunity sizes

OK, so we know the sales results that a particular store generates, and now we also know something about the store's performance based on the combination of average ticket and customer conversion. But how do we bring these ideas together in a way that makes the information meaningful and actionable?

We were working with a major luxury retailer when we were faced with this exact question. The results of our analysis were fascinating, but the retailer didn't know (and neither did we initially) what to do with it.

It occurred to us that the first step was to create a level playing field — to make the stores comparable — and to do that, we focused on traffic. Remember that stores don't control traffic. Some stores look like top performers, not because they are executing well, but rather because they have an abundance of traffic to sell to. Even with low average ticket and conversion rate, these stores look like winners. Comparing stores based on sales alone is like pitting a heavyweight boxer against a flyweight – not a fair contest.

We came at the problem by asking ourselves a very simple question: What would the sales results be for the stores if they all had the exact same traffic opportunity? In essence, we put all stores in the same "weight-class" by evaluating the average traffic volume received across the group of stores, then calculating the sales that each store would deliver based on this average traffic and on the store's actual average ticket and customer conversion rate. We then re-ranked the stores based on these normalized sales numbers.

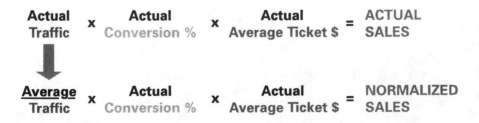

In the case of our district of ten apparel stores, the average daily traffic across the group of stores ranged from a high of over 1,000 counts per day to a low of less than 100 counts per day. If this doesn't constitute a heavyweight versus a flyweight mismatch, I don't know what would. The average daily traffic across all 10 stores was 350 counts per day. So we took the 350 counts per day average, applied the average ticket and customer conversion rate for each store, and then calculated the sales for each store, ranking them from high to low.

We called these normalized sales results the "In-store Performance Rank" – the true performance of the store, regardless of the traffic it receives. The results were mind-blowing. Take a look.

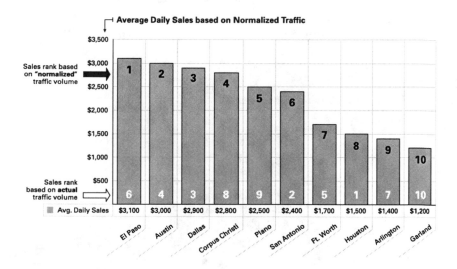

When we strip away the influence of traffic, store performance becomes clearer. The real insight comes from comparing the actual sales results and rank to the normalized results. As you can see from the chart above, there are three types of stores:

(1) **high-performance stores:** a high in-store performance rank but relatively low actual sales performance and rank;

(2) **opportunity stores:** low in-store performance rank but relatively high actual sales performance and rank; and

(3) **traffic-neutral stores** (i.e., unaffected by traffic): the same or similar in-store performance rank, as well as the same actual sales performance and rank.

Let's examine these three in more detail.

# High-performance stores

When the in-store performance rank is high but overall sales rank is low, the store is performing well, but the lack of traffic volume is stunting its sales performance. Based on actual sales, the El Paso and Austin stores were ranked #6 and #4, respectively. However, if these stores had the same average daily traffic as all the other stores (350 counts in this case), their sales ranks would be #1 and #2 respectively. These are great-performing stores, but they just don't receive enough traffic to realize their sales potential.

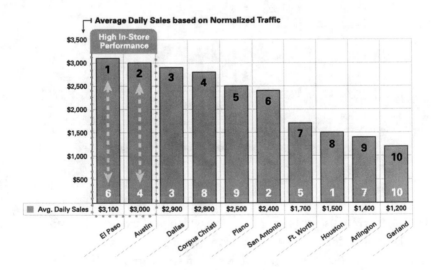

So now, instead of viewing these stores as middle-of-the-road performers, senior management understands that these are actually top performing stores that are being held back by a lack of traffic! *The bigger the gap between the in-store performance rank and the actual sales*

*rank, the more the key driver is traffic.* The implication is that in order to boost sales results in these high- performance stores, management needs to focus on driving more traffic into these stores. Traffic is the key lever.

# Opportunity stores

These stores are characterized by relatively low in-store performance rank but high actual sales rank. In this case, the store is generating high comparative actual sales by virtue of high traffic volume and not necessarily as a result of an effective in-store performance. This situation makes the store's performance look better than it actually is. More importantly, it's not as good as it could be.

The reason we refer to these stores as "opportunity" stores is that they have an abundance of traffic, but unfortunately too much of it is leaving without making a purchase. In the chart below, the San Antonio store is ranked #2 in actual sales, but only #6 in performance.

The Houston store is another, even more dramatic example. Its rank based on actual sales is stellar – it's the #1 store in actual sales. But again, if we strip away the windfall benefits of the traffic this store receives and hypothetically give it the same traffic as all the other stores, its in-store performance rank drops to #8.

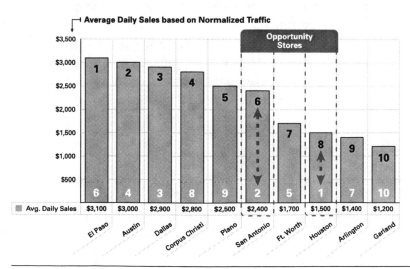

With opportunity stores, the bigger the gap between actual sales rank and in-store performance rank, the bigger the store's opportunity. These stores have plenty of traffic. Now management's imperative is to come up with strategies to improve customer conversion rates and (secondarily) average ticket. Driving more traffic into these stores is not going to be an effective use of the funds – they already get more traffic than they can apparently manage.

By breaking out the underlying sales drivers we are able to explore the key questions about the store's performance. Is the store understaffed? Is scheduling misaligned? Perhaps it's a training issue. Maybe the store is poorly merchandised. Maybe it lacks inventory. The point is that now management actually knows what it's solving for and can take steps to try to improve performance. Without the benefit of traffic and conversion analytics, these stores would likely continue to plod along, with senior managers well satisfied with the sales results and completely oblivious to how the stores are actually underperforming — and to what's truly possible.

## Traffic-neutral stores

When the in-store performance rank and the actual sales rank are the same or very close, we conclude that the store's performance is not being overly influenced by traffic. For example, the Dallas store has a sales rank of #3 and an in-store performance rank of #3. Compared to the other stores, it's performing well, and traffic has nothing to do with it. The Garland store is ranked dead last (#10) in actual sales and in-store performance – you can't blame lack of traffic on that. As the in-store performance index proves, even if this store had the same traffic opportunity as every other store, it would still be dead last.

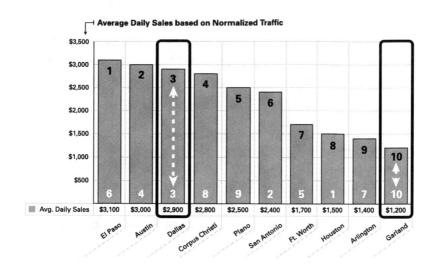

Average Daily Sales based on Normalized Traffic

| | Avg. Daily Sales | El Paso | Austin | Dallas | Corpus Christi | Plano | San Antonio | Ft. Worth | Houston | Arlington | Garland |
|---|---|---|---|---|---|---|---|---|---|---|---|
| | | $3,100 | $3,000 | $2,900 | $2,800 | $2,500 | $2,400 | $1,700 | $1,500 | $1,400 | $1,200 |

# Driving sales performance

*You cannot effectively drive sales if you don't know what you are solving for, and without putting sales results in the context of traffic, conversion and average sale, you can only speculate about what you need to do in order to drive sales.*

As I mentioned earlier, sales are a function of three variables: traffic, customer conversion rate and average ticket. If you want to drive comp sales, you need to influence one or all of these variables. Traffic typically requires some form of investment, so while it is a legitimate way to drive sales, there's a cost. Furthermore, if you drive all kinds of traffic into your stores, but the stores fail to convert the traffic into buyers, you get a dose of insult to go along with your helping of injury.

*Stores don't control traffic — but they do control what they do with the traffic they receive.* In order to drive performance, stores need to focus on average ticket and customer conversion rate. While average ticket has always been and will continue to be a critical performance metric, stores can't rely exclusively on it to improve overall sales results. Given the time and energy that retailers have already spent on driving up average sale, there's only so much more that can realistically be squeezed from this approach.

As important as average sale value is to driving results, retailers can be too focused on this one metric, and if they take it to the extreme, they could even be sub-optimizing sales. There is only so much up-selling and cross-selling Associates can do.

Customer conversion is the third — and in many ways the most powerful — factor in store sales performance.

Why? First, the opportunity: most retailers today don't calculate customer conversion, so it's completely uncharted territory, representing a whole new way to think about performance and opportunity. Second, conversion is something that store-level Associates actually control and influence; that's why it's among the purest measures of in-store performance. Third, as I mentioned earlier, the notion of "converting" traffic is conceptually easier for Sales Associates to understand and achieve (e.g., just sell to one more person per hour).

There are other reasons why customer conversion is such a revealing performance metric. But you can't influence it if you don't measure it! And, to their detriment, most retailers today don't measure it.

As I've shown, customer conversion rates and average ticket values are not mutually exclusive. The best performing stores are good at both, and the worst performing stores tend to be bad at both. *The combination of the customer conversion rate and average ticket combined provides the best, most reliable measure of true in-store performance.*

It is absolutely imperative to view store performance in the context of traffic, conversion and average ticket together in order to truly understand not only how your stores are performing but, more importantly, what you need to do to drive sales. Looking at store performance by sales results alone can mislead you about the store's true performance.

Each store is unique, and while you need to view each one individually to drive performance, it's useful to compare performance across stores. However, to do this in a meaningful way, you need to view in-store performance separately from overall sales results.

To elaborate: Traffic volume can make underperforming stores look like top performers, and vice versa, so it's vital to normalize traffic volume to get a clear picture of how your stores are truly performing. Normalizing traffic levels and calculating the resulting sales results helps management see how each store is actually performing. Like an MRI scan, it looks beneath the skin to provide a clear image of what's driving sales in the store.

Furthermore, normalizing traffic volume puts all stores on the same level playing field and enables  managers to understand what the sales drivers are and to take steps to improve results.

Without traffic and customer conversion data, none of these insights would be possible. But a great deal depends on the mindset and behavior of managers throughout your organization. These are the subjects of the next chapter.

# Chapter 3.2

## Getting Managers to Consume Conversion Insights

Across the boardroom table sat four key stakeholders from a large apparel chain: the CEO, CFO, Operations Director and a lowly District Manager. The DM – responsible for a mere 20 stores – was way out of his weight-class in this meeting, but the executives rightly thought it would be helpful to have some information from the field. We were there to talk about traffic and conversion analytics and how my company could help them potentially get more out of the data they were collecting.

This chain had installed traffic counters in all their stores and had been collecting and analyzing data for more than a year. Top managers felt they had a pretty good handle on things but were intrigued by our proposition to discuss the idea of getting more out of the data. So they agreed to the meeting.

As I looked across the table, the stakeholders were perfectly arrayed, from CEO to District Manager, as if the seating arrangement were dictated by formal protocol. As we launched into our discussions in earnest, I learned that this retailer was actually doing a pretty good job of collecting and analyzing traffic and conversion data – at least at the Head Office level. However, as we moved on to the topic of how the data is actually being used (or "consumed," as I like to refer to the process) particularly at store-level, our discussion took a curious turn.

Naturally, the CEO went first: "Conversion is an important initiative for us and it has been communicated throughout the organization." In a tone that suggested that he was mildly offended by my question, the CFO chimed in, "Of course our managers understand what conversion is and what to do with the data — it's part of their job." The Operations

Director, though somewhat subdued and less emphatic, was quick to add his support to the CFO, with a simple "I agree." Last, but not least, the District Manager spoke: 'Well...the store managers are seeing the data, but I'm not too sure they all know what it means or what to do with it."

Awkward silence.

As this real-world example illustrates, the store managers clearly weren't consuming the insights. Worse, the senior team believed they were. Getting field management to comply with a new policy, execute a new plan-o-gram, or even follow a new procedure is a challenge. Getting them to consume traffic and conversion analytics is certainly no different. But it can be done, and some retailers have found ways to make it work. It's worth the effort.

## Consumption → Action → Results

Consumption is what characterizes the retailer leaders who make the most of traffic and customer conversion insights in their business versus those who do not. They consume the insights in a deep and meaningful way. While getting meaningful consumption of new ideas and practices across the entire organization is among the most critical success factors, it is also most often the area where I see retailers struggling.

The leaders realize that these aren't simply additional metrics clogging up an already jam-packed dashboard; they're two of the critical metrics that help guide the operation of their business on a day-to-day basis. And everyone from the store Associate to the CEO knows and understands this fact.

Owning a piano and playing great music are two very different propositions. The same principle applies to traffic and customer conversion analytics. Buying traffic counters and collecting traffic data is easy. Comparing traffic data to transactions in order to calculate customer conversion rates, then producing charts and reports — pretty straightforward. But taking this information, making it meaningful, and then having your entire organization consume the insights in a way that truly makes a difference – that's hard. But worth it.

The driving of results can happen only if the insights that come from traffic and conversion analytics are <u>consumed</u> by the stakeholders. In this chapter we will more fully examine this most vital component of a successful traffic and conversion program – consumption.

*"Consumption" means that the insights are being used by all stakeholders across the organization, because they understand what the insights mean and how they can take action on them.* "Consumption" means that managers use the insights that come from these data, that they <u>actually do something</u> with the information – make decisions or change behaviors,  so that the ultimate outcome is better sales results and/or lower expenses.

It is an oversimplification to call this a "communication" issue – it's much more than that. Managers need to know what the information means to them and how they can act on it. Traffic and conversion analytics must become a part of the operating fabric of the organization. They must become as pervasive and meaningful as same-store sales and average ticket are today.

How do you make all this happen? There are four dimensions to effective consumption of traffic and conversion insights:

1) **communication:** As obvious as it is, it's worth stating for the record. If traffic and customer conversion analytics are going to be effectively consumed, then all stakeholders need to hear about them. Traffic and conversion need to become part of the company's everyday vocabulary. From the CEO and his/her team to the functional Head Office managers and ultimately, and maybe even most importantly, the regional, district and store-level personnel, everyone needs to learn what traffic and conversion are about and why they're important to the company, to customers and to him or herself as an individual performer. Retailers who make the most of these metrics have learned to "talk traffic" and "converse in conversion" as part of their daily interactions. As a senior executive of a shoe store chain once told me, "When the CEO talks to me in our weekly phone calls, he doesn't ask how sales are. He asks me about traffic and conversion rates."

2) **education:** Hearing it is the first step, but it has to go beyond the words. Managers need to know what these concepts mean; they need to know how it relates to the success of their store and the chain as a whole. Including traffic and conversion as part of an overall training program is a great place to start. However, a one-time training session alone will go only so far and likely won't be enough. Merely providing managers with data or stats without context will definitely not deliver results.

3) **engagement:** Even if a manager understands what traffic and customer conversion is, even if he/she realizes that it's important to the company, progress will not be made unless the manager is engaged with the analytics on a regular basis – daily, at least. There are lots of ways to keep stakeholders engaged with the analytics, but simply providing access to a data portal with a cornucopia of stats, tables and charts is not going to be effective. Providing the right amount of detail, in the right format, at the right time is key. Too much information is distracting and frustrating; too little information limits consumption and usefulness.

4) **action:** Pretty graphs and charts are easy to come by. While well-designed reports and easy-to-digest charts are vital to effective communication, managers still need to know how they can take action on the insights. What specifically can or should they do with the information?

The objective in all this is clear: to use traffic and customer conversion to help managers make better decisions and ultimately drive comp sales. Traffic and customer conversion can help them do that, but they need assistance and nurturing to know how to do it. If managers understand what customer conversion analytics are and how to use them, if they're engaged with the analytics as part of day-to-day operations, and if they're willing and able to put the insights to action, the result will be better store performance.

# Turning insights into action

A dealer of a large general merchandise retailer installed a traffic counter in his store. He thought there was merit to the insights that he could gain from traffic and customer conversion, so he thought he'd give it a try.

The traffic counters were installed, and the information started to roll in. It kept coming and coming. An array of wonderful graphs and charts filled his in-box with all kinds of insights. After about eight months of this, the dealer cancelled the service and had the traffic counters removed from his store.

When asked why, he said, "I've been looking at these graphs and charts, and it's all interesting, but nothing really changes. The patterns are the same month after month, so I guess I've learned all I need to learn from this." When he was asked what actions he took with the data or changes he made based on the insights, he said, "Changes? I haven't made any changes."

I was stunned. What did he expect? Magic? Miracles?

There's no magic to this. Installing traffic counters in your stores, collecting data and then waiting for sales to improve is analogous to installing a new POS and somehow hoping that this too will make sales go up. How can it? The only way for performance to improve is to change behavior or take an action that results in a better outcome. Without action, nothing changes.

Reviewing the traffic and conversion trends for a luxury retailer revealed that the conversion rates were consistently sagging between the hours of 6 PM and closing at 9 PM. A deeper analysis of the data showed that this evening-hour drop in conversion rate was not happening during the weekends, but only during the regular work week. In a follow-up discussion to review these findings with the store manager, it was clear that he couldn't explain why conversion rates were sagging.

After discussing the issue in detail, it was hypothesized that the conversion rate sag might be a result of senior staff leaving by 5 PM, leaving less experienced staff to run the store during these later hours.

Great hypothesis. But the only way to know for sure is to test it. It seemed like a pretty straightforward exercise: ask some of your senior people to change their shifts to work the later hours for a couple of weeks to see if conversion rates improved during the 5 PM to 9 PM daypart. The store manager's reaction was surprising: "Change staff schedules? Are you kidding me? It would take an act of Congress to get people to change their schedules. I can't do that!"

> *"Change staff schedules — are you kidding me?*
> *It would take an act of congress to get people*
> *to change their schedules — I can't do that!"*

The entire point of consuming the insights is to ultimately take action – to change a behavior or make some other change that will result in better performance. If a manager does not have the authority or the will to make a decision or to test his/her theories, then there's not much point to having the insights.

## Data presentation and detail

Having the right level of detail and presenting it in a meaningful way is critical if managers are going to consume the data. The table below is very typical of the data that many store managers have access to via the company data portal or ERP system. How could anyone reasonably be expected to make sense of this much data? When the information is presented in this way, even a trained data analyst would have a hard time finding the trends. And a store-level manager? Not a chance.

| Store | Date | TY-Sales | LY-Sales | % | TY-YTD | LY-YTD | % | UPTS | ASP | TRAFFIC | CONV % |
|---|---|---|---|---|---|---|---|---|---|---|---|
| #333 | 1-Jun-01 | $1,130.85 | $1,164.78 | -3% | $203,553.00 | $213,730.65 | -5% | 1.75 | $21.54 | 250 | 21.0% |
| #333 | 2-Jun-01 | $1,538.70 | $1,523.31 | 1% | $276,966.00 | $279,735.66 | -1% | 1.50 | $22.30 | 300 | 23.0% |
| #333 | 3-Jun-01 | $1,512.00 | $1,527.12 | -1% | $272,160.00 | $266,716.80 | 2% | 1.10 | $22.50 | 320 | 21.0% |
| #333 | 4-Jun-01 | $1,210.68 | $1,186.47 | 2% | $217,922.40 | $213,563.95 | 2% | 1.05 | $21.60 | 295 | 19.0% |
| #333 | 5-Jun-01 | $1,138.20 | $1,092.67 | 4% | $204,875.57 | $202,826.81 | 1% | 1.40 | $21.88 | 289 | 18.0% |
| #333 | 6-Jun-01 | $1,795.31 | $1,885.08 | -5% | $323,155.98 | $323,155.98 | 0% | 1.40 | $22.05 | 354 | 23.0% |
| #333 | 7-Jun-01 | $1,728.75 | $1,746.04 | -1% | $311,175.00 | $304,951.50 | 2% | 1.85 | $23.05 | 300 | 25.0% |
| | Week #1 | $10,054.49 | $10,125.46 | -1% | $1,809,807.95 | $1,822,582.56 | -1% | 1.44 | $22.13 | 301.14 | 0.21 |
| #333 | 8-Jun-01 | $1,865.76 | $1,828.44 | 2% | $335,836.80 | $332,478.43 | 1% | 1.90 | $24.00 | 299 | 26.0% |
| #333 | 9-Jun-01 | $2,203.74 | $2,159.67 | 2% | $396,673.20 | $392,706.47 | 1% | 2.05 | $23.85 | 385 | 24.0% |
| #333 | 10-Jun-01 | $2,419.20 | $2,395.01 | 1% | $435,456.00 | $448,519.68 | -3% | 1.85 | $23.04 | 375 | 28.0% |
| #333 | 11-Jun-01 | $1,189.65 | $1,189.65 | 0% | $214,137.00 | $209,854.26 | 2% | 1.80 | $22.66 | 250 | 21.0% |
| #333 | 12-Jun-01 | $1,127.11 | $1,104.57 | 2% | $202,879.80 | $202,879.80 | 0% | 1.50 | $20.95 | 269 | 20.0% |
| #333 | 13-Jun-01 | $1,209.60 | $1,197.50 | 1% | $217,728.00 | $224,259.84 | -3% | 2.10 | $21.00 | 288 | 20.0% |
| #333 | 14-Jun-01 | $1,224.94 | $1,212.69 | 1% | $220,488.75 | $218,283.86 | 1% | 2.10 | $20.85 | 235 | 25.0% |
| | Week #2 | $1,1240.00 | $1,1087.53 | 1% | $2,023,199.55 | $1,995,755.03 | 1% | 1.90 | $22.34 | 300.14 | 0.23 |
| #333 | 15-Jun-01 | $1,740.64 | $1,792.86 | -3% | $313,315.20 | $316,448.35 | -1% | 1.85 | $23.00 | 344 | 22.0% |
| #333 | 16-Jun-01 | $1,768.90 | $1,733.52 | 2% | $318,402.00 | $312,033.96 | 2% | 1.75 | $24.50 | 380 | 19.0% |
| #333 | 17-Jun-01 | $1,400.70 | $1,400.70 | 0% | $252,126.00 | $242,040.96 | 4% | 2.00 | $21.75 | 322 | 20.0% |

Providing store managers access to a data portal with tons of tabular data like this is problematic for several reasons: (1) there's too much data for the manager to process; (2) data presented in a tabular, numeric format make it virtually impossible to pick out any trends; (3) there is no hourly data, which is what store managers need in order to schedule staff; and (4) it's not portable. These types of systems are often only accessible in the store. So even if store managers intended to spend some time trying to decipher the data, they could do it only in the store.

The needs of managers throughout the organization are very different. What the CEO and his/her team look at is obviously different from what a store manager needs to look at, and traffic and conversion data need to be provided in a way that meets these unique needs. Here are the factors to consider in the preparation and presentation of traffic and conversion data to management stakeholders:

- amount of data
- level of data granularity (e.g., hourly, daily, weekly)
- data presentation (graphical, tabular, raw data dumps)
- timing (e.g., every morning by 9 AM)

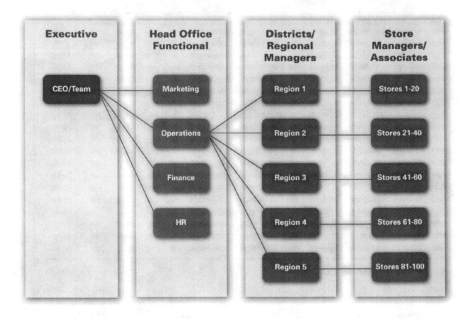

Let me elaborate on the needs of each key consumer.

**CEO and Executive Team:** The amount of data flowing into the executive suite is almost mind-boggling. Traffic and conversion data presented to this group usually works best as a weekly dashboard that includes top-level summary data, showing long, medium and short-term trends for the overall chain, with breakouts by district, region and major media markets. The presentation needs to be <u>clean</u> and <u>simple</u> – these executives already have too much data to look at and they have no patience for digging through tables or raw data to get answers. They want to know, concisely, how well their stores are performing relative to the opportunity.

**Head Office Functional Management:** Each functional head office department will have different needs, and so the amount of reporting and level of detail will vary. From Human Resources analyzing hourly patterns to optimize staff schedules, to Marketing measuring the impact of the latest promotional campaign, or Finance's building the latest revenue forecast, these power users will need virtually constant access to all traffic and conversion data, with daily and even hourly granularity.

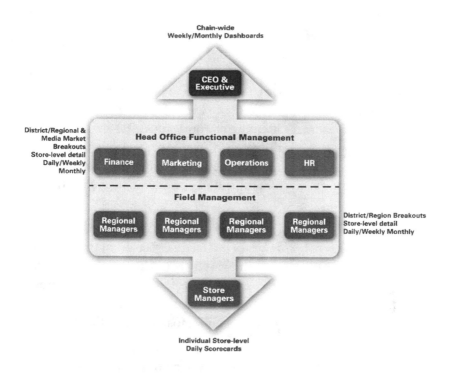

Chain-wide
Weekly/Monthly Dashboards

CEO &
Executive

District/Regional &
Media Market
Breakouts
Store-level detail
Daily/Weekly
Monthly

**Head Office Functional Management**

Finance    Marketing    Operations    HR

**Field Management**

Regional
Managers    Regional
Managers    Regional
Managers    Regional
Managers

District/Region Breakouts
Store-level detail
Daily/Weekly Monthly

Store
Managers

Individual Store-level
Daily Scorecards

**Field Management:** District and Regional Managers will need to see breakouts for their respective regions and districts. These managers are key users, and while their focus is on their respective regions or district, they need to be able to quickly scan across their store results, look for anomalies and drill down to store-level results.[1] As enablers for the Store Managers, the field managers are critical users of traffic and conversion data. They usually need daily and weekly reporting that provides deep store-level detail, so that they can understand performance across their stores and be able to engage Store Managers in a meaningful way about each store's trends, opportunities and challenges.

**Store Managers:** As with the executives, the traffic and conversion data for Store Managers needs to be simple to process – these managers are running the store and don't have time for a lot of analysis or digging. They need simple, clean graphical data showing them current results, short term trends, and performance relative to plan and opportunity. Store Managers need hourly traffic and conversion data, every day.

# Field management – critical consumers

As with many corporate initiatives, there tends to be a lot of thought and energy at the Head Office – developing the ideas, building programs, and launching them in the stores. Often the energy wanes after the program is launched. And, because it is legitimately difficult to effectively propagate programs from Head Office to the stores and ultimately the Associates, programs often lose momentum. Traffic and customer conversion are no different.

That's why *effective traffic and conversion programs must be implemented from stores up to Corporate Head Office* – not the other way around. Of course, ideas often and rightly come from the top, but in order for traffic/conversion to have a real impact on the business, store-level personnel need to understand what it's all about, what it means to them, what they can do to influence it – and, most importantly, that they can influence it.

Some retailers misguidedly believe that they should "shield" Associates and even Store Managers from this data – they have enough to worry about. They say, "We don't want to distract them from the day-in-day-out work of serving customers."

While I do understand where this paternalistic approach comes from, I believe it's misguided and ultimately misses the point. If you examine retailers who use traffic and customer conversion to the greatest benefit, you will discover that their store-level personnel are all well versed in what it is and how to put it to use.

> *"We don't share traffic or conversion results with our store managers...we don't want to distract them with the data."*

# Head Office "hoarding"

Some retailers go to all the trouble and expense of collecting traffic and conversion data — but then hoard the analytics at Head Office. These retailers misguidedly believe that they can influence store-level results without fully engaging field management. While there are many stakeholders in a retail organization when it comes to driving customer conversion, field managers are among the most important, and to exclude them from the process is a big mistake.

Conversion happens in the store. Store Managers and Associates are the people directly responsible for making customer conversion happen, so it's critical that they understand what conversion means and how significant it is; it's critical that they consume the insights.

The District and Regional Managers play a vital role, first in helping store-level personnel interpret the results and formulate hypothesis about what's influencing conversion, then in guiding the process of turning insights into action.[2] So while I will discuss the importance of having the entire senior executive team consuming traffic and conversion insights (Chapter 3.3), field managers and Associates require some additional consideration.

- **District and Regional Managers:** In many ways, the District and Regional Managers are the real linchpins in the effective use of traffic and customer conversion insights, just as they are in helping run the chain in general. Retailers who don't provide traffic and customer conversion analytics for these managers are asking them to almost do the impossible – find ways to improve store performance – without fully understanding what's driving the results.

  It is impractical for DMs and RMs to visit all their stores on a regular basis, yet it is vital for them to keep their fingers on the pulse of what's happening in their stores every day. While mystery shop and other customer experience measures can help, DMs and RMs have to rely on sales results to help them set priorities and focus attention where it's needed most – and to most managers, that means stores that are under-performing based on sales.

Almost more than any other stakeholder, DMs and RMs need to consume traffic and conversion analytics. They need to understand the patterns and trends for their stores, look for the opportunities, and then engage Store Managers and Associates to find answers and help them action the data. Customer conversion doesn't happen by accident. There are reasons why customer conversion rates go up and down in stores, and it's the DMs and RMs who need to dig into the results to find out why.

- **Store Managers:** Every retailer knows that great store performance starts and ends with a great Store Manager.[3] Store Managers are the unsung heroes of retailing. From recruiting and training, to merchandising and loss prevention, these often overburdened managers are called upon to do it all – and deliver positive comp sales. Unlike the DMs and RMs, they are in the store virtually every day. They do know what's going on. They see it and live it. But, just like the DMs and RMs, they need to understand what's driving sales results in their store and validate and quantify what they already intuitively know.

More than anything, traffic and conversion insights help create a platform on which to engage with DM's and RM's. It clarifies what the drivers are and enables the store manager to converse with the DM or RM in a meaningful way about what needs to be done – and without all the speculation that takes place when these managers have only sales results to rely upon.

Once again, because it bears repeating: stores generally don't control traffic. The focus of Store Managers and Associates is to convert the traffic they do receive. If sales are down because prospect traffic has dramatically deceased in the store, it's not likely the store's fault. So when a DM calls his/her Store Manager and asks why sales are down and the Store Manager says "the store is dead," it's hard to know whether the store is really dead — or the store staff is not executing. After all, it's the oldest excuse for poor sales in retailing.

But with traffic and conversion data, there's no guesswork. It's not opinion or speculation, but quantitative data – yes, I see, store traffic is actually down 15%, I need to let Marketing know.

Another critical factor in helping Store Managers consume traffic and conversion insights is to recognize that each and every store in your chain is unique. Like a fingerprint, each store has a its own traffic and conversion profile. It's not hard to understand why. Each store has a different location, competitive environment, geography, physical structure, and most importantly, staff. Everything about each store is different. And, while it's hard to not compare groups of stores, *when it comes to driving customer conversion at store level, the only numbers a Store Manager needs to focus on are his/her own.*

If Store A is converting at 20%, the focus should be on how to move it up to 22%, 24% or higher; if Store B converts at 40%, then the focus should be on getting it to 42%, 44% or higher. It's neither helpful nor instructive to remind Store A that Store B has a significantly higher conversion rate.

As I've said, conversion rates happen for reasons. If there is a 20-point difference in conversion rates between two stores, there's probably a good reason.

Personalizing traffic and conversion to the individual store and engaging the Store Manager on his/her results makes for the most meaningful and effective discussion. It makes consumption easier.

- **Associates:** While it is important to keep Associates focused on tasks and serving customers, far too often they are kept entirely in the dark about customer conversion. Given that Associates are one of the most important determinants (if not the most important) in customer conversion, it's important for them to understand what it is and why it's important.

Ultimately, customer conversion is a measure of how well the store collectively is serving customers. Even if overall sales are down because of lower traffic in the store, the Associates may be doing an excellent job of converting the traffic they do get – they may be performing very well, notwithstanding the lower traffic levels that might be driving the poor sales results. Instead of focusing on the poor sales results, it might be helpful for these Associates to hear about how well they're doing despite the low traffic.

# The act of consumption

Store Managers often ask me, "How do I improve my conversion? What exactly should I do with the information?" The most important thing a Store Manager can do is to compare traffic and conversion data to sales results and ask why.

Why did sales go up or down? Was it traffic that drove the results or conversion? Who was on shift? Were there extenuating circumstances like bad weather or a major shipment or promotion that impacted results?

Here's a summary of the important ways Store Managers should be using traffic and conversion analytics to improve results in their stores:

> ## Driving Customer Conversion...
>
> - Compare sales results to traffic and conversion – ask, What drove results?
> - Look for conversion "sags" and ensure you match staff schedules to traffic
> - Share results and set targets with the store team
> - Make "conversion" part of your everyday language
> - Understand why people don't buy in your store
> - Review results daily, make adjustments, share learning's
> - Think about conversion as an ongoing PROCESS not a one-time PROJECT

# Getting true alignment

There is a big difference between imposing a policy or operating principle and getting true buy-in and alignment. If leadership deems that traffic and customer conversion are important, managers will align – it's their job. They have no choice. However, this is not the same as getting true buy-in, where people truly understand the purpose and benefits for the organization and themselves personally. Here are some ways that I have found to work:

- **Keep it simple and level-appropriate.**
  Obviously managers have different skills and experience. The way our company communicates with a Store Manager is different than the way we explain things to a Regional Manager or a Head Office executive. Traffic and customer conversion must be framed in a way that makes sense to and is digestible by the manager and relevant to his/her rank. Store Managers need the simplest, most actionable data. Higher-level personnel will hear about the strategic importance of traffic/conversion.

- **Educate managers.**
  Providing meaningful training to managers is a significant challenge in retailing. But in order for managers to truly consume traffic and conversion insights, they need to understand what it is. Inundating managers with analytics (or, worse, access to web portals for analyzing data themselves) is not going to lead to meaningful consumption. Why should the leadership expect field managers to understand this stuff when many in the executive suite struggle with it?

  With Web-based learning tools, there's really no excuse for not providing all managers with some basic training on what these metrics are and how they get used. Basic education is critical to facilitating consumption.

- **Personalize it to make it more meaningful.**
  Getting some form of general training is an important first step, but it can't stop there. Because every store is unique, generalized training can only go so far. I have conducted a considerable number of Store Manager group training sessions. And while these sessions are an important vehicle in getting managers on the same page, invariably as the group session wraps up, you'll hear a Store Manager whisper, "Yeah, this is all good stuff...but my store's different."

Whoever said that is right. Your store is different, and that's why some form of training needs to get down to each Store Manager individually. Instead of generalizations, training should ensure that each manager understands the practical application of traffic/conversion data to his/her particular store and its actual results.

- **Be continuous and consistent.**
  Field managers are bombarded with programs and initiatives. There seems to be no shortage of programs, campaigns, initiatives, and policies, all urgent. While these all make sense on the whiteboards in the various functional departments at Headquarters, it all comes together at the stores. Traffic and customer conversion cannot be a program *du jour* – if it's treated as such, it won't take hold.

- **Incentives make it tangible.**
  Incentivizing customer conversion can be a very effective way of driving results and ensuring that managers stay engaged. Obviously not every retail chain is able or willing to create incentives based on customer conversion, but for those who are able (notwithstanding the above-mentioned pitfalls which management needs to avoid in designing incentive programs),  such incentives can have a powerful and lasting impact,  creating a customer conversion-centric organization.

# Conversion as stick or carrot

Customer conversion rate is a powerful metric. It measures how effectively staff is collectively serving customers who enter the store every hour of every day. Retailers who truly understand the importance of this metric realize that every customer counts and that delivering a great customer experience and serving the customer in a way that results in a sale is a never-ending process. A prospect that comes into the store at 10 AM is just as important as a prospect that comes into the store at 1 PM or 8 PM – they all count; they're all equally important, and customer conversion measures every one of them.

Customer conversion rate doesn't measure whether or not your staff acknowledged the prospect or asked if he/she needed assistance... or whether or not the Associate helped the prospect find an item. It simply and eloquently measures *the only thing that really counts – did the prospect make a purchase?* This isn't to say that acknowledging prospects, asking if they need assistance, or helping them find an item aren't important. These may very well be important aspects of delivering a great customer experience that ultimately leads to customer conversion, but they are simply a means to an end. Conversion is the goal.

Once retailers discover the tremendous impact on sales that improvements in customer conversion rates can have, they sometimes get over-zealous in trying to improve conversion. In fact, some retailers have gotten so aggressive about it that conversion rate becomes a performance stick with which managers are regularly and unfairly beaten. I have yet to see a case where using customer conversion rate punitively produces optimal results.

Retailers who use conversion rates as a stick create a negative feeling about them and management measures in general. And, instead of leading to improved performance, such incentives tend to create environments where staff is more apt to game the system or become more adept at creating excuses for why their conversion rates may be sagging.

When conversion rate is used punitively, managers tend to lose sight of what the metric is measuring and turn their energy to making the pain go away. For example, in an effort to increase conversion rates in her store, a Store Manager blocked the beam sensors at the entrance periodically throughout the day. The net effect of this behavior was that there were fewer traffic counts logged, and conversion rates miraculously increased. Of course overall sales didn't improve.

Creating incentives to improve customer conversion is a great way to not only drive sales performance but also to keep managers and Associates engaged and focused on customer conversion and consuming the insights in a constructive way. While much has been said and written about creating performance incentives in retail, here are a few things to consider about conversion rate incentives:

- **balanced targets:** Naturally, and as with any incentive program, some people will try to take advantage of the system. As the above example illustrated, if the only focus is to drive up conversion, there are ways to achieve higher conversion rates – as crude and simple as blocking sensors — that won't ultimately deliver better store performance. A balanced incentive program that includes average ticket, customer conversion rate, and, most importantly, overall sales works best. With this kind of program, gaming the system by driving up conversion rate if total sales don't improve won't result in a benefit. Average ticket and customer conversion rate are the two variables that store personnel can influence that ultimately drive sales performance, and these are the key behaviors that should be incented. Sell more to more people.

- **total store versus individual:** Because conversion rates in many retail environments cannot be easily attributed to individual Associates, developing overall store conversion targets is a great way to keep all Associates and Managers engaged. If you think about it, converting a prospect to a customer may take the effort of more than one Associate, so it stands to reason that an incentive program based on overall store performance makes great sense. Of course, this incentive program can be used in conjunction with individual performance programs you may already have in place.

- **realistic targets:** Setting targets in any performance program is critical. While it is important to set targets that encourage Managers and Associates to strive and aspire to levels of higher store performance, targets set too high can have the opposite effect. Given that each and every one of your stores is truly unique, the most effective way of setting conversion targets is individually by store rather than a chain-wide average. If you're going to create incentive programs based in part on customer conversion, it's critical to get targets right. Realistic and achievable targets help encourage consumption; unrealistic and unachievable targets impede consumption.

This topic is worth exploring further. The following real-world example will show you what I mean.

# Setting conversion targets to win or lose

I was discussing the idea of setting conversion targets with the CEO of a sporting goods chain when he emphatically declared, "The conversion target for all the stores should be 35% — period." The average conversion rate across his chain was about 30%. The majority of his stores were located in power centers or major strip plazas, and a handful was located in major shopping malls. While the chain's overall average conversion rate was 30%, conversion rates across the stores ranged from 20% (in the mall stores) to as high as 40% in his best performing store.

The CFO, who also sat in on the meeting, raised the concern that some stores might have a hard time achieving the 35% conversion rate target. The CEO's response was unequivocal: "I don't give a damn – I want them to strive. I see no value in setting targets too low."

Setting conversion targets is an important part of any successful traffic and conversion program. However, serious consideration needs to be given to how these targets are set and how conversion rate fits into an overall balanced performance scorecard. Setting a chain-wide conversion target is not advisable because conversion rates can vary so much across a chain.

The sporting goods chain nicely illustrates the problem. A sample of these stores is shown in the chart below. Increasing the overall conversion rate average from 30% to 35% represents about a 15% increase. But achieving this target by requiring each store to increase its conversion rate to 35% isn't realistic. The mall stores located in Santa Fe, Reno, and Carson City would need dramatic conversion rate increases of 75%, 67% and 59%, respectively, in order to achieve the new 35% chain-wide conversion target.

The CFO was absolutely correct. This target is not at all realistic, and if the CEO pushes for it, these Store Managers are understandably going to feel defeated.

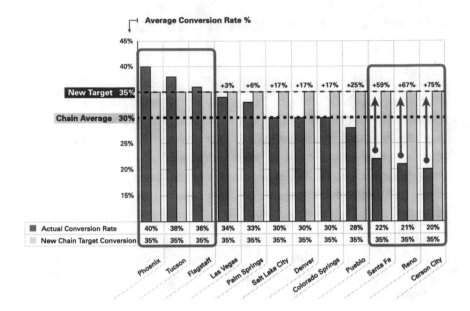

Average Conversion Rate %

| | Phoenix | Tucson | Flagstaff | Las Vegas | Palm Springs | Salt Lake City | Denver | Colorado Springs | Pueblo | Santa Fe | Reno | Carson City |
|---|---|---|---|---|---|---|---|---|---|---|---|---|
| | | | | +3% | +6% | +17% | +17% | +17% | +25% | +59% | +67% | +75% |
| Actual Conversion Rate | 40% | 38% | 36% | 34% | 33% | 30% | 30% | 30% | 28% | 22% | 21% | 20% |
| New Chain Target Conversion | 35% | 35% | 35% | 35% | 35% | 35% | 35% | 35% | 35% | 35% | 35% | 35% |

New Target 35%
Chain Average 30%

At the other end of the scale, the high converting stores like Phoenix, Tucson, and Flagstaff were already achieving conversion rates above the target – the new target is no big deal for them.

I have no concern with the CEO's desire for a 35% "stretch" conversion target for the stores to try to achieve. My concern is with how he's trying to get there. Given that each store is unique, it's vital that targets consider the unique characteristics of each store. Beyond the obvious mall versus off-mall difference (malls will almost always have higher traffic and lower conversion rates than off-mall locations), each store is completely unique, and the conversion targets should take this inequality into account.

One of the most effective ways to get Store Managers to buy in is to set customer conversion targets uniquely for each store. While this is more work, it's also the only way to adequately account for all the nuances and subtleties of each store. Furthermore, Store Managers tend to be significantly more motivated to pursue a target when they believe they have a realistic chance at achieving it.

Instead of requiring all stores to achieve a 35% conversion rate as the CEO demanded, the better way to get to the 35% overall conversion rate goal is to require each store to improve its own conversion rate by 15%. If each store increases its own rate by 15%, the overall chain average moves up to 35%, as the CEO had wanted, but now the Store Managers have a realistic chance of achieving the goal.

In general, *setting realistic, achievable conversion targets is critical to getting managers to buy in.* When they do, they are more apt to consume the insights and act on the data – and that's what ultimately leads to better performance.

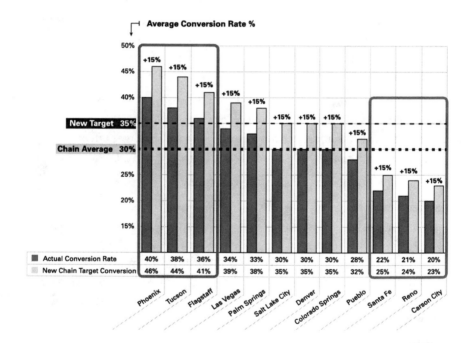

# Managers revolt: getting all stakeholders on board

It never ceases to amaze me how difficult it can be to get stakeholders onboard with traffic and customer conversion. Resistance can come from just about anywhere in the organization – from non-sponsoring senior executives to store-level personnel. It is absolutely vital to get all stakeholders aligned with the importance and value of these critical metrics. So why do managers push back?

On the surface it may appear that these managers are simply being difficult and or irrational. Useful metrics that provide powerful insights into your business – what's not to like? However, after having witnessed the push-back many times in different organizations from different sources, I've concluded that this isn't just a matter of bad attitudes with a few managers.

There are reasons why managers resist, and it is important for senior executives to understand the underlying causes and sources of the resistance so that they can address the issues and get effective organizational alignment, adoption and, ultimately, true consumption.

Here are some possible causes for the resistance:

- **resistance to change**
  Every new initiative creates tension, even those that are beneficial for the company and even the manager him/herself. People generally don't like change, and it's no different with traffic and conversion analytics. If the implementation of a traffic and conversion program creates additional work or distraction, it's not hard to understand why managers might push back.

- **resentment of additional scrutiny**
  Historically, the only way the Head Office could understand what was happening at store level was to look at the sales receipts. Today, with connected, real-time POS systems, Head Office executives have instantaneous access to sales results. And, beyond the sales data, executives have a whole host of other ways to understand what's happening in their stores, from mystery shop and customer experience tracking to sophisticated loss prevention surveillance

cameras that spy on managers. Store Managers have never been more scrutinized in the history of retailing, and for some of them, traffic monitoring and customer conversion analysis is just another variation of Big Brother.

- **potential to reflect negatively**
Traffic and conversion analytics put sales results in context. They clarify how results are being driven and where the shortcomings may be. If we break sales out into its underlying drivers (traffic x conversion rate x average ticket = sales), what works and doesn't work becomes brutally obvious.

For example, if an advertising campaign didn't generate the sales that were expected, the Marketing VP or Advertising Director cannot simply conclude that the stores dropped the ball if customer conversion rates are up, but store traffic volume has not increased — because that would mean that the advertising was ineffective at driving prospects into the stores. Or a Store Manager who was highly regarded as a top performer based on high store sales might now be viewed as an underperformer because traffic and conversion analysis revealed that the high store sales are more a function of windfall traffic in the store rather than brilliant execution. In this case, the Store Manager had the good fortune of managing a store that was located in a busy mall. Despite his poor customer conversion rate and average ticket, his sales results looked comparatively great. Traffic and conversion would show him to be underperforming compared to his traffic opportunity, regardless of his sales results.

- **unconvinced of the value**
Sometimes managers simply don't get it. They are not opposed to having additional measures in the business, and they are sincerely focused on delivering better performance. These are good managers. But as much as they try, they just can't seem to understand what traffic and conversion analysis will do for them or the business. And, misguidedly, they can't understand why the company would invest in traffic and conversion analysis over training, merchandising or other more "useful" initiatives. There are several reasons why retailers haven't fully embraced traffic and conversion analysis, and I discuss these in more detail in Chapter 3.4. This is the part where leadership

comes in. Not every field manager or functional manager is going to get this stuff, so leadership needs to <u>tell</u> them it's important. That's what you get paid the big bucks for, after all.

- **unpleasant past experience**
  Some managers are understandably gun-shy about how traffic and conversion might be implemented, and feeling this way can cause them to resist. This is how one Store Manager put it to me when I asked why he was against traffic counters being installed in his store: "I used to work for a chain that put traffic counters in the stores. At first it was OK. Then the DMs started harassing us about conversion rates. Why are they so low? What are you doing all day? It got so bad I quit, and so did a lot of other managers."

Leadership needs to understand that there likely will be some resistance to the implementation of a traffic and conversion analytics program – it's perfectly natural. Overcoming the objectives and getting alignment is not difficult, but it takes time and effort. If managers are well intended and truly want to see the company improve sales, reduce expense, and perform better, they will embrace traffic and conversion analytics. However, the efficacy of the program will ultimately be determined by how leadership executes the program – there is a right and a wrong way to do it.

# Making conversion "cultural"

One of the fundamental mistakes retailers make is to treat traffic and conversion like a discrete project. Step 1: buy traffic counters. Step 2: generate lots of reports. Step 3: watch for better results – done. Move on to the next project. One of the hallmarks of the companies that are effectively using traffic and conversion is that they don't treat it as a project. They treat it as a process – an ongoing process.

*"Conversion has become part of how our store staff speak about and understand what's happening in their stores...customer conversion has become as normal as putting on a staff t-shirt."*

As one thoughtful retail executive said to me, "Trying to get the organization to focus on customer conversion is nothing short of cultural change." This is a profound and accurate view of what it takes to really make a difference with customer conversion.

Every retail organization is unique – different culture, operations, opportunities and challenges. While I am not suggesting that retailers should subscribe to a particular cultural framework or schema, I do know that retailers who fully embrace these analytics and consider customer conversion broadly across their organizations come to realize that it does impact their culture – it changes how they think about and manage their business.

Retailers who make the most of traffic and conversion analytics realize that they need to have an organizational culture that encourages and reinforces effective consumption of traffic and conversion insights. The deeper and more broadly traffic and conversion insights are consumed, the more they influence the organization's culture, as these critical metrics become part of the operating DNA of the company. The insights permeate every aspect and every level of the organization; traffic/conversion analytics become a part of how the business is operated at a very fundamental level.

# Counter-culture: offending your cultural sensibilities

I've met retail executives who told me that they are concerned that bringing conversion into their organization will somehow negatively impact their corporate culture. "We are not that type of retail organization," they say. For some reason, these retailers have convinced themselves that "conversion" is synonymous with "aggressive selling techniques" – which, of course, it's not.

Creating a culture of conversion is not so much the objective as it is a consequence. The broad and effective application of traffic and conversion analytics has as much to do with modifying corporate culture as a focus on average ticket or comp sales do. Performance metrics alone don't change culture – even great ones like conversion rate – but what they do is create an operational context for the company.

The retailers who use these metrics best will often say that they've become woven into the fabric of their organizations so much that they're part of the corporate culture. They didn't set out to change their culture — it happened as a consequence of effectively deploying traffic and customer conversion in their organizations.

# Consumption is the key to success.

If there is one attribute that most clearly defines retailers who use traffic and conversion data to great advantage — compared to those who dabble with it or have tried and failed — it's their ability to consume conversion insights across the entire organization. In these leading retailers, everyone understands the importance of traffic and conversion, from the CEO and the executive team through every layer of the organization and ultimately right down to the sales floor.

When everyone in the company "gets it," when everyone talks about it every day, and when compensation and performance are measured, in part, by conversion results, the concepts naturally become part of the company culture. This is a good thing. Only a truly great metric can have this magnitude of impact on an organization – and conversion rate can.

As is the case with any significant initiative, fully realized success with traffic and conversion analytics depends so much on the CEO and the executive leadership team. It takes senior executive clout to knock down the barriers and overcome the objections that will inevitably challenge a fledging traffic and conversion program.

But it's not just the CEO or a single senior executive who should shepherd the program – everyone seated around the executive boardroom table plays a role in a successful implementation, and that's the topic to which we next turn our attention.

# Chapter 3.3

## Implications 'Round the Executive Table

If it's used at all, traffic and conversion can often be relegated to the less-than-high-profile bastion of "tactical" management. OK, you can optimize staffing; yes, you can gauge the impact of advertising, and you can calculate conversion rates – great stuff. Traffic and conversion analytics is a useful tool that helps a Store Manager run his/her store better.

But it's not something senior executives need to concern themselves with. After all, senior executives need to focus on the big picture. They need to take a broader, longer term perspective on the business. In short, they need to be "strategic." Traffic and customer conversion aren't strategic — are they?

The insights that come from traffic and customer conversion data should be of interest to every executive sitting around the boardroom table. Unfortunately, that's not how it usually works and, as a result, many retailers are not getting the full value from their traffic and customer conversion analytics (if they have any at all).

The vast majority of the presentations I deliver are to senior executives. When I get invited to speak, I sometimes get asked, who should attend? My answer is always the same – the entire executive team.

I find it curious that when I present to executive teams, I will often see them all nodding enthusiastically in agreement with the ideas and insights I present, saying things like "this is great stuff" or "fascinating insights." But as the meeting concludes and I ask whom I should follow up with for further discussion, for some reason, there can be a tremendous amount of reluctance to "own" these critical analytics.

So it goes around the executive board room table, "This is more of a Marketing thing, isn't it?" says the CEO. The CMO turns to the VP of

Sales Operations: "Doesn't this make more sense in Ops?" "There's a lot of data here, maybe Finance is the better fit," says the Ops VP. Everyone loves this stuff, but no one wants to own it.

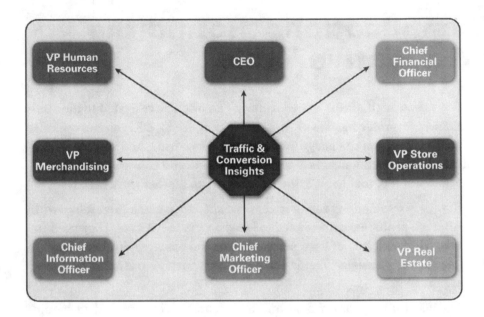

So who's responsible for traffic and customer conversion in your organization? Sadly, for most retailers, it's no one. Part of the dilemma could be that traffic and customer conversion can fit in so many places. When effectively implemented, traffic/conversion analytics should be broadly consumed across the entire organization. If your organization is not leveraging the insights across all the functional departments, then you are missing out on ways to improve your business.

*"The entire organization understands their role in helping drive conversion. The merchandising team looks at conversion...the marketing team looks at traffic and conversion...the product team looks at conversion. Everybody knows what their role is in driving conversion."*

— Senior Vice President of Operations

The simple fact is that every executive is a stakeholder and can and should be using traffic and customer conversion insights in his or her respective area of responsibility. So, for those executives who believe traffic and customer conversion is an "Operations thing" or a "Marketing thing," I'll briefly go around the executive table and discuss the key areas of importance and the implications for the use of traffic and customer conversion in each functional area.

# Finance – CFO/Vice President Finance

Of all the executives, the CFO should be among the most interested stakeholder in traffic and customer conversion insights. If there is one department where it is critical to understand what lies beneath the sales results, it is Finance. While the CEO has to keep his eye on the big picture, the CFO is paid to dig deeper, to understand the minutiae, and provide the CEO and all internal and external stakeholders with the hard facts.

Presenting outcomes isn't good enough; the CFO needs to provide the "color" around the numbers. What drove the results? Where is the business trending? Listen in on the quarterly earnings call of any publicly traded retailer, and you will hear CFOs facing a barrage of questions from a mob of Wall Street analysts who spend all their days, and their Ivy-League brain power, dissecting the retailer's financial statements, press releases and any other morsel of information they can find about the chain.

When comp sales are up, these calls are breezy and upbeat – lots of congratulatory comments from the analysts. "Great quarter, guys!" But when comps are down, or the results fall short of the Street's expectation, look out. Awkward silence, terse responses and a vow to do better next quarter are typical – usually followed by a slump in stock price.

Regardless of whether you are the head of Finance for a large publicly traded retailer or a small chain, it's your responsibility to understand the numbers, and traffic and customer conversion are two very important numbers that you need to understand.

Traffic and conversion analytics won't turn bad financial results into good results, but they will help management (and the CFO in particular) explain what drove the numbers. And, when effectively used, they might even help avoid poor results in the first place. Here are some of the specific ways the Finance team can use traffic and customer conversion insights.

- **financial reporting; explaining results:** Yes, the results are the results and traffic and customer conversion data won't change them. However, understanding the underlying drivers completely changes the interpretation of the results.

  If overall sales are down, it is far easier to discuss the problem if, at the same time, the CFO can speak to the underlying drivers. For example, reporting that year-over-year sales are down 3% is not something any CFO would look forward to reporting. However, what if the CFO could explain the results this way: "While it is true that our comps were down 3%, the fact is, store traffic was actually up by 8%. Our buyers did a great job picking the latest trends – maybe a little too good. Unfortunately, our supply chain and logistics let us down, which resulted in stock-outs and a decrease in our conversion rates. We've got these worked out, and I'm sure we'll see the results improve going forward."

  Traffic and conversion data, along with the other traditional financial measures, enables the Finance team to speak confidently about what drove the results. Even when results aren't great, the fact that management understands the drivers provides some comfort. OK, they dropped the ball but at least they know what went wrong.

- **calculating ROI and investment assessment:** There is no shortage of places to spend money in a retail enterprise. From new killer promotions, to requests for more labor hours, new in-store digital signage, updating security systems, store renovations – you name it; the demands on the financial resources are relentless. Someone has to play financial traffic cop and that's the CFO and his/her team's job.

So what's the CFO to do when these stakeholders come looking to secure funding for all these seemingly important and worthwhile investments? It's tough. While traffic and conversion data won't miraculously provide absolute clarity for every financial decision managers need to make, they do provide valuable context that can go a long way towards helping all parties involved better understand if investments are having an impact. Here are just a few examples:

» The marketing team just invested in a major campaign, sales didn't go up, but store traffic was way up. It worked, but we didn't execute at store-level.

» We invested in additional labor hours, and customer conversion rates increased– OK, good decision on the extra labor.

» We tested new digital signage in some stores, but conversion rates didn't increase at all like the vendor said they should– let's not roll out until we do more testing.

You get the picture.

While traffic and conversion insights won't turn bad investments into good ones, virtually any investment meant to drive sales or reduce expenses in the stores can benefit from the context that traffic and conversion data provide.

Traffic and customer conversion insights enable managers to be more accountable for the money they spend and to better understand the return on their investments. By understanding the underlying drivers, managers have the critical context they need but that sales results alone cannot provide. Investing money in programs that work and spending less on programs that don't work can have a profound impact on the bottom line. It may not be perfect, but it is significantly better than the alternative: counting the money in the till and guessing.

- **budgeting, planning and forecasting:** Every aspect of the planning, budgeting and forecasting process can benefit from the additional insights that come from traffic and customer conversion data. Ostensibly, budgets and forecasts are based on historical business results – actual sales and expenses. Not only do traffic and customer conversion data help the Finance team understand the underlying sales drivers explaining the historical results, but they can also be used to refine future forecasts.

Store traffic is a leading indicator that provides critical insights into future results that current sales results alone cannot. If year-over-year chain-wide traffic volume is trending down, this is a very ominous sign that indicates that the collective sales opportunity in the stores is shrinking – fewer prospects are coming to your stores. Ironically, in the short-term, sales results may actually increase, as customer conversion rates often go up when traffic levels fall. This dynamic can mask the true and more concerning underlying trend.

With traffic data, the systematic traffic decreases would show management that it has potentially a far more serious problem to deal with than the sales results alone would indicate. If executives are armed with traffic trend data, a decision to increase advertising spending in order to drive traffic volume could more easily be justified, and the inevitable decrease in sales might be avoided or at least mitigated.

Just as forecasts and budgets are created to provide targets, so too should they be developed for traffic and customer conversion. Instead of merely forecasting out based on historical sales results, Finance should include the underlying drivers in the forecast model.

Let's say the Finance team analyzed the year-over-year traffic, conversion, and average ticket results for the prior quarter, as shown in the table below. Compared to last year, during Q1, on average, traffic was up 2%, conversion was up 3%, and average sale was flat. After consulting the business leaders, it was decided that these year-over-year variances were reasonable for the coming quarter, so the team applied these same factors to the last year's traffic, conversion, and average ticket for Q2 to build the forecast. The net result is that overall sales should be up 5% if this forecast holds. Without traffic and conversion data, the forecast would be based on sales data only.

| Y.O.Y. Rolling Previous Three Months | | | | |
|---|---|---|---|---|
| | Jan | Feb | Mar | Avg |
| Traffic | 0.93 | 1.10 | 1.03 | 1.02 |
| Conversion | 1.00 | 0.93 | 1.17 | 1.03 |
| Avg. Sale | 0.96 | 0.94 | 1.09 | 1.00 |

**Based on Three Month Rolling Comp Average**

| | Traffic | | | Conversion | | | Average Sale | | | Days in Period | SALES | | Y.O.Y. Sales Variance |
|---|---|---|---|---|---|---|---|---|---|---|---|---|---|
| | Actual 2010 | Factor | Est. 2011 | Actual 2010 | Factor | Est. 2011 | Actual 2010 | Factor | Est. 2011 | | Actual 2010 | Est. 2011 | |
| April | 661 | 1.02 | 674 | 4.7% | 1.03 | 4.8% | $94 | 1.00 | $94 | 30 | $87,609 | $92,042 | 5% |
| May | 702 | 1.02 | 716 | 4.6% | 1.03 | 4.7% | $100 | 1.00 | $100 | 31 | $100,105 | $105,171 | 5% |
| June | 705 | 1.02 | 719 | 7.0% | 1.03 | 7.2% | $72 | 1.00 | $72 | 30 | $106,596 | $111,990 | 5% |

# Human Resources – Vice President, HR

As I explained in Chapter 2.3, the importance of traffic and customer conversion insights to the HR team is significant. Today more than ever, HR departments are being asked to assess organizational capability, find ways to optimize labor costs, execute incentive programs, and create training initiatives that help deliver better results. The task of HR is to build organizational capability. However, without traffic and customer conversion sights, HR Staff lacks the critical context it needs in order to understand underlying drivers and develop programs that make a difference.

Launching a chain-wide sales training program will not improve sales if traffic in the stores is systemically down and declining. If the HR team did launch a program in conditions like this, it would, on the basis of sales results alone, probably look ineffectual. Traffic and customer conversion would reveal the underlying conditions that sales results could never show. In this case, HR might see that customer conversion rates are up, suggesting that the training is making a difference, but that the sales results are not materially improving because of the reduced traffic.

Or the HR department may be asked to create a sales incentive program that encourages up-selling by associates. A well-designed and executed program may indeed deliver higher average ticket and UPTs as hoped, but if customer conversion rates sag as Associates strive to earn their incentive while inadvertently leaving some prospects unserved, the end result might be that, despite meeting the program objective, overall sales results didn't improve.

Here are some of the areas where traffic and customer conversion insights could greatly assist HR:

- labor scheduling optimization;
- performance management;
- training program development and assessment;
- incentive programs and rewards.

## Merchandising — Vice President, Merchandising

At first glance it may seem that traffic and customer conversion have less relevance to the head of Merchandising. However, just as with operations and marketing, the insights that come from traffic and customer conversion analytics are vitally important to the Merchandising team.

These people are responsible for ensuring that the stores have the right product in the right place in the right quantity. It's a challenge. Getting it right is critical. When a hot selling item stocks out, or simply doesn't make it to store in time for the advertising, there are all kinds of implications— none of which are good.

Given that one of the key drivers of customer conversion is prospects finding the product they're looking for, the Merchandising team has a critical role, especially in big-box stores, where navigation and effective product display can be the difference between success and failure in making a sale. If people can't find the product they're looking for, they leave without buying, and this is directly reflected in customer conversion rates.

If store traffic volume is high, prospects are visiting the stores. If, when they get there, they don't make a purchase, merchandising could be directly responsible. Perhaps the store had plenty of product, but customers simply didn't care for it. Disappointment with the product often shows up as systemic conversion sags — conversion rates are down broadly across the chain or significant regions of the chain. If conversion is down only in some stores, rather than across a wide range of stores, there is quite likely a store-level execution issue. A product issue, beyond the initial conversion sag, will also, over time, impact traffic. Why bother going to that store? They didn't have anything I wanted last time.

There are many uses for traffic and customer conversion insights within the Merchandising department, and we'll explore some of them in more detail.

- **validating product mix and price discount decisions:** As I noted above, getting the right product to the right place at the right time is a critical part of the merchandiser's role. Merchandisers rely on mountains of POS data to help them understand sell-through down to the SKU level. In fact, all kinds of sophisticated merchandising systems have been developed to help merchandisers forecast demand, trigger discounts, and generally execute what is undoubtedly a challenging and vital role. While POS data ultimately drive merchandising decisions, traffic and customer conversion can provide the Merchandising team with valuable context that can help refine product mix decisions. For example, sell-through levels on what was expected to be a fast- moving featured item just aren't meeting expectations. Is the market just not buying? Are the stores not executing? How can the merchandiser know for certain?

  While sell-through is the ultimate determinant, what if the merchandiser knew that store traffic was materially down, that far fewer prospects are actually visiting the stores? Perhaps the lower sell-through is merely a result of the lower visitation and not a lack of interest in the particular SKU. On the other hand, if store traffic did not decrease — that is, the same volume of traffic is visiting the store — and sell-through is still low, perhaps in-store execution issues are responsible, or prospects simply aren't buying. Maybe it's time for a mark-down. In either event, traffic and customer conversion provide additional insights that POS data alone cannot.

- **measuring in-store merchandising effectiveness:** From self-checkout to digital displays and store atmospherics, merchandisers today have a wide variety of devices at their disposal to motivate customers to buy. It seems that retailers are investing in these sophisticated and expensive systems as never before, ostensibly to help drive sales results. But how can they know for certain what impact they're having?

For example, a retailer tests new digital displays in a number of locations. It's a significant cost, but research suggests that the digital displays, compared to traditional displays, are more compelling and encourage people to buy more. So the head of Merchandising gets approval to pilot the displays in a number of stores in a region. The displays are installed, and the program is executed. After a few weeks of monitoring, the head of Merchandising pulls the sales data for the test stores – and finds that despite a flat average ticket, comp sales are up by 5% in the test stores, compared to other stores in the chain. On the surface, this looks like a win. Sales have increased, and it appears as though the digital displays made the difference. The Merchandising executive recommends that the program be expanded.

This is all very reasonable, but before moving too fast, the merchandiser needs to understand traffic and customer conversion rates in these test stores. Digital displays aren't going to compel more prospects to visit the stores, so one should expect that if these displays were making a difference, then conversion rate and or average ticket values should be going up. That is, people who are already in the store should be buying more. However, what if we knew that store traffic in the test stores was actually up 10% — that is, more prospects were visiting these stores, and in fact, customer conversion rates were down? The higher traffic drove the sales increase, suggesting that the digital displays probably had very little to do with the sales lift. Knowing this, would you expand the program?

On the other hand, if traffic levels in the test stores remained constant, but customer conversion rates were measurably higher compared to the stores that didn't have digital displays, then one might fairly conclude that the displays had something to do with driving results. The point is, without traffic and customer conversion data, critical context is missing to support decisions like this one. Relying on POS data alone isn't enough.

- **inventory management and logistics systems:** One of the key drivers of customer conversion is product availability. If customers stream into the stores looking for the hot item and can't find it — or the store simply doesn't have it — the results will show up very clearly in the traffic and conversion data: traffic will be up, and customer conversion will drop significantly. Without traffic and customer conversion data, these insights may be masked or muted. With the data, not only will the results be clear, but merchandisers will actually be able to quantify the conversion loss.

- **store layout, redesigns and renovations:** Retailers spend a considerable amount of time, energy and money on store designs, layout configurations, renovations and refresh updates. While there are plenty of good reasons to make these investments, improving store productivity and driving sales are always underlying motivations. If these investments don't have a financial return, why do them? Like the examples above, traffic and customer conversion insights help put the financial outcomes in context and provide a perspective on what's really behind the sales results. For example, an entirely new change-room design might be tested to encourage customers to try on clothing, in the hope that the new design will translate into higher overall sales. It may be that the new design is very effective and customers are trying on more clothing and buying more, but because overall store visitation is down, sales may look flat or even down, leading the merchandisers to believe the program didn't deliver results.

# Information Technology – Chief Information Officer/VP, IT

Like any data system in the organization, the IT department is often called upon to own and manage traffic counters and the resulting data. While the CIO and his team are not business users of the data, they often play a critical role in procurement of the systems and the ongoing management and maintenance and, ultimately, the stewardship of this vital information.

I discussed some of the key IT issues related to traffic counters in Chapter 1.5, but here's a summary of other things the CIO should keep in mind regarding the company's traffic and conversion analytics program:

- Who is the business owner and who are the other key stakeholders for the traffic and conversion analytics? What are their specific and unique requirements?

- What is the ongoing involvement of IT in maintaining the traffic counting system (including monitoring data integrity)?

- What type of traffic counter technology will be best suited to the store environment? Different counting systems work better in certain store environments, so you may need different types of systems for different store configurations.

- Can traffic data be collected through an existing system, such as loss prevention surveillance?

- What other data streams (e.g., POS, marketing plans, labor hours) need to be combined with traffic data, and who is responsible for making this happen?

- How does the capture system for traffic data integrate with other internal systems such as ERP and labor management systems?

Over the years, I've been called on by IT departments looking to procure a traffic counting system. While technology procurement is a legitimate and important role of IT, often the IT managers are unclear about the business user's needs. This lack of clarity isn't IT's fault; the root of this problem is the general lack of ownership among the key stakeholders in the executive suite. Back to the original question: who owns traffic and conversion analytics?

When IT leaders don't have a clear sense of the business needs for traffic and customer conversion analytics, they run the risk of procuring a system that doesn't meet those needs. And, if the system doesn't meet the business needs, it won't get used (or at least not used as it should be) and inevitably will fall into disuse (and perceived irrelevance). In these cases, the retailer typically says, "We tried traffic counting, but it didn't work for us."

Not only is this a significant waste of precious budget, and the already over-taxed IT department's time, but, worse, the retailer gets turned off to the idea of traffic and conversion analytics. That's the biggest tragedy of all.

# Real Estate – Vice President, Real Estate

While I might not go so far as to argue that the old axiom about the three most important factors in successful retailing — location, location, and location — should be replaced by conversion, conversion, conversion, it's still undeniable that finding the best locations for new stores is vital to future growth of any chain. The cost of opening a new location is considerable, and the consequences of opening a store in a poor location very costly. Some might say that picking great locations is both an art and science, constrained by availability and affordability.

Real estate is an important component of any successful retail strategy. And it's a complex and high-risk effort. Traffic and customer conversion insights can provide the Real Estate team with useful decision support. Some examples:

- **understanding cannibalization of new stores on existing locations:** Obviously the idea of opening new locations is to reach prospects you might not have otherwise reached and to deliver incremental sales. When new stores are opened in markets where no existing stores are located, cannibalization is not an issue; however, when you open a new store in a market that already has an existing store or stores, you run the risk of shifting sales from an existing store to the new one. This is suboptimal at best and potentially even disastrous.

  Of course you cannot fully understand the cannibalization impact of a new store on existing locations until after the new store opens, and while this is technically too late, traffic and conversion data can help the Real Estate team better understand if indeed cannibalization actually occurred. Normally, the team would analyze sales results for the stores near the new one to see if sales were negatively impacted. If a new location is actually siphoning off business from an existing store, the process will first manifest itself as a decrease in traffic before it shows up as a decrease in sales. Makes sense, doesn't it? The new store opens, and customers from the existing store visit the new store; traffic in the old store decreases.

  So why not just rely on sales impact? After all, if traffic goes down, won't this be reflected in the sales results? Not necessarily. Here's why. Because traffic and conversion tend to be inversely related, in the short term, as traffic levels fall, customer conversion rates may actually increase. And so, despite the lower traffic, overall sales may appear to be unaffected by the new location. In this case, the true cannibalization impact of the new store is concealed by the increase in customer conversion. Over time, if traffic continues to wane in the old location, conversion rate increases will likely not make up the difference, and executives will be scratching their heads, wondering what went wrong.

- **providing negotiating leverage on lease renewals:** Finding great new locations is one thing; keeping them – at a reasonable cost – is another. Depending upon the size of chain, there can be a constant stream of lease renewals and negotiations that need to be conducted every year. Of course, the Real Estate team is trying to beat the lease costs down as much as possible, and the property owners are trying to justify their rates. These are often very tough negotiations.

One way the Real Estate team may try to argue for reduced lease rates is to use traffic data. For example, if a retailer claims that his/her rent should be reduced, in part because sales at the store in the mall are declining, the mall operator might point out that the sales decrease could be a result of numerous factors, including poor staffing, inventory, or product mix issues – that is, things that have nothing to do with the mall or location. However, if the retailer could provide traffic data, showing how traffic in this particular store is down, while traffic at his stores located in other malls is up, he/she might be able to make a more compelling case to the mall operator. I'm not suggesting that traffic data alone will cause property owners to surrender, but it may give your Real Estate team an edge.

- **understanding the impact of competitors on existing locations:** As important as it is to understand the impact of your own new stores on existing locations, it's just as important to understand the impact your competitors' new locations may have. When a competitor opens a new store right beside one of your existing stores, it's reasonable to think that it's going to impact your business. Sales may go up, go down, or stay the same, but understanding the effect of traffic and conversion enable management to better understand the true impact. When a competitor opens a store near yours, traffic levels in your store can actually increase. This happens because the new competitor creates additional drawing power, bringing more prospects to the trading area, and your existing store can see a lift in traffic as a result. If a traffic lift occurs but your store is not prepared for it, conversion rates could sag, giving the impression that the competitor is stealing sales, when in fact, you missed a great opportunity.

# Marketing – Chief Marketing Officer/ VP, Marketing

Given that I devoted an entire chapter to the topic, I think you already know how I feel about the importance of traffic and customer conversion to the Marketing department. As I discussed in Chapter 2.3, Marketing is one of the critical stakeholders of traffic and customer conversion insights. It's hard for me to imagine that marketers can even do their jobs without the benefit of traffic and customer conversion insights to help them understand if their investments in advertising and promotions are having any impact. How do these executives justify the investments they make? How do they calculate the return on these investments?

If you could cut your advertising spend by 5%, and still get the same volume of traffic in your stores, would you do it? Or if you could invest the same budget but drive up traffic by 10%, wouldn't you want to do that?

Retail marketers have taken solace in the now infamous John Wanamaker adage "Half the money I spend on advertising is wasted, and the trouble is, I don't know which half." When marketers are asked to explain their ROI or quantify impact of the investments they're making, it can sometimes seem like an exercise in excuse management. The fact is, if you are looking in the till to justify your marketing investments, you're looking in the wrong place. Traffic and customer conversion can provide marketers with the insights they need to help make better decisions and justify their investments.

While I won't rehash everything I stated in Chapter 2.3, here again are some important ways Marketing can and should use traffic and conversion insights:

- measuring the impact of advertising and promotions;
- calculating marketing ROI;
- assessing competitor impact;
- conducting advertising and promotion testing;
- determining traffic acquisition cost;

- targeting and refining programs;
- providing context for customer experience scores and measures.

Of the many places traffic and conversion analytics could reside in the organization, given all the direct uses for these insights, Marketing is certainly one of these places. The only department who might want it more is Sales Operations.

# Sales Operations – Vice President, Operations

Notwithstanding the above, traffic and conversion most naturally fits in Sales Operations. As Peter Scully, one of our conversion champions from Chapter 1.2 said, "Every Operations leader should be a conversion champion!" He's right.

In many ways everything the organization does is in support of the Sales Operations function – to serve customers and sell product. There is no one department that needs traffic and customer conversion insights as much as this team does. Not only should Sales Operations own it — they should be demanding it. Traffic and customer conversion are basic inputs that they need to run their stores on a daily basis. Without it, they are being asked to do the impossible – deliver sales growth without fully understanding how to do it.

Think about it. Every day these managers need to deliver the sales targets, despite difficult economic conditions, a tough competitive environment, and limited resources. No matter how hard these managers look at the mountains of POS transaction data, they just won't find the answer to the all-important "How do I drive sales?" question. Mystery shop and customer experience information helps, but the information is often not conclusive, specific or actionable.

These managers know the "what" – sales are down, and we need to get them up. But, unfortunately, they simply don't know the "how." Maybe it's a training issue. Maybe it's a recruiting issue. Maybe it's a customer service issue. Maybe, maybe, maybe.

So the Store Managers discuss it with their District Managers, who discuss it with their Regional Managers, who in turn discuss it with the VP, and still no obvious answers. Maybe it's a marketing issue – over to you, Chief Marketing Officer.

The fundamental problem these managers face is that they simply don't know what they are solving for. But traffic and customer conversion insights can fill in some of the most critical blanks. Having the benefit of traffic and customer conversion insights won't magically make sales go up, but at least the Sales Operations team will understand what they're solving for, and they'll have a fighting chance at influencing the outcomes.

## The politics of "owning" a traffic and conversion program

At the end of the day, it doesn't matter who owns traffic and customer conversion, as long as <u>someone</u> owns it. The entire organization will be better off, regardless of where it resides. Budget (or lack thereof) is often the root cause for why executives don't sign up to own traffic and customer conversion. If you own it, you pay for it. Which executive is willing put up his or her hand to take a budget hit when they're all already struggling to make ends meet with the budgets they do have? Not many, it seems.

The investment in traffic and customer conversion analytics is as fundamental and as critical as point-of-sale or loss prevention. These are systems that serve the greater good of the entire organization — and so do traffic and conversion analytics.

Another problem that can arise: the traffic and customer conversion data gets stuck in a particular functional department silo. "Owning" is not the same as hoarding data. If one department hoards, the insights don't get fully leveraged, and the company doesn't realize the full value of the investment. While the investment in traffic and conversion analytics could easily be justified on its value to the Sales Operations team alone, the ROI is profoundly positive when the insights are leveraged across all functional departments and stakeholders. It's worth exploring the ROI question a little further.

# Calculating the value of a traffic and conversion program

I'm often asked, "What's the ROI of implementing a traffic and conversion program?" A fair question that any executive should ask. However, given the way I see retailers struggle with this question, it seems that ROI stands for "really often incalculable."

It doesn't have to be that way. There are both direct and indirect benefits of successfully implementing a traffic and conversion analytics program. It's not like the old finance textbook examples of calculating the ROI of a new piece of equipment churning out so many more widgets. Calculating ROI is easy – cost of equipment, revenue from incremental widgets being produced, and presto, you have your return on investment.

The reality of calculating an ROI on a traffic and conversion program is not so easy. The key problem seems to be identifying and assigning the value of the benefits.

# All cost but no benefit

Consider the cost of traffic counters, ongoing maintenance, hiring analysts to extract the insights, developing reports, delivering them to stakeholders, and then finally training staff. It's significant. So the costs are well understood, but what about the benefit? What quantitative benefit should you use to calculate the ROI against the costs incurred for your traffic and conversion program?

Here's a basic ROI heuristic that works for most retailers. Calculate the incremental gross margin you would generate from a one-point increase in overall conversion rate for the chain. Now calculate your ROI against this incremental gross margin. The increase in gross margin based on a one-point lift in customer conversion alone should deliver a healthy ROI to almost any retail organization, with a payback in less than 12 months.

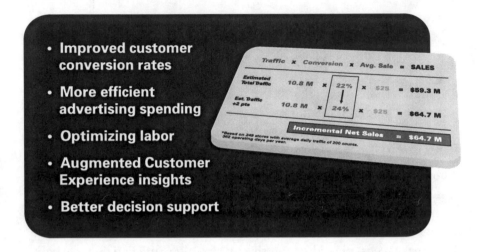

- Improved customer conversion rates
- More efficient advertising spending
- Optimizing labor
- Augmented Customer Experience insights
- Better decision support

But the ROI benefit isn't limited to the gross margin impact of an increase in conversion rate. There are other legitimate benefits that should be factored into the ROI calculation, including:

- cost savings related to more efficiently spending advertising dollars;
- cost savings related to more effectively scheduling staff;
- cost savings from optimizing labor hours;
- cost savings from precision targeting your mystery shop program;
- expenses that can be avoided by just making better decisions because you and your Managers understand the underlying drivers of the business.

These are all legitimate benefits that should be factored into your ROI calculation, but because you would be hard pressed to precisely value these indirect benefits, I say, forget them. That's right. Don't bother. Just treat these additional benefits as pure upside.

# What ROI do other retailers get?

"What kind of payback do other retailers get?" is another question I often get. This is a difficult if not impossible question to answer. Frankly, I'm not sure why it's even relevant. The success or lack of success is entirely contingent upon the retailer's own ability to implement the program, embrace and consume the insights, and ultimately action the information. The results vary from stellar and game-changing to dead-on-arrival, but this has nothing to do with traffic counters, data or analytics — and everything to do with the retailer's own ability to execute.

Customer conversion is a great metric, but metrics alone won't make you great. Only you can make yourself great. You have a significantly better chance at doing that with the benefit of traffic and conversion analytics than if you don't. So to the retailers who constantly ask me, "What is the ROI of a traffic and conversion program?" I tell them: it's entirely up to you.

So, now that we've gone 'round the executive table examining how each executive can and should leverage traffic and conversion insights, let's turn our attention to the retailers who are actually doing this – and those who don't.

# Chapter 3.4

## Why Some Retailers Get it – and Others Don't

Some of you might be thinking that up to this point, I have made some fairly reasonable arguments for why traffic and customer conversion are important. In my wildest dreams, some of you might even be willing to give these issues serious reconsideration and actually start to look at traffic and conversion in your stores – a big victory, I would say.

However, others might be thinking that they haven't yet heard the other side of the argument. Considering the collective wisdom of the massive retail industry, if traffic is so vital and conversion so great, why haven't they taken hold? Why aren't they as pervasive as POS?

You might be thinking that the retail industry has already collectively voted on this, and the low penetration rates of traffic counters and overall lack of attention paid to conversion rate tells you everything you need to know – it's not important, no matter what I say. The comment below, which is what an executive vice president of a major department store chain said to me, perhaps sums up the quiet consensus of the industry:

*"We don't have interest in pursuing traffic and conversion analysis as we have our plates full with other work."*

— Executive Vice President of Stores

OK, fair enough. The million dollar question is: If this stuff is so damn great, why doesn't everybody already do it?

In this chapter, I'll explore the question further, and I promise you some answers.

I'll explain it in the very words senior executives say to me to answer the "why" question. While I admit that some of the objections are reasonable, many are lame, and some are outright ridiculous. The things some executives say...well, you'll see.

Before we get to the executives, I want to talk about market penetration rates of traffic counters and what this tells us about retail technology priorities. If retailers are not all buying traffic counters, what are they spending their precious budgets on every year? We'll have a quick look.

Then I will introduce you to my traffic/conversion adoption curve, which shows the varying degrees of acceptance and leverage of traffic/conversion data in the industry. You can look at the curve and compare your chain's position to the others.

From there, we'll get into the objections – the not-so-compelling arguments for not using traffic and conversion analytics.

Finally, I'll talk about retailers who truly lead in the understanding and application of traffic and conversion analytics — and what they say. As part of this discussion, I'll share some of what I have discovered are the best practices of the retail leaders who use these critical metrics.

# Technology investments – follow the money

A recent survey of retailers indicated that technology investment priorities were as follows:[1]

- 58% "providing Associates with better tools"

- 50%: Payment Card Industry (PCI) compliance

- 40%: loss prevention

- 30%: inventory management

- 25%: customer relationship management (CRM) tools.

Part of the challenge is to decipher what this means. For example, what does "providing Associates with better tools" exactly mean? I'm not suggesting that these are important areas that retailers should be investing in, but you will be hard pressed to find anything related specifically to traffic and conversion analytics.

I was able to find one study that included a direct reference to "brick and mortar traffic counters" as a technology investment. I had to dig all the way back to a retail technology study from 2001,[2] but I thought the results were intriguing. This survey set out to discover how the benefits from various technology investments compared to retailers' expectation. The survey looked at benefits versus expectations in two dimensions: effectiveness for increasing sales and decreasing expenses. As the charts below show, relative to other technologies, traffic counters seem to meet retailer expectations on both fronts.

# Applications' Effectiveness
# for Increasing Sales

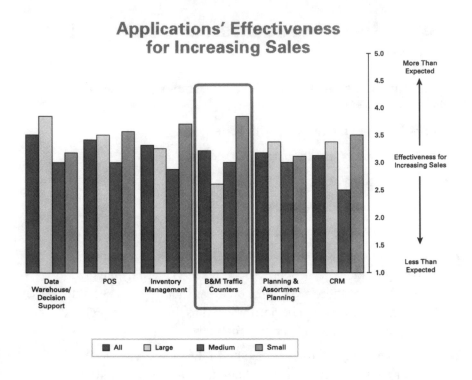

Legend:
- All
- Large
- Medium
- Small

# Applications' Effectiveness
# for Decreasing Expenses

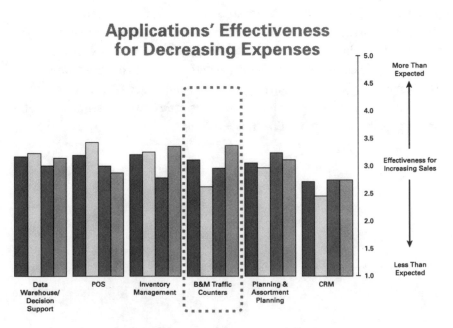

According to this survey, traffic counters delivered the same or better benefits relative to expectations as other important technologies, both in terms of increasing sales and decreasing expenses, yet traffic counter penetration is very low compared to these other technologies and don't have anywhere near the profile.

While this study might not provide the conclusive, compelling proof some retailers might be looking for in order to make the plunge, the fact is that there is a dearth of industry data available on traffic counters and conversion analysis – believe me, my research team and I have looked!

Does it matter that the industry doesn't talk about or include traffic counters in its annual surveys? Yes, actually, it does. Lots of retailers use these benchmarks to compare their priorities to the industry's in order to think through their investment decisions. So when traffic counters aren't part of the dialog, when they're not included in surveys, they just don't seem important. If retailers are looking for validation of the use and criticality of traffic counters, they won't find it in industry surveys.

And now that the lexicon has shifted to "business intelligence" and "analytics," you'll see it even less. While traffic and conversion belong in business intelligence and analytics, these are big, vast domains, and so lowly traffic counters and conversion just don't get the same attention. They get lost in the cacophony of analytic stuff.

I believe the lack of industry attention has contributed to retailers' general disinterest in traffic counters, which translates directly into low traffic counter penetration rates. No traffic counters, no traffic data; no traffic data, no conversion metric.

# Traffic counter penetration

Hard data on traffic counter penetration is difficult if not impossible to find, so we conducted our own survey to try to find the answer. We sent auditors to major malls across North America and had them visit each tenant in the mall to see if the store had an electronic traffic counter installed. We visited thousands of stores.

Not only did we get data on overall traffic counter penetration, but while we were at it, we noted variations by category as well. While our study wasn't exhaustive or perfectly scientific, the results were fascinating.

According to our study, overall traffic counter penetration was about 35%.[3]

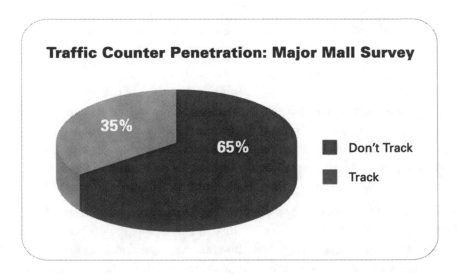

**Traffic Counter Penetration: Major Mall Survey**

Now as you consider these results, keep in mind that the malls we visited represented some of the biggest and best: Mall of America in Minnesota, King-of-Prussia near Philadelphia, the Galleria in Houston, Woodfield Mall in Chicago, West Edmonton Mall in Edmonton, and Yorkdale Mall in Toronto, to name a few.

The tenants of these malls represent some of the best and most successful retail brands in the world. So it's reasonable to assume that these retailers would be more inclined to adopt technology than, say, smaller regional chains located off-mall or in less prestigious venues.

My point is this: if we observed only a 35% penetration rate of traffic counters among some of the biggest and most successful retailers, it's not unreasonable to assume that overall market penetration, taking all retail categories and sizes into account, would be lower than 35% — my best guess is around 25%, and to be just a little optimistic, I'll say 30%.

Beyond measuring overall market penetration during our visits, we noted the retail categories, so that we could determine whether there was higher or lower penetration by category. From our results, shown in the chart below, it's clear that traffic and conversion analytics are more important to some categories than others.[4]

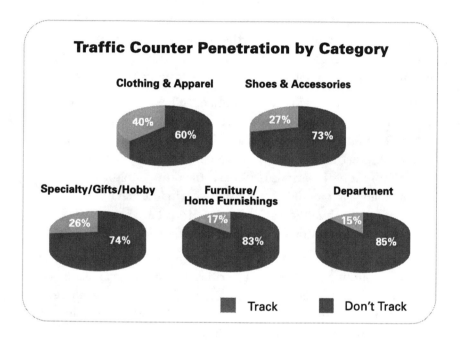

The category with the highest penetration of traffic counters was apparel retailers, followed by shoes and accessories, specialty/gifts/hobby, home furnishings, and department stores. Again, keep in mind that these were mall retailers only, so lots of categories have limited representation – or none at all.

But the key point is clear: penetration rates of traffic counters is staggeringly low.

# Why traffic and customer conversion are not more pervasive

While it's difficult to say exactly why traffic and conversion analytics has not become at least as pervasive as POS, ERP, CRM, or other technologies and measures, there are some clues that suggest an explanation:

- **lack of appreciation for importance:** While virtually every retailer has heard of traffic and conversion, many do not fully appreciate their importance. Furthermore, many retailers have erroneously concluded that their sophisticated POS system, with detailed transaction data, provides all the insights they require.

- **capital cost barrier:** Given that almost all retailers live in a perpetual state of limited resources, the substantial investment in traffic counting technology is a legitimately difficult decision. Implementing traffic counting equipment across a large chain can cost hundreds of thousands of dollars. In addition to the investment in technology, the retailer must also invest in internal resources to effectively analyze the traffic data and translate the results into meaningful information for decision makers.

- **lack of internal expertise:** Even if a retailer makes the investment in traffic counting technology, it's critical to have internal expertise that can analyze the data, interpret the results, and ultimately see to it that the insights are turned into action. Unfortunately, finding these skills in the market are difficult.

- **lack of educational support:** A review of the materials and concepts taught in undergraduate and grad level retail programs shows a clear lack of support for traffic and conversion analysis. Simply put, traffic and conversion are rarely, if ever, taught in retailing education; consequently, graduates have no point of reference. They don't know what they don't know.

- **lack of will and discipline:** Despite the abysmal penetration rates of traffic counters in retail stores, the actual percentage of retailers who are using their traffic and conversion data in a meaningful way is probably significantly lower. For many of the reasons stated above, while retailers may have made the financial investment to purchase equipment, some (perhaps most) may not have made the commitment to use the insights – they have lost their will.

- **fixation on comp sales and other traditional measures:** If the retail industry is not concerned with traffic and conversion, why should any individual retailer be concerned with them? This seems to be particularly the case for publicly traded retailers, who are most concerned with what the stock analysts are concerned with — and this, as you will know if you have listened to an analyst call lately, is not customer conversion rates.

# Traffic and conversion adoption curve

As telling as the penetration results are, they're not the whole story. The mere fact that some retailers have traffic counters doesn't mean they have them installed in all their stores. And even if they have traffic counters installed in every store, they're not necessarily using the data in a meaningful way.

Knowing what I know about penetration — and after literally hundreds of interviews and meetings I have had with retailers who track traffic and customer conversion and those who don't – I believe that the Traffic and Conversion Adoption Curve looks like this:

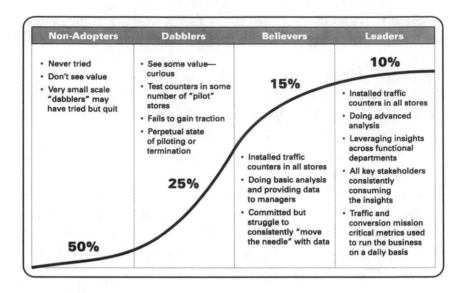

| Non-Adopters | Dabblers | Believers | Leaders |
|---|---|---|---|
| • Never tried<br>• Don't see value<br>• Very small scale "dabblers" may have tried but quit | • See some value—curious<br>• Test counters in some number of "pilot" stores<br>• Fails to gain traction<br>• Perpetual state of piloting or termination | • Installed traffic counters in all stores<br>• Doing basic analysis and providing data to managers<br>• Committed but struggle to consistently "move the needle" with data | • Installed traffic counters in all stores<br>• Doing advanced analysis<br>• Leveraging insights across functional departments<br>• All key stakeholders consistently consuming the insights<br>• Traffic and conversion mission critical metrics used to run the business on a daily basis |

10%

15%

25%

50%

Retailers fall into one of four categories: Non-adopters, Dabblers, Believers and Leaders. I'll discuss each type in more detail.

## Non-Adopters

The largest group by far — I estimate 50% of all retailers. I often think of this group as "the great unwashed." At least half of all retailers don't track traffic and by default can't measure conversion.

Non-adopters have either never tried traffic counting or measuring conversion rates or have perhaps conducted a pilot test so minuscule and so lacking in executive support it was virtually dead-on-arrival or quickly terminated.

As you'll see later in this chapter, there's a litany of reasons why they don't adopt. But the reasons don't really much matter. The fact is, these retailers just don't, and many of them simply won't – at least not anytime soon. Traffic counting and customer conversion just doesn't seem to make sense to these executives – or at least not enough sense.

These retailers say things like, "We've been thinking about traffic counters for years...but have just never done anything about it." Or "We're not sure this is right for our business."

## Dabblers

If the moniker seems mildly pejorative, you would be correct. These are retailers who have tried traffic counting, but for some reason, it just didn't seem to get any traction. These are executives who generally say things like "We tried it and it didn't work" and "We're still testing it in a small number of stores and we don't have the results yet...." It's unclear to me exactly what results they're waiting to see, and often it seems unclear to them as well.

The Dabblers in particular need to be reminded that traffic and conversion analysis is not some form of magic. It's as if they're waiting to see sales "pop" just because they're tracking prospect traffic in some number of their stores. What results are they expecting?

The more Dabblers I talked to, the more I came to realize that part of the blame should be laid at the feet of the traffic counting industry – the companies that are out there selling electronic traffic counters to retailers.

The argument for tracking traffic and customer conversion is conceptually compelling to a lot of retailers – who doesn't want to know how many people are visiting their stores? It's so compelling that many retailers undertake a pilot project in some of their stores to test the counters.

But that's often when things go wrong.

It's not unusual for projects to lose traction and then get terminated. When you consider the versatility and depth of insights that come from analyzing traffic and conversion data, it just seems such a tragedy that these retailers were so close; they actually tried it – but in the end let unarticulated objectives, sloppy execution, or perhaps lack of will rob them of this information that's so critical to the success of their business.

To add insult to injury, many of these retailers are quite poisoned by this experience and go on to perpetuate this "it doesn't work" mentality to other retailers they come into contact with, or other retail organizations they might join after they leave their current employer. The sad refrain of "we tried it and it didn't work" continues and spreads.

Given that this seems to happen so frequently, I'd like to explore in more detail the questions of why and how these Dabblers lose traction.

# Losing traction – what goes wrong?

Making the transition from Dabbler to Believer or Leader is a significant challenge for many retailers. Obviously someone thought it was important enough to try – good grades for the attempt!

However, as with an unwatered sapling, roots won't take hold, growth is stunted, and the project will eventually wither and die. I've worked with a great many retailers – smart and thoughtful ones at that – who got stuck in what I refer to as "a perpetual state of piloting." These pilots can languish on for many months, even years before someone finally (and mercifully) pulls the plug.

The problems are several: (1) it's often unclear exactly what is being tested and what the specific goals or objectives for the test are; (2), related to (1), is lack of owner (often the IT department gets conscripted to lead the investigation and implementation of the traffic counting test – it's a piece of technology, so why wouldn't IT be leading it?); and (3), again related to (1), because traffic counter companies are in the business of selling traffic counters and not typically in the business of helping retailers drive business results, there is no follow-up. Management, when it finally gets around to even looking at the project again, deems the exercise to be pointless and traffic/conversion dies a slow, painful death.

Here are some additional issues that can derail even a well-conceived traffic and conversion program, causing it to stall or fall short of the full value it can deliver:

- **data integrity issues:** Traffic counters and traffic count data are fallible. While traffic counter technology has continued to improve, it's not perfect. Sensors fail, collector units get unplugged, the Internet connection goes down – stuff happens. These normal technical failures can lead to gaps in the data that wreak havoc on reporting. If these issues persist, the data (rightly so) falls out of favor with its management users or becomes just plain unreliable. The net result is that the key insights are not being extracted.

- **waning executive support:** In some cases, even when the information has some credibility in the executive suite, support wanes, because either the data are being only partially used, or the lack of tangible results keeps them off the radar screen of many in the senior ranks. Yes, they collect the data, and yes, the districts or even some of the store operations people use it, but it's not something that the senior executives of the company need to concern themselves with on a regular basis.

- **lack of action or consumption:** Lack of consumption is the root of all evil when it comes to ineffectual traffic and conversion programs. Traffic and conversion data are just that — data. Data alone won't defeat an aggressive competitor; it won't add luster to your brand if it's falling out of favor with the coveted 18-25 year old demographic; it won't make your advertising more effective; and it won't improve sales. It's just data. *Only the retailers who understand the insights and act on them can make a difference in business.* Many, many retailers struggle with how to consistently take action on the insights.

- **regime change:** Some retailers were well on their way to becoming Leaders when the unthinkable happens – the CEO or senior-executive-in-charge leaves the company. The new executive comes in, reviews the existing programs (having come from a Non-adopter or a Dabbler company) and just doesn't see the benefit – program terminated.

I've talked to retailers who describe the sometimes all-out effort on the part of some or all the current traffic and conversion stakeholders, using all their powers of persuasion to convince the new executive of the value of traffic and conversion and plead with him or her to keep the program alive.

If there's enough will, the program may live, but it's often still a very tough battle to keep the senior executive engaged with the insights, and the eventual result is a total discontinuance of the program.

While regime change can have a tragic result when the incoming executive just doesn't see the value, it should be noted that the opposite is also possible. A retail organization has never used traffic and conversion data, and a new executive comes in and mandates that it be used. Rare, but it can happen.

## Believers

These are retailers who have made the decision to implement traffic counters in all their stores, who strongly believe in their value, and who sincerely work toward fully consuming and using the insights. However, for various reasons they struggle with how to get the maximum benefit from the data.

Unlike Dabblers, Believers see the light; they get it. Theses retailers understand the business knowledge that the traffic/conversion insights can provide, and they've made a significant capital commitment to purchase traffic counters, the IT time to implement the counters, and varying degrees of management's time – from executives to functional managers to District/Regional managers and even Store Managers.

These retailers have done all the obvious things with traffic and conversion data. They use them to schedule staff; they know their customer conversion rates across the chain and by store; they may be using the data to understand the impact of marketing and promotions.

After capturing some of the low-hanging fruit with the data, and after several years of working with it, they struggle with trying to move the sales performance needle further. They get frustrated with the lack of results, and traffic and customer conversion become just another initiative, still part of the "dashboard" — but something that can get prioritized and lose executive attention.

Believers are generally very thoughtful and strategic retailers. They do care. They want to get more out of their traffic and conversion insights; they see the value, but they bump up against the bounds of their own analytic and operational capabilities and fail to squeeze all they can from this treasure trove of data.

Believers do so much right, but in my experience the key stumbling block often relates to consumption, or more precisely, lack of consumption. They struggle with getting the message down to store-level effectively and consistently. So while there is relatively good usage at the higher levels of the organization, it doesn't completely connect in the stores and consequently falls short of achieving the cultural impact Leaders do. The points I made on "consumption" and creating a conversion culture in chapter 3.2 may be worth revisiting.

## Leaders

As the name clearly suggests, these are retailers who have discovered the profound insights that can come from understanding traffic and customer conversion in their stores. These retailers consistently consume the insights and are exceptionally adept at using them to understand results and underlying performance drivers. They're willing to act on the data and to adopt behaviors that drive sales performance improvements and expense savings.

Leaders have traffic counters installed chain-wide and use the insights broadly through the organization, from senior executives to Store Managers and even Associates. Everyone knows what traffic and conversion are and how vital they are to his/her own area of the business. For the very best of this group, traffic and conversion have become components of the culture. These companies don't just talk traffic/conversion; they live it every day.

These Leaders have turned traffic and conversion into a significant competitive advantage. Later in this chapter, I'll explain more about what Leaders do with traffic and conversion data and what they say about it.

Now what about the barriers that have prevented traffic and conversion from being as pervasive in the industry as POS? Let me share with you what some executives have said to me about traffic and conversion – it's both amusing and disturbing.

# Why retailers say they don't track traffic

Over the course of many years and hundreds of meetings with retail executives, I've had the opportunity to ask them point-blank why they don't track traffic and measure customer conversion. The responses are curious, sometimes perplexing, and sometimes even ridiculous.

Some retailers even go so far as to suggest that while customer conversion is worth measuring, traffic counts alone aren't particularly useful. The fact that they entirely miss the not-so-subtle point that without traffic data you can't actually calculate customer conversion tends to get lost in their well-articulated but completely misguided objection. Some of the more popular objections retailers have to traffic and customer conversion analysis are listed below.

### "We've thought about it for years...but..."

Since the publication of my first book, *When Retail Customers Count*, I've spent the better part of the last six years meeting with retail executives. I have had countless conversations with retailers from all across North America, representing every imaginable retail category, size, shape and level of sophistication. In my experience, most retailers have considered counting traffic in their stores at one point or another. It's something that they say they have been thinking about...but. Here's the "but" part.

### "Traffic counters are too expensive."

Undeniably every capital investment needs to be scrutinized and evaluated. If an adequate return cannot be achieved, then the capital should be deployed elsewhere – this is obvious. The capital required to purchase traffic counters, have them installed, and then dedicate resources to manage the system, extract the insights, and ensure that these insights are consumed across the organization in a meaningful way – it's a significant commitment.

The investment in traffic counters and infrastructure can run thousands of dollars per store, and the ongoing staff resources to implement and manage this effectively will cost many times more.

The affordability objection is legitimate. However, as with any proper ROI calculation, the expense must be compared to the potential benefit, and herein lies the problem. As I said at the end of Chapter 3.3, much of the affordability objection is based on the lack of benefit attribution to traffic and conversion programs. Without an assessment of a potential benefit, the costs will always seem prohibitive.

Retailers generally get the cost part, but they struggle with determining the benefit and attributing a value to it.

## "Traffic counters are imprecise, therefore useless."

All data is imperfect —POS systems, inventory systems, financial systems, and staffing tools. All systems are fallible, but that doesn't mean they aren't helpful or shouldn't be used. Traffic counters are no different. There is no such thing as a perfectly accurate traffic count – all traffic data has impurities. To discount the value of traffic and conversion insights simply because you can't achieve a perfectly accurate traffic count is entirely misguided.

As I explain to executives, regardless of how technologically advanced traffic counters have become (and they have), they count all movements through the door, including staff, families shopping together (i.e., buying groups), deliveries, and other non-prospect traffic. Because of this, the absolute values are less important than capturing traffic counts consistently.

On any given day, there will be noise in the traffic data; the key is to follow the trends. So while the objection is often delivered with much conviction and righteousness (after all, they are technically correct), it misses the point. The traffic data may be a little noisy, but the real prospect counts are in there and with an experienced eye, the important insights can be extracted.

## "We're already inundated with data – we don't need more!"

This is an undeniable fact in many businesses today, maybe even more so in retailing. In a meeting with the CEO of a jewelry chain, this was exactly his point. When asked why his chain didn't track traffic and customer conversion, he said, "We have so much data, we almost don't know what to do with it all. The last thing we need is more data."

---

*"We collect lots of data...we have more data than we know what to do with!"*

– CEO Jewelry Store Chain

---

While the "data inundation" argument represents a legitimate challenge that executives face, it is not a valid argument against the importance or value of traffic and customer conversion metrics. It's simply an evasion. The real issue here is simply data <u>quantity</u> versus data <u>quality</u>. Producing mountains of data is easy; anyone can do it. This CEO almost sounded proud of the amount of data his company collected. Congratulations! You have piles of data — that you admittedly do a poor job of analyzing.

As I tried to convince this CEO that traffic and customer conversion metrics deserved a place on his dashboard as critical indicators, not only was he unmoved, but he displayed an even more disturbing objection: an utter lack of understanding of not only the value of these metrics but also, and even worse, of how they are calculated. In rebuttal to me, he said, "Besides, with all the data we collect, I'm sure we can figure out our conversion rate somehow...."

This was a startling profession of both ignorance and blind faith, but I kept my cool: "With all due respect, if you don't count traffic, you can't calculate customer conversion rates, and you don't currently count traffic in your stores, so no, there's no way you can calculate your customer conversion rate."

The meeting abruptly ended at this point. I don't go out of my way to challenge or make senior executives feel foolish, but when I get objections like this — from a CEO, no less — you wonder what retail executives are focused on. It's certainly not traffic and customer conversion.

## "Traffic and conversion don't apply to us – we don't need 'em."

Some retailers have nothing against these metrics *per se*. They simply don't believe that traffic and customer conversion apply to their business. So they fail to even consider the possibilities.

While it is quite true that the application of traffic and customer conversion does vary by segment and even by chain, the fundamentals apply to virtually every type of retailer, regardless of size and category.

One of the very few exceptions is pure-play grocery retailers. Practically everybody who visits a grocery store intends to buy, so this is the one category where transactions are a reasonably good proxy for traffic.

However, I would submit that today, there are far fewer pure-play grocery retailers than there used to be. As I suggested to the SVP of Operations for a major "grocery" chain, based on the product mix in your stores today, which now includes home electronics, home accents, books, and apparel, it would seem that traffic and conversion apply just as much to you as to Best Buy or Gap.

Sometimes executives mistakenly believe that because their Associates are compensated in whole or in part by commission, conversion is less important or simply not applicable. They argue that commissions create the incentive to convert as many prospects as possible, so conversion rate is naturally maximized as Associates sell to maximize their own earnings.

This logic is flawed. Here's why. This executive wrongly assumes that his Associates are constantly trying to maximize sales, but they aren't.

Let's say that the store has a massive sale; the store is overrun with prospects. The Associates are gorging on the windfall traffic, and it's a commissions bonanza. After the first two days of the event, some Associates, bloated with commissions, are perhaps less inclined to deliver the stellar service they might have otherwise. In other words, the financial incentives lose steam, and while the Associate did maximize the benefit for him- or herself personally, the company's benefit was not maximized. Customer conversion would have revealed that opportunities were missed and that the company didn't get all that it could have.

Another misconception is that "destination" retailers don't need to track traffic and conversion. Some of these executives believe that just because their stores are not mall-based, they are therefore a destination; they have no incidental traffic, and everyone who sets foot in their stores is there to make a purchase.

If your store is the only store at the top of a mountain, then yes, I agree, you are a destination and any prospect determined enough to come to your store is likely a buyer. But for everyone else, you're not.

Retail categories have become so blurry — and competition so fierce and unforgiving — that any retailers today who delude themselves into thinking that their stores are "destinations" are seriously underestimating the competition and overestimating their position in the market.

## "We've been successful to this point. Why start now?"

If you've never tracked traffic or calculated customer conversion rates in your business, you may well ask why you should start now. After all, you've grown your chain into a leader in your category; you know your business; you consistently deliver solid results; and your chain is flourishing.

---

*"We're an extremely successful company...we've come this far without it, why do we need it now?"*
— Senior VP Operations General Merchandise Chain

---

Sure, the competitive landscape is getting crowded, and you have to work a little harder to keep the growth going, but overall business is going well. Why change focus now?

Not only does change suggest some element of risk – what if this doesn't work? – it can be distracting. All true. The downside of the "if it ain't broke, don't fix it" argument is complacency. Success breeds complacency, and that is certainly the case here.

During a meeting with the Senior Vice President of Store Operations for a major North American discount merchandiser, I was simply told that "Look, I believe in the virtues of traffic counting and measuring conversion, but frankly, we're a huge and successful chain...we've come this far without looking at traffic and customer conversion, so why should we bother now?" End of meeting.

---

A few weeks later, I was back in my home town, shopping with my 10-year-old daughter. She asked me about how my meeting with the retailer in question had gone, because we both liked to shop at the chain and were fans. "Sadly, Taylor, it didn't go well. They basically said that they didn't need to count traffic because they were so successful without it, they didn't feel that they needed to start now." My daughter looked at me quizzically.

> *"Daddy, I would say that you should track traffic so that you can be even better!"*
> — Taylor Ryski, 10 years old

I asked her what she would have said to them, and her answer surprised me. With the enthusiasm and sincerity that only a ten-year-old could muster, she said, "Well, Daddy, I would say that you should track traffic so that you can be even better!"

How is it that the answer is obvious to a 10- year-old, but not to a Senior Vice President?

## "This is for small retailers, not sophisticated ones like us."

I was taken aback by this response from the CEO of a men's clothing chain. "I've looked at traffic and conversion, but it's just too simplistic for us. We are a major chain; we have Ph.D.'s on staff to help us understand our business and develop performance programs. This traffic and conversion stuff may make sense for a smaller retailer, but not a sophisticated retail operation like us." The issue underlying this objection lies in the fact that traffic counters have been around retailing for decades – they're not a new or "sexy" idea.

The notion of counting prospects seems passé, unglamorous and therefore, as the flawed logic goes, pointless. Sadly, too many retailers are bedazzled by the latest trend and would rather pursue this than something as basic and old-fashioned (and fundamental and critical) as counting traffic and measuring customer conversion.

This objection is based on a fundamental lack of appreciation for what traffic and customer conversion insights can offer. If you simply don't understand how these critical metrics can be used, or even what they mean, you'll naturally be skeptical about the incremental value they can deliver.

To repeat (because it's so important and fundamental): *without knowing traffic and customer conversion, retailers have no way of knowing how well their stores are performing relative to their unique sales opportunity; they cannot understand what's driving the sales results (traffic, conversion or both), and they will have no way of knowing what they need to do to improve.*

When I explain this to skeptical retailers, an alarming number remain unconvinced. Given the significant investments that retailers have made in enterprise resource management systems, inventory management, workforce management, measuring customer experience, and labor management, I do understand how they might believe that the incremental value of traffic and customer conversion would be nominal.

But it's not. In fact, traffic and customer conversion make many of these other systems even more meaningful and productive!

## "Traffic and customer conversion are just not a priority for us."

If you accept the premise that traffic and customer conversion are critical performance measures, what could possibly be a higher priority?

While this is a quick and convenient objection, the underlying issue, again, is the utter lack of appreciation of what traffic and customer conversion can reveal.

In any business there will always be multiple competing priorities, as well as emergencies and distractions that management has to deal with. Retail executives don't have a monopoly on these. Competing priorities are especially nerve-wracking when the retailer is already struggling with results and is searching for a silver bullet. "I need better results – now!"

But implementing a solution when the problem is not yet defined or fully understood is tantamount to ready-fire-aim.

Traffic and customer conversion data help you understand the underlying drivers; they help you better understand the problem and formulate an appropriate remedy. *Traffic and conversion analytics don't distract you from your priorities. They help you set priorities.*

## "We tried it, and it didn't work."

While I'm never surprised to hear that retailers have installed traffic counters (often at significant expense) and then struggled with collecting, analyzing and operationalizing the insights to produce meaningful results, this is clearly a baby-and-bath-water situation. While it's completely understandable that these retailers would be reluctant and even skeptical about the value of traffic and customer conversion, the problem does not lie with the data or the metrics, but rather with the retailer's ability to consume the insights and put them to practical use.

Metrics are metrics – data, measures, insights. To look for better performance from a metric alone would be tantamount to buying AC Nielsen market share data and expecting your market share to improve. It obviously won't improve unless you do something to effect change.

The same holds for traffic and customer conversion analysis. Retailers who have installed traffic counters in their stores, collected some data, and produced a few charts may be dismayed to find that no matter how hard they study their pretty PowerPoint slides, performance won't necessarily improve. And then, tragically, they conclude that traffic and customer conversion were ineffectual.

Weak leadership is another sad condition I see in some C-suites. One of the most disturbing objections I get from some "we already tried it" senior executives is related to their inability to get the lower-level managers to buy in.

> *"I like it, but my team just doesn't see the value, so what's the point?"*
>
> — CEO Furniture Store Chain

Executives who delegate leadership should not be in positions of authority. Do patients tell doctors what medicine to prescribe? Do students tell teachers what to teach? Of course not, and neither should lower level managers decide if traffic and conversion is right for the chain.

As we saw in the stories of the Customer Conversion Champions, in almost every case, it took the leadership of a strong executive to make the decision and then stay the course, despite the resistance that so often accompanies change.

## "We don't know what to do with the data."

This is another objection that I find hard to comprehend.

I remind executives who say this that every day, their managers are making decisions to try to deliver better results. Developing new training programs, refining inventory and logistical systems, creating and launching new promotional campaigns, sourcing and buying new product lines...the list is endless. All of these initiatives are to help move the performance needle – to drive chain performance.

> *"We like the reporting and analytics, it's great stuff, but we just don't know what to do with it."*
> – Senior VP Sales Specialty Confectionary Chain

Traffic and conversion analytics put these decisions in context. Investing in advertising to drive more traffic into a store that has low conversion is a bad decision; initiating a sales training program in a store with high conversion will not likely deliver better sales results. *If all you do is assess your decisions in the context of traffic and customer conversion, you will be better off than what you are doing today, which is largely flying blind.*

## Traffic and conversion as a competitive advantage

In a meeting with the CEO of a large apparel chain, I was pleasantly surprised at just how much this CEO got it. It was great! We talked enthusiastically about the many uses of traffic and customer conversion insights, agreeing on almost every point. I had finally found a retailing executive who was willing to give traffic and customer conversion the credit they deserve. While the CEO admitted that as an organization they hadn't fully exploited the insights, they were continuing to make progress. I was impressed. This company was well on its way to becoming a Leader.

While it was clear that this retailer didn't need my help to advance his traffic and customer conversion program, our conversation turned to the industry's general indifference to these critical metrics. I asked him straight out, "You obviously understand the importance of traffic and customer conversion, so let me ask you: Why doesn't the rest of the industry get this stuff?"

> *"I don't like to talk to other retailers about what we do with traffic and conversion...it's a competitive edge."*
>
> – CEO Apparel Retailer

His answer surprised me.

"Well, I get asked about traffic and conversion all the time at conferences and other functions, Executives from non-competitor chains approach me and ask, "What do you make of this traffic and customer conversion stuff?" And I always reply the same way: "It's OK."

Incredulous, I ask, "What do you mean, It's OK. Just OK? I thought you got it. You sounded like you were using traffic and conversion in a meaningful way...that you understood the importance, so why would you say it's just 'OK'"?

He leaned back in his chair, striking a Lee Iacocca pose of self-confidence, and calmly said, "I don't like to tell other retailers what we're doing with traffic and conversion because I see it as a competitive advantage. There are so few exploitable advantages in retailing that I don't want to give anything away – not even to a non-competitor retailer."

While I do understand this executive's motives for not shouting the virtues of traffic and conversion from the rooftops, and I appreciate that there is no direct incentive or benefit in his doing so, I think he's overstating the value his words could have on other retailers' ability to be successful with traffic and conversion analytics.

It's as if Tiger Woods described his golf swing to me in great detail, there's no risk that this information will enable me to win major golf tournaments. I can "know" what to do, but results come only from doing, and I certainly can't execute like Tiger. And so it is with traffic and conversion analytics.

Lots of retailers have installed traffic counters, collected a bunch of data, and then tried to make some sense out of it, but they just couldn't get traction. Those retailers who have persevered, honed their skills, and worked hard at using the data have reaped the rewards.

Let's examine these Leaders a little further.

# What Leaders say and do

The more I learn about retailers who use traffic and conversion analytics effectively (and those who don't), the more I'm convinced that retailers themselves are not completely to blame, though many wounds are indeed self-inflicted.

The traffic counter industry consists fundamentally of companies in the business of selling store traffic data collection systems and software tools for analyzing the data. The problem is, of course, that data collection systems and tools alone won't change your business.

Just like buying a new POS system will not improve comp sales; putting traffic counters in your stores alone won't give you an edge. So retailers are attracted by the benefits that the vendor's brochure promises but then fail to realize those benefits because of their own inaction.

It's analogous to purchasing a Steinway grand piano and somehow expecting to compose music like a grand master. Traffic counters are simply an instrument that you need to play. If you commit to it, work hard, and practice, you will compose beautiful music in the form of better sales results and expense savings.

## Real results

The undeniable fact is that some retailers are running their operations better – optimizing expenses, allocating resources more efficiently, and delivering better results that are partly or entirely attributable to actions taken on the basis of traffic and customer conversion analytics. It's not a fluke. These retailers are truly competing on analytics — and winning.

And so, when I meet one of these retail leaders, we often talk enthusiastically and at length about all the great ways traffic and conversion analytics can be leveraged. Optimizing staff? Check. Measuring advertising impact? Check. Business forecasting and planning? Check. And on it goes.

Another curious trait of these leaders is that they are always looking to improve. Even though they already seem to be doing everything possible with traffic and conversion data, they are always willing to talk to me. When I ask why, they simply say, "Because we wanted to make sure we're not missing something," or "We want to learn about more ways we can leverage this data."

It's also become a habit of mine to ask leaders I meet why they think more retailers don't use traffic and conversion analytics. Almost without fail, I get the same answer: "I can't imagine running our stores without traffic and conversion data, and I can't understand how anyone else could either."

*"Next to sales, conversion is the metric that the top executives talk about most — our senior executives talk about conversion every single day."*

— SVP Operations

> *"We improved our conversion rates from 42% to 48% in four years."*
>
> – Executive VP Operations Specialty Gift Retailer

---

> *"Traffic and conversion are becoming <u>religion</u> in our company!"*
>
> – CEO Shoe Store Chain

---

# Traffic and conversion best practices

There really is no magic here, but invariably, curious retailers will ask what the best practices are for the use of traffic and conversion analytics – the practices that will deliver the best results. The answer is contained in the entirety of this book, but for those who prefer a quick checklist, I offer the following in what I believe are order of importance:

1) executive sponsorship/ownership;

2) willingness to act on insights and change behaviors;

3) consistently viewing <u>all</u> aspects of the business in context of traffic and conversion to better understand drivers and set priorities;

4) leveraging the insights across organization ( it's not just a Marketing or Operations thing);

5) allowing time for the new way of thinking to take root and become part of the corporate culture;

6) treating it as an ongoing process, not a one-time project.

# Convinced yet?

If traffic counter penetration rates, along with the lack of mention of conversion in industry media or in the public disclosures of major chains, were the litmus test for importance of traffic and customer conversion, then the results are clear: traffic and conversion are irrelevant.

Furthermore, if one were to take to heart the comments of the many senior executive naysayers who have written these vital measures off for various and sundry reasons, it would indeed be the path of least resistance to focus attention on other, more popular initiatives like customer experience, loyalty, social media, or mobility, to name a few.

While it's not at all my intention to suggest that these aren't important initiatives – they are – I can't overemphasize the point that traffic and customer conversion help you get so much more out of them that it makes more sense to focus on traffic and conversion first. Furthermore, I would argue that *traffic and conversion offers more leverage and is so much faster in terms of measuring and driving results than so many other initiatives that it should be given high priority.* Traffic and conversion analytics can make a difference in your business – on Day One.

If by this point in the book you're still not convinced that traffic is vital and customer conversion is the last great retail metric, then I'm not sure that the conclusion of this book will change your mind. If skepticism is still coursing through your consciousness unabated, then I urge you to revisit the Customer Conversion Champions in Chapter 1.2 and carefully reread the last section of this chapter on what leaders say and do.

Once you've done that, I ask you to simply consider this one last question: is it possible that these executives just might be right?

Now, on to my closing arguments.

# Conclusion

# Conclusion

## Chief Conversion Officer

We seem to want to add the "chief" prefix to any position that is of significance in business today. The corporate landscape is cluttered with "chiefs." Here are a few of the more exotic I've found:

- Chief Brand Officer
- Chief Creative Officer
- Chief Innovation Officer
- Chief Learning Officer
- Chief Listening Officer
- Chief Privacy Officer
- Chief Process Officer
- Chief Procurement Officer
- Chief Product Officer
- Chief People Officer
- Chief Sales Officer
- Chief Strategy Officer
- Chief Supply Chain Officer
- Chief Experience Officer

Perhaps it's time for a Chief *Conversion* Officer. Imagine. One executive who has complete oversight and responsibility for ensuring that customer conversion (and traffic, while we're at it), get measured, tracked, and most importantly, consumed and leveraged across the entire organization. It seems apropos for the kind of profound knowledge revealed by the last great, retail metric, doesn't it?

When you consider the executive attention we assign to other areas of our business, as we see from the number of "chiefs" who populate corporate tribes today, the idea isn't completely far-fetched.

It may be fanciful to think that a role like Chief Conversion Officer will ever exist. I've never seen or heard of one, and I probably never will. Designating an executive as a Chief Conversion Officer might give this vital metric the profile it rightly deserves if nothing else, but a title alone won't improve conversion rate.

## This is *not* about analytics; it's about leadership and change

As you reflect on what you have just read, I hope you come to realize that *Conversion: The Last Great Retail Metric* is not an analytics or a business intelligence story, despite the abundance of graphs, charts and data I present.

This book is about **leadership and change**.

Traffic and conversion data, like a keg of gunpowder, cannot deliver the desired outcome without an accelerant. If you don't have traffic and conversion data, you don't even have a keg. But if you have traffic and conversion data without the leadership and will to use it as an accelerant, you'll get the same result: no bang for your buck.

The fact is, change is hard – especially when you're already successful. Even if traffic is vital and conversion is the last great retail metric, incorporating these into your existing business operation is messy – you need to invest in traffic counters, you need to analyze data, re-think processes, deal with push-back, train people…the list goes on.

The only way this could ever make any sense is if you truly believe that you have a realistic chance at reaping the rich benefits for your business – benefits that come from the successful application of traffic and conversion data insights. You can do it, but it's entirely up to you.

## Retailers who know vs. retailers who act

There's a book by Jeffrey Pfeffer and Robert Sutton entitled *The Knowing – Doing Gap*, which really resonated with me as I struggled to get retailers to buy in to the idea of traffic and conversion. As I reflect on the countless discussions I've had with executives, it occurs to me that almost every one of them knows about traffic and conversion – they just don't seem to <u>do</u> anything about it.

It gave me some (cold) comfort knowing that it wasn't just in traffic and conversion that executives don't act on the data – they don't act on lots of things they know they should.

At the risk of soundly overly self-assured, I believe that it would be difficult for anyone who understands retail business to completely reject the evidence I presented for the value and importance of traffic and customer conversion.

This is where I believe most retailers are today – they know, they just don't do. It's my great hope that this book encourages more of those who know...to <u>do</u>.

## Well within any retailer's grasp

The simple truth is that <u>any</u> retailer can use traffic and conversion analytics successfully. It's within the budget and organizational capacity of even the smallest retailer as long as there's the leadership to try — and the determination to work through the inevitable short-term resistance to change.

The Conversion Champions in Chapter 1.2 are the proof. Are these retailers simply spectacular outliers, generating results that could never be achieved by mere mortals? I doubt it – because in fact these retailers also struggled, had doubts, persevered, and then delivered meaningful results.

You can too.

## Do it for field managers if no one else.

While the application and use of traffic and customer conversion analytics will not guarantee business success, it will provide clarity, a certainty of knowing what makes your business move and what does not. You'll have a better understanding of the result of your actions to drive the business.

Conversion data enable you to think and talk about your business in completely new ways. You can engage Managers and Associates in a way that helps them understand how they can -and do — influence business outcomes <u>every day</u>.

Every department and executive should be using these insights. But if you use them for just one group, do it for your field management. These people need all the help they can get. Consider how frustrating their lives must be – *they're expected to drive sales results in the stores, without fully understanding what they need to do.*

If you provide traffic and conversion analytics to your field management alone, you'll realize a healthy ROI. If your Marketing team leverages it, you'll be ahead of the pack. If you use it beyond these two groups, you will be among the leaders and well on your way to champion status.

## The last great retail metric

We conclude where we began: is customer conversion the last, great retail metric?

I vote "yes," but I would be delighted to hear the case for any other metric that might deserve the honor.

It might seem inappropriate to bestow "greatness" on a something that is not recently discovered or invented – after all, conversion has been around retailing for decades. But that's what I think makes it especially remarkable – it's been here all along, right under our noses. It's stood the test of time, but it's never been fully understood or leveraged – until now.

And the best thing about this last, great retail metric is that it can help make *you* great.

# Acknowledgements

# Acknowledgements

The first thanks often go to the author's family –and for good reason! Writing a book is a truly laborious process, and as it nears completion, it can become all-consuming. Even when you love the topic (as I do), it gets to be a grind, and you can lose your sense of humor (as I did, occasionally). So to my wife Corine, daughter Taylor, and son Cole – thanks for your patience and support.

To the Conversion Champions — Diane Blois, Eric Wagstaff, Peter Scully, Larry Leibach, Kevin Graff, Dr. Bernard Lefang, and Dr. Jayashankar Swaminathan – thank you all for sharing your wisdom and experiences. You are all true champions, and I am eternally grateful for your contribution. Thanks also to Vy Hoang for sharing his technology and industry expertise.

I'm also grateful to have worked with so many talented people on this book. First, Dr. Alan Perlman, a brilliant linguist, editor and author in his own right, who edited the book. Next, Joanne Meredith and Jessa Dupuis of vrse design inc., who took on the herculean task of creating and manipulating the many images, charts, graphs and photos that populate this book, then putting them all together in a wonderful way. I'm indebted to Blaine Bertsch and Tom Dodd, friends and mad creative geniuses, along with the FISSION Media gang, and especially Cameron Wakal for his work on the book cover. Next, Julie Olsen, my researcher extraordinaire for her great work in finding the facts. And, finally, Jeremy Haeseley, Ryann Jacoby, and the team at AuthorHouse.

I'd like to thank the whole HeadCount team, especially, Jesse Robbins, Richard Sefcik, Sheryl Burry, and Jim Kiddoo for their hard work in keeping our business moving forward while I was distracted with the book — and for their unwavering belief that conversion truly is the last great retail metric.

Thanks also to Dr. Paul McElhone from the School of Retail at the University of Alberta for being a constant source of insight, advice and friendship. Also, to my dear friends Debra Greig, Dan Finkelman, Peter Smith, Steve Wezerek, Rebekah Sterr and Corine Tamiko Matsuda for taking the time to review the manuscript and provide thoughtful and helpful comments.

Finally, a special thanks to Bruce Johnson – the guy who just won't stop believing in me even when I occasionally do.

# Photo Credits

page 18: © Jeff Hinds | Dreamstime.com; page 25: © sweetym | istockphoto.com; page 99, 101, 106: © Valariej | Dreamstime.com; page 120: © 123render | istockphoto.com, © sweetym | istockphoto.com, © CostinT | istockphoto.com, © luismmolina | istockphoto

**End Notes**
**Appendix**
**Index**

# NOTES

## Chapter 1.1

1. J.A. Petersen et al., "Choosing the Right Retail Metrics to Maximize Profitability and Shareholder Value," *Journal of Retailing 85*, no. 1, (2009): 95-111.

2. P. Underhill, *Why We Buy: The Science of Shopping* (New York: Simon & Schuster, 1999).

3. W. Eckerson, Pervasive Business Intelligence: *Techniques and Technologies to Deploy BI on and Enterprise Scale*, (Washington: The Data Warehousing Institute, 2008), TDWI Best Practices Report, 3rd quar.

4. ABI Research: Research News. *Spending on Retail Technology Systems Will Exceed $20 Billion in 2014*, (March 18, 2010), http://www.abiresearch.com/press/

5. B. Kilcourse and P. Rosenblum, *Walking the Razors Edge: Managing the Store Experience in an Economic Singularity*, (Research Systems Research LLC, 2009), Benchmark Study.

6. T. Davenport and J.G. Harris. Competing on Analytics: The New Science of Winning. (Boston: MA, Harvard Business School Press, 2007); T. Davenport, J.G. Harris, and R. Morrison. Analytics at Work: Smarter Decisions, Better Results. (Boston, MA: Harvard Business Press, 2010).

7. P. Conroy and S. Bearse, Customer Conversion: *The Changing Nature of Retail, Planting the Seeds of Growth*," (Consumer Business Industries Practice, Deloitte & Touche USA LLP, 2010), Retail Growth Challenge Framework 3rd ser.

8. G. Lawrie, M. Gilpin, and A. Knoll, *Store-Traffic Technologies to Drive Revenues*," (Forrester Research Inc., 2009): 1-8.

9. Peterson, E.T., *Website Measurement Hack: Tips & Tools to Optimize Your Business*. (Bejing: O'Reilly, 2005).

# Chapter 1.2

1. Eric Wagstaff (Director, Organizational Development, ALDO Group), interviewed by author, March 2011.

2. Diane Blois (Vice President of Human Resources, HMV), interviewed by author, December 2010.

3. Peter Scully (Senior Vice President of Sales and Operations, Black's Photo Corporation), interviewed by author, March 2011.

4. Larry Leibach (Principle, Workforce Insight), interview by author, December 2010.

5. Kevin Graff (President, Graff Retail), interview by author, December 2010.

6. Bernard Lefang (Vice President of Research & Analytics, Market Force), interview by author, December 2010.

7. Dr. Jayashankar Swaminathan (Senior Associate Dean, Academic Affairs and Glaxo Distinguished Professor, Global Business and Operations, Technology and Innovation Management, Kenan-Flagler Business School), interview by author, January 2011.

# Chapter 1.3

1. P. Farris, et al., *Marketing Metrics: 50+ Metrics Every Executive Should Master*, (Upper Saddle River, N.J.: Wharton School Pub., 2006), 106-107.

2. K. Perkins, Retail Metrics, About Retail Metrics, (2011), http://www.retailmetrics.net/corp.asp

3. PetSmart Inc., 10-Q Quarterly Financials (November 24, 2010), http://investing.businessweek.com/businessweek/research/stocks/financials/secfilings.asp?ticker=PETM:US

4. Coldwater Creek 2009 Annual Report, http://phx.corporate-ir.net/phoenix.zhtml?c=92631&p=irol-reportsannual

5. dELiA*s, Inc., 10-K Annual Financials, (April 15, 2010), http://investing.businessweek.com/research/stocks/financials/secfilings.asp?ticker=DLIA:US

6. Motley Fool. *Foolish Fundamentals: Same-Store Sales*, (September 5, 2007), http://www.fool.com/investing/general/2007/09/05/foolish-fundamentals-same-store-sales.aspx

## Chapter 1.4

1. Hart Associates, "Mystery shopping industry to send teams to Capitol Hill in attempt to preserve jobs for millions," *Mystery Shopping Providers Association*, (April 28, 2009), http://www.mysteryshop.org/news/article_pr.php?art_ID=100

2. M. Michelson, "Taking the Mystery out of Mystery Shopping," Mystery Shopping Providers Association, (January 1, 2004), http://www.mysteryshop.org/news/article_pr.php?art_ID=22

3. P. Singh, "Opinion: Why Mystery Shopping Isn't Enough for Retailers," Retail Customer Experience, (May 25, 2010), http://www.retailcustomerexperience.com/article/21751/Opinion-Why-mystery-shopping-isn-t-enough-for-retailers

4. Singh, "Opinion"

## Chapter 1.5

1. Vy Hoang (Executive Vice President, i3 International), interviewed by author, January 2011.

2. E. Woyke, "Attention Shoplifters," *Bloomburg Businessweek*, (April 3, 2011), http://www.businessweek.com/magazine/content/06_37/b4000401.htm

# Chapter 2.1

1.  Conroy and Bearse, *Customer Conversion*

2.  B. Orr, E. Nelsen, and R. Sahota, "Customers Want a Consistent In-store Experience," *Mercer Management Journal* 22 (2006), 41-46, http://www.oliverwyman.com

3.  Conroy and Bearse, *Customer Conversion*

# Chapter 2.3

1.  D. Brady and D. Kiley, "Making Marketing Measure Up," *BusinessWeek* 3912 (2004): 112-113.

2.  Petersen et al., "Choosing the right retail metrics"

3.  S. Lam, et al., "Evaluating Promotions in Shopping Environments: Decomposing Sales Response into Attraction, Conversion, and Spending Effects," *Marketing Science 20*, no. 2 (2001): 194-215.

4.  Lam et al, "Evaluating Promotions"

5.  Petersen et al., "Choosing the right retail metrics"

# Chapter 2.4

1.  S. Lam, M. Vandenbosch, and M. Pearce, "Retail Sales Force Scheduling Based on Store Traffic Forecasting, "Journal *of Retailing* 74, no. 1, (1998): 61-88.

2.  Lam et al, "Retail Sales Force Scheduling"

3.  Lam et al, "Retail Sales Force Scheduling"

# Chapter 3.1

1.  I.D. Amir et al., "Relative Effects of Store Traffic and Customer Traffic Flow on Shopper Spending," *International Review of Retail, Distribution and Consumer Research 20*, no. 2 (2010): 237-250, doi: 10.1080/09593961003701841

# Chapter 3.2

1.  B. Robinson, "Empowering Store Operations with Analytics and Business Intelligence," *National Retail Federation* (June 2010), http://www.nrf.com/modules.php?name=News&op=viewlive&sp_ id=953

2.  Robinson, "Empowering Store Operations"

3.  B. Kilcourse, "The NRF Mood Ring," *Retail Systems Research* (January 19, 2010), http://www.retailsystemsresearch.com/_ documents/summary/1044

# Chapter 3.4

1.  J. Sheldon and G. Buzek, *Store Systems Study 2009: Retail Technology Spend Trends*, (Randolph, NJ: Research Information Systems, 2009), 6TH ann.

2.  Retail Council of Canada. *The Canadian Retail Technology Survey*, (July, 2001).

3.  Headcount Corporation, "Proprietary Mall Audit Study" (on-site observations of traffic counter use), 2008.

4.  Headcount Corporation, "Proprietary Mall Audit Study"

# Appendix A

HeadCount Data Survey of 140 Publicly Traded Companies for the terms "traffic" or "conversion" found in Published Annual Reports and Q-10's during Nov-Dec 2007 and Nov-Dec 2010

| Retail Chain | Y2007 "Traffic" | Y2010 "Traffic" | Y2007 "Conversion" | Y2010 "Conversion" |
|---|---|---|---|---|
| 1 99 Cents Only Stores | no | no | no | no |
| 2 A.C. Moore Arts & Crafts, Inc. | yes | yes | no | no |
| 3 Aber Diamond Corporation | no | no | no | no |
| 4 Abercrombie & Fitch | yes | yes | no | no |
| 5 Aeropostale, Inc. | no | yes | no | no |
| 6 American Eagle Outfitters, Inc. | yes | yes | yes | yes |
| 7 American Greetings Corporation | no | no | no | no |
| 8 Ann Taylor Stores Corp. | yes | yes | yes | yes |
| 9 BabyUniverse, Inc. | no | yes | no | no |
| 10 Barnes & Noble Inc. | no | yes | no | no |
| 11 Bassett Furniture Industries | yes | yes | no | no |
| 12 bebe stores, inc. | yes | yes | no | no |
| 13 Bed Bath & Beyond Inc. | no | no | no | no |
| 14 Best Buy | Yes | yes | No | no |
| 15 Big 5 Sporting Goods Corporation | yes | yes | no | no |
| 16 BJ's Wholesale Club, Inc. | yes | no | no | no |
| 17 Bon-Ton Stores, Inc. (The) | yes | yes | no | no |
| 18 Brown Shoe Company | no | yes | no | no |
| 19 Build-A-Bear Workshop, Inc. | yes | yes | no | yes |
| 20 Cabela's Incorporated | yes | yes | no | no |
| 21 Cache, Inc. | yes | yes | no | no |
| 22 Callaway Golf Company | yes | no | no | no |
| 23 Carter's, Inc. | no | yes | no | no |
| 24 Cato Corp. | yes | yes | no | no |
| 25 Charles & Colvard | no | no | no | no |
| 26 Charming Shoppes, Inc. | no | no | no | no |
| 27 Chico's FAS, Inc. | yes | yes | no | no |
| 28 Children's Place Retail Stores, Inc. (The) | yes | yes | yes | no |
| 29 Christopher & Banks Corporation | yes | yes | no | yes |
| 30 Coach, Inc. | no | yes | no | yes |
| 31 Coldwater Creek Inc. | yes | yes | no | yes |
| 32 Columbia Sportswear Company | no | no | no | no |
| 33 Conn's, Inc. | yes | yes | no | no |
| 34 Cost Plus, Inc. | yes | yes | no | no |
| 35 Costco Wholesale | yes | yes | no | no |
| 36 CSK Auto Corporation | yes | yes | no | yes |
| 37 dELIA*s Inc. | yes | yes | no | yes |
| 38 Dick's Sporting Goods, Inc. | no | yes | no | no |
| 39 Dillards, Inc. | yes | yes | no | no |
| 40 Dover Saddlery, Inc. | yes | yes | no | no |
| 41 Dress Barn, Inc. (The) | yes | YES | no | no |
| 42 DSW Inc. | yes | yes | no | no |
| 43 Eddie Bauer Holdings, Inc. | yes | yes | yes | yes |
| 44 Ethan Allen Interiors Inc. | yes | yes | no | yes |
| 45 Family Dollar Stores Inc. | yes | yes | no | no |
| 46 Finish Line, Inc. (The) | yes | yes | no | yes |
| 47 Finlay Enterprises, Inc. | no | no | no | no |
| 48 Foot Locker, Inc. | no | yes | no | yes |
| 49 Fossil, Inc. | no | yes | no | 0 |
| 50 Fred's, Inc | yes | yes | no | no |

| Retail Chain | Y2007 "Traffic" | Y2010 "Traffic" | Y2007 "Conversion" | Y2010 "Conversion" |
|---|---|---|---|---|
| 51 Furniture Brands International, Inc. | yes | NO | no | no |
| 52 GameStop Corp. | yes | yes | no | no |
| 53 Gaming Partners International Corporation | no | no | no | no |
| 54 GAP Inc. | yes | yes | no | no |
| 55 Genesco Inc. | no | no | no | no |
| 56 Goldas Jewelry | no | no | no | no |
| 57 Guess? Inc. | no | yes | no | no |
| 58 Gymboree Corporation (The) | no | yes | no | no |
| 59 Harley-Davidson, Inc. | no | no | no | no |
| 60 Hart Stores, Inc. | yes | no | no | no |
| 61 Haverty Furniture Companies Inc. | no | no | no | no |
| 62 Heely's, Inc. | yes | yes | no | no |
| 63 Hibbelt Sports, Inc. | no | no | no | no |
| 64 Home Depot Inc | no | no | no | no |
| 65 Hot Topic, Inc. | yes | yes | no | no |
| 66 J. Crew Group, Inc. | yes | no | no | no |
| 67 J.C. Penny Company Inc. | yes | yes | no | no |
| 68 Jo-Ann Stores, Inc. | yes | yes | no | no |
| 69 Joe's Jeans Inc. | no | no | no | no |
| 70 Jones Apparel Groups Inc. | no | no | no | no |
| 71 Jos. A. Bank Clothiers, Inc. | yes | yes | no | no |
| 72 Kirkland's, Inc. | yes | yes | yes | yes |
| 73 Kohls Corporation | no | no | no | no |
| 74 La-Z-Boy Inc. | yes | yes | no | no |
| 75 Limited Brands, Inc. | yes | yes | no | no |
| 76 Lithia Motors, Inc. | no | yes | no | no |
| 77 Liz Claiborne Inc. | yes | yes | no | no |
| 78 Lowe's Companies, Inc. | no | no | no | no |
| 79 lululemon athletica, inc. | no | yes | no | no |
| 80 Macy's Inc. | no | yes | no | no |
| 81 Men's Wearhouse, Inc. | yes | yes | no | no |
| 82 Monro Muffler Brake, Inc. | no | yes | no | no |
| 83 Mother's Work, Inc. | yes | yes | no | no |
| 84 Nam Tai Electronics, Inc | no | no | no | no |
| 85 Natuzzi S.p.A. | yes | yes | no | no |
| 86 Nautilus, Inc. | no | no | no | no |
| 87 New York & Company, Inc | yes | yes | no | yes |
| 88 Nike Inc. | no | no | no | no |
| 89 Nordstrom Inc. | yes | yes | no | no |
| 90 Office Depot Inc. | no | no | no | no |
| 91 OfficMax Incorporated | no | no | no | no |
| 92 O'Reilly Automotive, Inc. | yes | yes | no | yes |
| 93 Pacific Sunwear of California, Inc. | yes | yes | no | yes |
| 94 Palm Harbor Homes, Inc. | no | yes | no | no |
| 95 Pantry, Inc. (The) | yes | yes | no | no |
| 96 Payless Shoes | Yes | yes | Yes | yes |
| 97 Pep Boys Manny Moe & Jack | yes | yes | no | no |
| 98 Perry Ellis International | no | yes | no | no |
| 99 PETsMART, Inc. | yes | yes | yes | yes |
| 100 Pier 1 Imports Inc. | yes | yes | no | yes |

| Retail Chain | Y2007 "Traffic" | Y2010 "Traffic" | Y2007 "Conversion" | Y2010 "Conversion" |
|---|---|---|---|---|
| 101 Polo Ralph Lauren Corporation | no | no | no | no |
| 102 Procter & Gamble Co. | no | no | no | no |
| 103 Quiksilver Inc. | no | no | no | no |
| 104 RadioShack Corporation | yes | yes | no | no |
| 105 Retail Ventures, Inc. | yes | yes | no | no |
| 106 Rex Stores Corporation | yes | yes | no | no |
| 107 Rock of Ages Corporation | no | no | no | no |
| 108 Ross Stores, Inc. | no | no | no | no |
| 109 Saks Incorporated | yes | yes | no | no |
| 110 Sally Beauty Holding, Inc. | yes | yes | no | no |
| 111 Sealy Corporation | no | yes | no | no |
| 112 Sears Holdings Corporation | yes | yes | no | no |
| 113 Shoe Carnival, Inc. | yes | yes | no | no |
| 114 Shopper's Drug Mart Corporation | yes | yes | no | no |
| 115 Signet Group plc | yes | yes | no | no |
| 116 SKETCHERS USA, Inc. | yes | yes | no | no |
| 117 Sony Corporation | no | no | no | no |
| 118 Sotheby's | no | no | no | no |
| 119 Sport Chalet, Inc. | no | no | no | no |
| 120 Stage Stores, Inc. | yes | no | no | no |
| 121 Staples, Inc. | yes | yes | no | no |
| 122 Steve Madden, Ltd. | yes | YES | no | no |
| 123 Tandy Leather Factory Inc. | yes | yes | no | no |
| 124 Target Corporation | yes | yes | no | no |
| 125 The Buckle, Inc. | yes | yes | yes | yes |
| 126 The Talbots, Inc. | yes | yes | no | no |
| 127 The Walt Disney Company | no | no | no | no |
| 128 Tiffany & Co. | yes | yes | no | yes |
| 129 Timberland Co. | no | no | no | no |
| 130 TJX Companies Inc. | yes | yes | no | no |
| 131 Tractor Supply Company | yes | yes | no | no |
| 132 Trans World Entertainment Corp. | yes | no | no | no |
| 133 Tuesday Morning Corp. | yes | yes | no | no |
| 134 Urban Outfitters, Inc. | yes | yes | yes | yes |
| 135 Walgreens | yes | no | no | no |
| 136 Wal-Mart Stores | no | yes | no | no |
| 137 Williams-Sonoma Inc. | yes | yes | no | no |
| 138 Wolverine World Wide Inc. | no | no | no | no |
| 139 Zale Corporation | yes | yes | no | no |
| 140 Zumiez Inc. | yes | yes | no | no |

# Appendix B – Featured Experts

  Workforce Insight, Inc.
1600 Wynkoop, Suite 5B
Denver, CO 80202
Toll Free: (800) 394-5516
www.workforceinsight.com

 Graff Retail
114 Lakeshore Road East
Suite 100
Oakville, Ontario L6J 6N2
Email: solutions@graffretail.com
Phone: (905) 842-1275
Toll Free: (888) 263-1835
www.graffretail.com

 Market Force Information Inc.
Headquarters
Colorado Office
Post Office Box 270355
Louisville, CO 80027
Phone: (303) 402-6920
www.marketforce.com

The University of North Carolina at Chapel Hill
Kenan-Flagler Business School
Campus Box 3490, McColl Building
Chapel Hill, NC 27599-3490
Phone: (919) 962-5327
www.kenan-flagler.unc.edu

i3 International
Head Office
780 Birchmount Rd, Unit 16,
Scarborough, Ontario M1K 5H4
Phone: (416) 261-2266
Toll Free: (866) 840-0004
www.i3international.com

Kiosko Inc.
36 Precision Drive, Suite 100
North Springfield, VT 05150
Phone: 802-886-3030
Toll Free: (866) 554-6756
www.kioskousa.com

**Head**Count

HeadCount
Research Center One
9419-20 Avenue
Edmonton, Canada T6N 1E5
Phone: (780) 463-7004
Toll Free: (877) 463-7004
www.headcount.com

# Index

CPSIA information can be obtained at www.ICGtesting.com
Printed in the USA
239816LV00004B/2/P